The Male Factor

THE
MALE
FACTOR

■ ■ ■

The Unwritten Rules, Misperceptions,
and Secret Beliefs of Men in the Workplace

■ ■ ■

SHAUNTI FELDHAHN

BROADWAY BOOKS • NEW YORK

Library of Congress Cataloging-in-Publication Data
Feldhahn, Shaunti Christine.
   The male factor : the unwritten rules, misperceptions, and secret beliefs of men in the workplace / Shaunti Feldhahn.—1st ed.
   p. cm.
   1. Sex role in the work environment. 2. Men—Psychology. 3. Men—
Attitudes. I. Title.
   HD6060.6.F45 2009
   650. 1'3—dc22
                                                          2009027276

ISBN 978-0-385-52811-5

Printed in the United States of America

Design by Gretchen Achilles

1   3   5   7   9   10   8   6   4   2

First Edition

To Calvin and Nerida Edwards
for twelve years of life-changing
collaboration and friendship

Contents

The Male Factor Research Team

Front, left to right: Jenny Reynolds, research analyst; Shaunti Feldhahn, author; Linda Crews, director of operations; Karen Newby, research assistant. Back, left to right: Kim Rash, content advisor; Vance Hanifen, research assistant; Calvin Edwards, content advisor; Jeff Feldhahn, content advisor; Leslie Hattenbach, research assistant. Not pictured: Jackie Coleman, research assistant; Ann Browne, cofounder, Human Factor Resources.

ABOVE LEFT: Decision Analyst team, left to right: Ramiro Davila, senior research analyst; J. Scott Hanson, PhD, vice president, Client Service; Felicia Rogers, executive vice president, Client Service.

ABOVE RIGHT: Analytic Focus team, left to right: Charles Cowan, managing partner; Mauricio Vidaurre-Vega, research assistant.

CHAPTER 1

A New Skill Set

"Are you saying women don't already know that?"

The charismatic African-American businessman sitting next to me in first class looked at me in disbelief. We were only a few minutes into the usual "What do you do?" airplane conversation when I shared something that apparently stunned him.

I had explained that I was a financial analyst by training, had worked on Wall Street, and was now, unexpectedly, a bestselling author and speaker about relationships.

His inevitable question: "What's your main topic?"

"Men." I grinned at his wry expression. "I spent a few years interviewing and surveying a few thousand men. My last book identifies some ways that men tend to privately think and feel, that women tend not to know."

He folded his arms across his chest, and it was his turn to chuckle. "OK," he said, "hit me with one."

So I shared one of my findings about men—one that I will share with you in the following pages—and that is when the amusement turned to disbelief.

When I confirmed that even the most astute women may not know that particular truth about men, I could see that suddenly, his thoughts were off in a universe of their own. If he hadn't been strapped in his seat, I think he would have gotten up and started pacing.

"That explains something!" he finally said. "You see, I'm a corporate trainer and consultant. Fortune 100 corporations bring me in to help with leadership and strategy at the highest levels of the organization. And all too often, I see skilled and talented women sabotage their careers because they treat the men they work with in a way that no man would treat another man."

He looked at me with awakening interest. "But from what you're telling me, these women probably don't even realize that that is what they are doing."

It was my turn to be interested, and my notebook and pen were already out. "Can you give me an example?"

"I'll give you an example of something that just happened a few hours ago." For the next few minutes, he told me his story (which I'll relay in a later chapter), and concluded, "I was so puzzled why this female executive would shoot herself in the foot like that! But perhaps she simply didn't understand how her actions would be perceived by her colleagues—colleagues who were mostly men."

THE HOLE IN THE BUCKET

The range of what we think and do is limited by what we fail to notice. And, because we fail to notice that we fail to notice, there is little we can do to change until we notice how our failing to notice shapes our thoughts and deeds. —R. D. LAING

Over the last few decades, corporations across America have developed a bucket of programs to help advance or retain women. Many approaches have been quite effective; others, better in theory than in practice. We've seen a surge in management attention to work/life balance issues—particularly to retain working moms—and a corresponding surge in flextime and telecommuting options. Businesses and industry groups are increasingly fostering female networks and mentoring relationships as an alternative to playing golf with the guys, and are emphasizing professional development for rising women. Organizations large and small have studied and trained their people on avoiding sexual harassment, and on the unique needs of female workers, customers, and stakeholders. Gender-equity task forces have proliferated.

But as valuable as that effort is, I've come to realize that it has a significant hole. We as women can be skilled, talented, highly educated, mentored, networked—and yet trade all of that away by unintentionally undermining ourselves in our interactions with male colleagues. As my new friend on the airplane put it, we can still sabotage ourselves simply because we do not understand the "male factor": some relevant truths about how the male half of the population thinks—and thus how they may be perceiving (or misperceiving) our words and actions.

Even without that potential trap, we may be missing some important insight, effectiveness, and tactical advantage through a simple gap in information—a gap exacerbated by the fact that (as you will see) men often have clear internal expectations but don't feel able to openly share what they are privately thinking. So the end result is the same: A woman can all too easily be missing valuable information that might be helpful or important for her—information that she would presumably *want* to know in today's market. One senior executive put it this way:

Women in business have seen some tremendous opportunities open up, but have also seen that it is still a man's world in many ways. What I mean, though, is different than you may think. What I mean is that, historically, for better or for worse, men pretty much created what we mean by "the business world" today. And since men still tend to hold most of the top-level positions, their subconscious ideas about how things should work are still framing the debate.

It would be extremely helpful for women to have insights

into what it's like to be a man in that business world. When men say things like, "It's not personal; it's business," it would be helpful for women to understand what "it's business" actually *means* in the minds of the men whose ideas originally defined that business world.

Based on everything I have heard from men about how they think and feel—and how surprising some of those facts have been to the millions of women who have read my previous books or heard me discuss those findings—I would argue that understanding men *in the ways that might impact us* is a career-critical skill set that women can develop, like any other.

Over the years, I've heard from hundreds of women readers who were validated that they had already recognized and incorporated some of these truths into their workplace approach—and from many others who wished they had learned these often-hidden truths earlier or better.

All of us want to be effective and be perceived as "getting it" instead of triggering the unspoken question, *Why would she do that?* While the need for understanding is most obvious among younger women who are still learning their way in the marketplace, a better understanding of men has certainly helped senior female professionals, as well. One senior vice president found her work relationships with men improving so much after she read my original book that she personally bought one hundred copies, one for every woman in her department.

If in your line of work you have any significant interaction with male superiors, coworkers, subordinates, customers, or other constituents, it is worth it to get inside their heads and better understand what they privately think—especially in areas that affect you, but that they would never tell you themselves. Not because their way is "right," or because you should necessarily adapt to their expectations, but because their perceptions exist and could be affecting you regardless of whether you know what they are. Far better to have full information, so you can make the *informed* decisions that are right for you.

MEN 101

You may have seen the humorous graphic comparing women and men to two different old-fashioned control panels. The one labeled "Woman" has dozens of random buttons, gauges, and circuit breakers. The one labeled "Man" has an on-off switch.

Pop culture suggests women are complex, while men are straightforward. And in some ways, that may seem to be true. But in other ways, I've found it to be quite misleading—and dangerously so. *Not taking into account the complexity and depth of men's thinking can put women at a significant disadvantage.*

How I Woke Up to What I Didn't Know

In 2001, I stumbled across some important facts about what men are often privately thinking and feeling, that women often never know.

I had recently moved with my husband from New York City to Atlanta, and was working as a financial and organizational analyst. In my spare time I was also writing fiction. One of my main characters in my second novel was a man, a good, decent husband and father and successful businessman. And I realized that although I could put on paper what my character was *doing* in my various scenes, I had no idea how to write what a man would be *thinking*. So I began asking male friends for help. I would describe a given scene, and then ask, "What would you be thinking in this situation?"

And I often found myself shocked. Over and over again, the men described foundational, private thoughts that I would never have guessed at. They described deep, daily ways of thinking and feeling that were a complete surprise to me—even after eight years of marriage. I kept thinking to myself, "Why have I not heard this before?!"

I started doing more and more of these interviews, hitting up everyone from my male colleagues to the guys behind the counter at Starbucks. And it soon became clear that what I was learning was too important to stop with creating a character in a novel. So once the novel was finished I began a more systematic approach to investigating the most important things that women just tend not to "get" about men. Over the course of several years, I interviewed and surveyed more than 1,500 men, conducting two professional, nationally representative surveys.

Very early on, I realized that what I was hearing related to either a man's personal life or his work life. The men would sometimes describe how they felt or thought in a given home-life scenario, and sometimes describe their private impressions at the office. Both were equally eye-opening to me. But I couldn't tackle both in the same book. So I started with the personal relationships, and wrote *For Women Only: What You Need to Know About the Inner Lives of Men*, which was published in 2004. Shortly thereafter, my husband, Jeff, and I teamed up to write the companion book, *For Men Only: A Straightforward Guide to the Inner Lives of Women*. The books instantly became bestsellers; in just four years they sold more than 1.5 million copies and have been translated into fifteen languages.

I became extremely busy with traveling and speaking, often at large women's conferences, churches, government workshops, or marriage seminars. And over the next few years, I continued the process of investigating the key surprises in our personal relationships, researching and publishing books for teenagers about how the opposite sex thinks, as well as a book for parents to help them understand how their teenager thinks (a scary prospect, I know!).

But as each year went by, I continued and expanded my research of men, with an eye toward a book that would help women understand men in the workplace, and, ultimately, help women advance.

In 2007, I turned my full attention to understanding men in the workplace. How do men privately think and feel about things at work that women don't already know? What do men privately say when they are promised anonymity and can be completely honest and candid, that we would never otherwise hear? What are the truths that seem common to most men, regardless of personality, industry, age, race, or any other differing factor—the private truths that we women often misunderstand, or miss completely, simply because we may be wired differently?

> *What do men privately say when they are promised anonymity and can be completely honest and candid, that we would never otherwise hear?*

Most important, what are the areas in which most men instinctively tend to act and think the same way, tend to subconsciously expect others to do the same, and view *not* doing so as anything from a confusing aberration to outright weakness? In other words, which of these inner truths about men might unwittingly trip women up without our ever realizing it—and which might help us to be even more effective once we understand them?

In pursuing these questions I found, as I had with the research on *For Women Only*, that my analytical training and Wall Street experience provided an important—if a bit unusual—foundation for uncovering, analyzing, and communicating hidden truths about how people think.

I have a master's degree in public policy with a concentration in business from Harvard University; my core classes in quantitative and qualitative analysis were taken at the Harvard Kennedy School, and my electives at Harvard Business School. After graduation, I became a financial analyst at the Federal Reserve Bank of New York, primarily investigating and analyzing what was going on underneath the surface of the Japanese financial meltdown, and sharing those findings at the highest levels of the Federal Reserve System.

I worked there for only three intense years, but it laid the foundation for an entirely new type of analysis of what was going on underneath the surface in relationships. I am forever grateful to my former colleagues and supervisors for throwing me in at the deep end and setting their expectations high.

THE RESEARCH BEHIND THIS BOOK

Reason is the slow and torturous method by which those who do not know the truth discover it. —BLAISE PASCAL

During the years of investigating how men privately think in the workplace, I interviewed every businessman I could, distilled the truths that I felt would be the most helpful to women readers, and then worked with professional survey designers to develop and conduct a nationally representative survey to test if what I was hearing was common to most men. That sounds simple, but it required an intense effort involving me, seven of my staff researchers and assistants, several corporate consultants, and a team of survey experts from two different companies over the course of eight years. In the end, well over 1,500 men provided input specifically for this book, in addition to the 1,500 men who had contributed their insights to my previous research.

Those numbers don't just include "official" surveys and interviews. I kept a notebook, pen, and digital recorder permanently by my side so I could capture informal interviews in the most unlikely places. I travel a lot, and on every flight, if I was sitting next to a man who was willing to talk (most were), I would ask him questions. At coffee shops, restaurants, on the subway, and in social gatherings, I looked for opportunities to strike up conversations with businessmen and conduct impromptu interviews. It continues to surprise me what a man will divulge when you don't know his name or where he works, and he's on a boring daily commute.

It is also amazing what a man will tell you when you do know his name and where he works—but he has been guaranteed anonymity. I guaranteed each man in writing that all quotes appearing in the book would be completely anonymous, and that they would never be able to be tied to a particular individual or organization. To ensure that anonymity, I promised to judiciously alter identifying details.

As a result, I got virtual—and often physical—access to the inner offices and leaders of dozens of household-name companies and organizations in every corner of the country (and a few beyond our borders). I interviewed hundreds of men—from entrepreneurs with a start-up staff of ten people, to businessmen who started some of our most recognized retailers. I heard surprising insights from both middle-level managers at small companies and C-level executives of the largest companies in the world. I sat down for interviews in cluttered, disorganized offices in remote suburbs, and in the most luxurious penthouse-suite offices I've ever seen. And I did several dozen conference calls with executives who were in cities beyond my immediate travel plans, but whom I couldn't afford to miss.

From Manhattan to Orlando, Omaha to Austin, Minneapolis to Los Angeles to Seattle, and of course in my current hometown of Atlanta, I was amazed and grateful for the breadth of input I was able to receive.

My main regret is that in the limited space of this book I am only able to pass along a fraction of what I have gathered. I can't, for confidentiality reasons, post full transcripts of these conversations. But if you go to TheMaleFactorBook.com, the website for this book, I will over time post as much helpful information as I can, scrubbed of all identifying information.

About a dozen senior-level businessmen proved to be particularly helpful and insightful and became more in-depth advisors during the process, agreeing to answer follow-up questions or sitting for multiple interviews. These advisors ranged from C-level executives at nationally recognized companies, to owners of thriving businesses, to partners at management consulting firms. Some of these men are quoted multiple times (although, like all others, they are identified by a fictitious first name).

You also will read a number of examples and stories relayed by a series of helpful female advisors, businesswomen who proved invaluable during this process. Some of these women signed confidentiality statements and spent hours reading through transcripts and draft chapters, setting up interviews with men, helping me develop and test the survey, and thinking through the application of what I was learning to their own experiences.

Identifying the Surprises and Testing the Survey

Each time I interviewed a successful businessman, I had to avoid the temptation to turn the interview into a crash course in business advice, and instead stay focused on what insight he had to share as a man, that a woman might never otherwise hear. As I listened to these men talk, I gradually came to identify a number of "truths" I felt were the least known, and thus the most helpful, to women today in the workplace; several specific hypotheses about how men think and feel in several specific areas.

Next I had to design a survey to test these hypotheses. Were these findings actually true and common to most men? Or, despite my often random sampling, had I gotten a skewed view of men's thinking?

Once again, Chuck Cowan of Analytic Focus came to the rescue. Chuck used to be the chief of survey design at the U.S. Census Bureau; he later worked at Price Waterhouse, and then founded the much-in-demand analysis firm Analytic Focus. I had relied on Chuck as my survey design consultant since 2003. He in turn had connected me with the renowned survey company Decision Analyst—one of the top companies in the world for conducting the sort of reliable, nationally representative online survey I needed for my books. Since people are less likely to be honest about certain personal subjects in a telephone survey, the project required a professionally conducted online survey with stringent quality controls to ensure reliability.

With Chuck guiding the process, I developed survey questions and tested them over and over again to ensure they were understandable, weren't leading, and that the men saw "their" answer choice represented. I did more than a dozen rounds of testing. The process of testing the survey itself led to some fascinating insights— not to mention some amusing situations. Like almost getting me and one of my research assistants arrested for criminal trespass on the subway. Apparently, according to a particularly intimidating urban police officer, even when men are voluntarily taking part in a survey it is considered "solicitation."

After the thirteenth round of testing, we were ready to conduct the official survey.

The survey had one primary goal: to test and quantify my hypotheses about men's thinking. I wasn't trying to develop an academic study of every possible permutation about how men think and feel. I was concentrating on the areas that women tend not to understand about men in the workplace. (If you would like to know more about our survey methodology, please see the appendix written by Chuck Cowan at the back of this book.)

The official survey included 602 men from around the country, including a panel of 100 executives. The survey included a nationally representative sample of men aged twenty-five to sixty-five, across all races and occupations, and provided a 95 percent confidence level, with a margin of error of 3½ percent. I also included a control group sample of 100 white-collar women.

In the end, the survey results confirmed the majority of my hypotheses. But as with each of my other surveys over the years, it was inconclusive on a few others. The confirmed subjects became the starting point of each chapter; the others were dropped from further research for now, and are not included in the book.

OUR STARTING POINT

The intellectual takes as a starting point his self and relates the world to his own sensibilities; the scientist accepts an existing field of knowledge and seeks to map out the unexplored terrain.

—Sociologist DANIEL BELL

My research was all about developing theories, testing them, and refining them to whatever degree that I could. But I also wasn't starting from a blank slate, nor can I do so in this book. In the chapters ahead, to allow me to reserve my limited space for the key findings about men, I will be starting with the following suppositions, which are based on prior research and information:

Gender Differences Exist

The most important starting point is the understanding that there are, in fact, fundamental differences between how men and women think. This seems like an obvious statement to many, but for many others it has become controversial to accept or even discuss. I don't pretend to know *why* some of these male-female differences exist, or which ones result from "nature" or "nurture"; that is a discussion that can be left for another book, and another author.

Rather, it is enough to recognize that many scientific disciplines—from clinical psychology to brain science to anthropology—have investigated and identified multiple differences between the sexes. Some of those clinical issues will be outlined in the pages ahead. But for the most part I will stick with focusing on how men think and feel in the workplace and let the men speak for themselves.

There Are Exceptions to Every Rule

Despite the real differences between men and women, everyone is an individual. When I say that "most" men appear to share a particular perspective, I mean exactly that—most men, not all. I will of necessity make some generalizations in the chapters ahead. One of the reasons I commissioned the survey was to understand what generalizations could be made, and what were the exceptions.

Some Generalizations Apply to Both Men and Women; the Differences Are Often in the Details

It is also important to explicitly say that, despite our differences, women can of course identify with many things that are important to men. For example, just because I say that men value a "suck it up" mentality (chapter 8) or look for a particular type of professional respect (chapter 9), it doesn't mean that women don't. Quite often, the differences—and the surprises—were in the details: the magnitude, frequency, or cause of a particular perception. For example, both men and women value respect, but it is surprising how unexpectedly easy it is for a man to feel that he's being disrespected by words or actions that women would never have seen that way.

In a similar way, I found that the more high-level a woman was, the more likely she was to share a viewpoint similar to men. Although men tended to answer questions the same way regardless of how senior they were, that was not the case for women. That leads to the intriguing question of whether certain women *became* more senior because they already thought "more like men," or whether the process of rising through the ranks caused them to change the way they thought—but that question, too, is going to have to wait for a different research project!

Explanation Is Not Endorsement

Over the past few years of sharing these findings, I have found that some women mistakenly assume that identifying and explaining a commonly held male thought means that I endorse it. As I make clear in the chapters ahead, I am not saying that men's assumptions are right (I've actually included quite a few that are wrong), or that women must change to fit into a "man's world." This book can and should be used as much to help men examine their thoughts and assumptions as to help women understand them.

> *I am not saying that men's assumptions
> are right, or that women must change
> to fit into a "man's world."*

MY GROUND RULES ON WHAT TO INCLUDE

It may be helpful to know some boundaries and ground rules I set for myself as I decided what could and what couldn't be included in the limited space of this book.

First, as noted earlier, I focused primarily on truths about how most men think that I felt would be surprising to women. I tried to stay away from general business advice, no matter how helpful. And if something about the way men thought was interesting but common knowledge to most women seemed more tied to individual personality than gender, or had been thoroughly covered elsewhere, I usually didn't include it.

Second, with hundreds or even thousands of fascinating comments and observations to choose from on any given topic, I decided to include quotes only from men whom I felt had a genuine desire to help women advance. If I felt a man was indifferent or perhaps even harboring some private animosity toward women, I continued to interview him, but didn't include his comments.

This was an admittedly subjective judgment. Obviously I had no way of evaluating the goodwill of the men providing comments on the survey. And the data and conclusions themselves cover all sorts of men, since women don't always have the good fortune to work only with men of goodwill. But for any actual interview quoted in these pages, I focused on men who seemed to care about women's advancement and were sincerely trying to help.

Third, that said, I didn't pull any punches. If many men in my interviews felt that women needed to know something about their thinking, I tried to make room for it—especially if it was backed up by the results from my survey. There may be times that you may not like what some of the men had to say. But *if* it is true that many or most men are privately thinking or perceiving things a certain way, it is in our best interest to know it. Knowing the truth is far better than operating based on wishful thinking.

> But if *it is true that many or most men are privately thinking or perceiving things a certain way, it is in our best interest to know it.*

Fourth, although nearly every man gave me multiple examples where female colleagues were effective and "did it right," I couldn't balance every negative with a positive. While I have tried to include some helpful positive examples, these findings may often be even more helpful when used to remove hindrances that stand in the way of otherwise-effective women. So I want to provide as many anti–self-sabotage principles as possible. This balance could leave the impression that "all women do it wrong all the time," and that is not at all what the men were saying. Very much the reverse, in fact. The men went out of their way to point out the many cases of women they worked with who were widely admired and respected by men.

Fifth, I tried wherever possible to not only provide information, but also to pass along the thoughts of the men on how we could apply that information. However, those ideas are much more subjective than the rest of my research and are included simply in case they are helpful to some. While there were common patterns in how men thought and perceived things, men's advice on how women might incorporate that knowledge was highly varied and often seemed to depend on personality, values, or circumstance.

In general, the application implications are reserved for the latter part of each chapter, since my goal in this book is not to advise women on "what to do," but to pass along the critical knowledge that women need to make their own informed decisions.

In the chapters ahead, I have tried to get you started by incorporating a representative sample of the application ideas and some general principles. Beyond the book, I have also worked with women's networks, training groups, mentors, and coaches in various fields to build materials for further development. In the end, everyone's situation is different, and you are far better equipped than I to observe how these foundational facts play out in your industry and circumstance, and develop strategies that work best for you. If you want to go further, and are willing to share those strategies with others, please go to my website, TheMaleFactorBook .com, and chime in to the discussion. I—and other women readers— would love to hear what has worked for you.

CHAPTER 2

Observations from the Research Process

The Big Picture of How Men View Women and Men in the Workplace

A few observations and much reasoning lead to error; many observations and a little reasoning lead to truth.

—Nobel Prize winner ALEXIS CARREL

You can observe a lot just by watching. —YOGI BERRA

In many ways, I found the process of conducting the one-on-one research for the book just as fascinating as the substance of what I was hearing. During the course of talking with and surveying men about how they think and feel in the workplace, and how they perceive female colleagues, I saw some unmistakable big-picture patterns that simply didn't exist when men were talking about their personal relationships.

As a result, although this wasn't originally in my plan for the book, I felt that ten of these big-picture observations were important to the conversation and critical to share.

TEN OBSERVATIONS

1. The men sincerely wanted to help women advance and were aware of the hurdles we face

With very few exceptions, the men I interviewed seemed to have a sincere desire to help women advance, both because they cared personally and because they knew it would be better for business in the end. Marty, the chief executive officer of a $5.5 billion medical-industry organization, had recently and substantially altered his organization's gender balance by bringing more women into top roles. As he put it, "Advancing women is an asset and good for us from a long-term perspective." I heard similar comments from a great many of the men I spoke with.

Most of the men were also surprisingly aware of the external hurdles women encounter in business—in many cases citing dilemmas faced by their wives, girlfriends, daughters, or female colleagues that a man would probably never have to deal with.

In most cases, a busy executive's willingness to carve out time for an interview seemed tied directly to that genuine goodwill toward women. Each man seemed to feel that even if some of those external hurdles still existed, he could at least help women avoid the internal ones caused by misunderstandings or gaps in knowledge about men, since, statistically, men were still likely to be in control at one time or another of the path upward.

One senior executive whom I will call Geoff, the worldwide chief marketing officer (CMO) of a Fortune 500 company, provided this fascinating if blunt input in an interview:

"Women have to tell themselves, in business, it's still a man's world. That's changing slowly *and you shouldn't accept it.* But you do have to accurately evaluate the landscape. The better the evaluation, the better the results. You have to conduct yourself accordingly and say, 'I won't compromise, but I will understand the rules.' And remember that the only way to change the company is to get higher up."

"But many of us think that competence should be the most important thing," I protested. "That's the way it should work. If we are highly competent we should be able to succeed, period."

Geoff shook his head. "No," he said. "Think about it. Generally, especially as you rise through the ranks, no one is *incompetent*—so it falls to those other factors. It's not just talent, because everyone has that. Instead it's the boss valuing trust, valuing people who fit with his own style, and valuing loyalty. It's so hard to break into those teams. You can have talent, but you have to earn loyalty."

"Especially as you rise through the ranks, no one is incompetent—so it falls to those other factors."

And that, of course, is one of the goals of this book: to help women see those crucial internal factors other than talent that tend to play a part in a man's perception of the work world—and of them.

Some readers might be skeptical that the men I interviewed were truly being altruistic. Could they have simply been assuaging subconscious guilt by speaking with me and thus feeling like they'd done something to "help women"? In fact, a few of the men *explicitly* volunteered that was the case! But even that minority dynamic was revealing. These men were aware of and felt a degree of guilt over instances where they had advanced in place of equally competent women. Now, years later, they wanted to help me identify and understand the often unseen factors that could have tipped the decision.

The vast majority, however, genuinely seemed to want to help me simply because they wanted to help and encourage women.

2. The men were eager to share

Once the men were convinced that what I was doing was genuine and that they wouldn't be quoted by name, I found them not only willing but eager to share their thoughts candidly.

Several times, when I was referred to an executive for a scheduled appointment, I showed up to find that he had a list of five or six things he absolutely *had* to tell me before he could let me out the door. Because those I made office appointments with tended to be more senior and more busy, I usually asked for only a twenty- or thirty-minute time slot. In more than half of those cases, the person I was interviewing became so engaged by our conversation that he ended up giving me far more time than he had originally intended—often forty-five-minutes to an hour.

In one case, I was interviewing the president of a Fortune 50 company in his executive offices, sandwiched between his return from Japan the day before and his departure for Germany that evening. He had to duck out of an executive committee meeting to make time for our interview. Yet even that interview went twice as long as expected. (Thirty minutes, instead of the fifteen his secretary had said was the most he could give.) I kept expecting a board member to show up and politely drag him back into the executive committee meeting!

3. The men agreed there was a real career and business need for women to better understand men (the reason for this book)

On the survey and in my interviews, a large majority of men said there were indeed areas in which women tripped themselves up, because they didn't understand some core truths about men or how women were being perceived by men. This is the core of "The Male

Factor"—the effect of a man's perceptions on a woman's effectiveness and prospects—and it can be qualified to some degree. First, on the survey, two out of three men believed that highly talented women sometimes shoot themselves in the foot due to not understanding how they are being perceived.

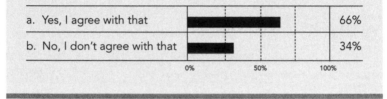

In your opinion, are there certain things that even skilled and talented women sometimes unintentionally do that undermine their effectiveness with men, simply because they don't realize how they are being perceived by the men they work with? Choose one answer.

a. Yes, I agree with that		66%
b. No, I don't agree with that		34%

It was telling that the agreement was even higher (77 percent) among the critical bracket of thirty-four-to-forty-four-year-old men who were more likely to be in the middle ranks of the organization, actually working with many female peers day to day, and competing with them for the path upward.

Even more important was the difference between men's and women's perceptions of the *type* of understanding needed. Among my control group of women, 71 percent agreed that women sometimes shot themselves in the foot with men. But the types of self-sabotage they mentioned were often those that women already know (for example, not to weaken yourself by turning a statement into a question). The types of self-sabotage the men mentioned were in most cases very different (not turning a statement into a question was rarely mentioned), and were largely perceptions that men rarely vocalize, so women don't usually hear.

On average, more than half (56 percent) of the types of self-sabotage mentioned by men as most critical, were not picked up on by any women. And more than a third (35 percent) of women's perceptions of what would hurt them most with men, were things that not a single man mentioned.

There simply are many things that men most value, and/or warn against, that women may miss. Most of those areas will be covered in the chapters ahead.

In men's minds, if a woman does *not* understand how men perceive things, it creates a frustrating dynamic. (Just as it does for us when the situation is reversed.) Again, most of the men I spoke with actively wanted to help women advance, viewed that advancement as a benefit to the company, and viewed the loss of female workers or their lack of advancement as a real problem for the business. But *these same men* also acknowledged that *if* a woman didn't understand how men perceived things, it created problems for the woman—and sometimes for the company—that wouldn't have arisen otherwise and that they would prefer to avoid.

A few pages back, I quoted Marty, a CEO who had made a successful effort to advance women. Yet the quote that appears earlier was only part of what he said. Here is how he finished his thought:

> I think advancing women is an asset and good for us from a long-term perspective. But sometimes . . . sometimes it can be a torturous process to get there.

This was very representative of what I heard from many of the senior men I interviewed. Geoff, the CMO I mentioned earlier, put it this way:

Women have always been two-thirds of my key positions because women give me more creativity and impact, and I think they generally produce a better product or service. Problem is, they also tend to give me more trouble; they create a lot of broken glass.

Now, obviously, we women may strongly protest the perception that promoting women can sometimes be a "torturous" process, or that "women create a lot of broken glass." I've seen many cases where men were more likely to be the culprits for both! As you will see a bit later, though, it is very much in our best interest to avoid the resulting temptation to write off those comments or this entire discussion.

4. The men were of one mind—about men

The men did sometimes contradict each other about women, about advice for women, and about thoughts on business in general—as one would expect of people with very different personalities and backgrounds. But I was struck that they very rarely contradicted each other about how men think.

In the chapters that follow, you will therefore sometimes see conflicting statements about women, such as "Women hesitate to speak their mind because they want to be liked" versus "Women are assertive and don't care how that is perceived."

Remember, the scope of this book cannot lead to conclusions about what is right or wrong in the men's perceptions of us, or analyze trends of how women actually do things. Instead, this research is about what men *think* of a woman (or a man, for that matter) who does or says a particular thing in a particular way. Whatever your work life is like, whatever your habits, patterns, words, or actions, this research will help you understand how they are perceived.

5. Even men of goodwill expressed uncomfortable perceptions about women. I found these were less the result of hang-ups about women than of an inner truth about men

As I mentioned in the introduction, I tried to relay interview quotes only from men whom I felt had genuine goodwill toward women and a desire to help women advance. But that doesn't mean that some of their comments weren't challenging.

Both my female research assistants and I sometimes found ourselves indignant when transcribing parts of the interviews I conducted. Many times I fundamentally disagreed when a man who otherwise seemed very progressive made a sweeping generalization such as "Women usually do such-and-such and men never do."

Now, such blanket statements were thankfully in the minority; it was much more common for men to be so judicious that it took a while to piece together the sometimes startling patterns in what they were saying. But for the purpose of understanding how men think, it really doesn't matter whether a man's perception is accurate and appropriately nuanced or not.

Even when women might roll their eyes over certain comments, should we completely ignore those perceptions or call them off-limits? Certainly, trying to *change* them may be valuable. And corporate America has done both.

A great deal of effort has been made to change certain perceptions about women through sensitivity seminars and the like, and those efforts continue to be very important. But I have come to realize that they can also backfire if they are not paired with a better understanding of *why* those impressions among men exist in the first place. Because many of those perceptions *don't* stem from individual chauvinistic hang-ups, but from deep, foundational needs, fears, and truths that are common to many men. If we summarily dismiss an unpalatable remark, we miss the opportunity to look past it to see if there is a deeper truth at work that women need to be aware of. Thus, our tendency to make certain discussions off-limits can actually end up *hindering* women's advancement instead of helping it.

We don't have to agree with certain privately held thoughts, nor do we have to accept them—but it does not demean women to go through the process of examining them. I've seen over and over again in my own life and work that it is in my best interest as a woman to identify and understand the impressions men have (and often don't feel that they can say), so that I can look beneath the surface to a helpful truth . . . and so I can work to counter inaccurate or unfair perceptions where necessary.

I've also seen that a parallel effort is needed for men in the workplace to better understand and correct common misperceptions about women, by presenting similar research on what female colleagues may be thinking and the deeper truths that will make men, in turn, more effective and understanding in their work with women. That research project is now under way as well.

6. The women most resistant to this discussion were often perceived as those who could most benefit from it

Over the past few years, I have conducted a number of corporate training sessions to share my emerging findings with professional women. In each case a handful in the audience were quite offended. They simply disagreed that there were facts they might not understand about the men they worked with, or that any lack of knowledge could be hindering them in ways that they didn't see.

One corporate training session stands out in my mind. The leadership of a midsize company had heard me speak elsewhere, and in turn invited me to train the women on staff on my findings. Over the course of several days, hundreds of women cycled through the training center for a two-hour session with me. While most were intrigued and saw how they could apply my preliminary findings, about five women in one session were quite vocal in their resistance to what I had to share.

After the session ended, one of the senior women in the company came up to apologize for some of the rather disrespectful things that had been said. "Those women," she sighed, "were the main reason we wanted to do this training in the first place. Jessica [not her real name] is a vice president, and most of the others who disagreed with you are her department heads. They are smart and talented—and most of the men here have some serious difficulties in working with them. Jessica has the potential to rise to a more senior position, but the executive team simply can't see promoting her if she doesn't get this. And today she just made clear that she has no interest in doing so."

In several cases I observed, and in many examples relayed by the men I interviewed, it seemed that, ironically, the women who found themselves most resistant to this idea were often the ones the men felt most needed to hear it—for the sake of the women's own careers and effectiveness.

One man in an international service business provided a helpful analogy:

You know, when you do business with the Japanese, they require it to be done in a certain way. So we have to accommodate that. It's the same thing doing business in other cultures. When you do things with them, you have to do it in a certain way to be really productive. *Especially* if your natural inclination is not built that way, you have to really be aware of it and be willing to work and learn what they expect—not just what you expect.

That's the way it works with what you're doing [helping women understand men]. In my previous firm, several of us spearheaded an effort to help change the good ol' boy culture to be more welcoming to women. But it works both ways. Just as if you were doing business with another culture, I would urge anyone, when in doubt, to be flexible and be willing to learn.

> *"Just as if you were doing business with another culture, I would urge anyone to be flexible and willing to learn."*

Having worked with Japanese businessmen myself for three years, I understood exactly what this man was saying. Some of the perceptions and suggestions in the chapters that follow may not follow our natural predispositions. And there almost certainly will be cases where we simply decide that adjustments in our behavior or approach aren't appropriate or necessary. But there may also be many cases where we recognize that, without compromising ourselves, it is in our interest to "be flexible"—or at least willing to learn.

7. The main hurdle: political correctness

The whole process of asking about men's innermost thoughts, feelings, and perceptions—including their candid perceptions of women—was fraught with a concern about political correctness. By even talking about these matters, nearly every conversation felt politically incorrect. And I was fascinated that the men clearly felt the weight of that fact.

Probably three out of every four men I spoke with were clearly trying very hard to be judicious in their use of words, sometimes with long pauses while they sought for just the right phrasing that would reassure me that they were trying to express politically incorrect sentiments in a way that was as respectful as possible. (The other one out of four were often quite blunt and didn't seem to care what they said or what I might think about it—but they were also more likely to be strangers on an airplane rather than someone whose name and business I knew.)

But interestingly, the men's caution wasn't just because they were saying these things out loud. Most had clearly absorbed an internal desire to not even think (much less express) something that might be perceived as disrespectful to women.

In fact, one of the reasons it took me so long to develop useful survey questions was the difficulty in getting men to set aside the issue of how their answer would be perceived, or their worry about whether they *should* feel a certain way, and just answer the question honestly. Even though the men knew the survey was completely anonymous, they were much more on their guard when sharing perceptions of the woman in the next cubicle than the *For Women Only* survey respondents had been when sharing perceptions about their wife or girlfriend. On test surveys, I was fascinated to see that several men refused point-blank to answer questions that asked how they would feel if a female colleague did or said such-and-such. I have collected a stack of test surveys where men left an answer blank, writing in the margins comments like, "I don't see why it is relevant whether or not the colleague is female." Interestingly, the *women* I tested the survey on had absolutely no problem answering those questions—and were often harder on their female peers than the men were!

Because of that "internal political correctness meter," it was much more difficult to develop appropriate questions for the survey. I had to build in more questions to catch internal contradictions, add more explanatory language, and be much more precise about what I was asking and what I wasn't.

Similarly, even when my male interviewees had a ton of insight and examples to share, they often were hesitant to identify particular actions or patterns as being more likely to occur with women than with men—even if that objectively did seem to be the case.

In quite a few cases, a man would give an example of something a female colleague did or said that interfered with how she was perceived, but was quick to add, "But that may not have anything to do with being a woman—that may have just been her personality." My next question was always, "OK, can you give me an example of when a man you worked with did something similar?" And most of the time the answer was "Well—no." Interestingly, where the answer was yes, my interviewee usually added that when a man *had* done it, he had been looked down on even more harshly because of it.

8. The men usually felt unable to address certain issues with female colleagues, and had instead stuffed their annoyance

In a similar way, where the men I interviewed were irked by something that they felt women tended to do that men tended not to do, they had often gotten used to sublimating or pushing their reaction down, or to simply ignoring their irritation. In a sobering number of cases, they felt the political climate was such that they couldn't address such an issue directly (or fully) without being misunderstood or even—in some cases—labeled a misogynist.

But of course their annoyance hadn't gone away: It was just simmering underneath the surface. Which was one reason why, when we started discussing these matters, their reactions at times erupted rather intensely as something that they had been wanting to share for a long time.

Perhaps because of this dynamic, I heard of many cases where a female colleague never realized she was being perceived a certain way—and then was utterly surprised at being sidelined, turned down for a promotion, or forced out altogether.

In some cases, men identified certain patterns that they viewed as foibles among their female colleagues but didn't seem to particularly resent—they seemed resigned to or "forgiving" of them. Many times, when I asked how a man felt about an example he'd just shared, I heard things like, "If you're going to work with women, you just have to get used to it." Or, more subtly, "As a manager, you make accommodations."

Personally, I was just as bothered by the fact that men were "making accommodations" for a woman's "foibles" as I was by the fact that they so often felt that they had to stuff or push down their annoyance.

I believe women need to know what these perceptions are and create a climate where we are able to hear them: in other words, a climate where both men and women feel able to share these things just as they would any other business issue. That is the only way women (or men) will be able to correct misperceptions, or address the issue if there is indeed something we need to hear.

> *I believe women need to know what these perceptions are and create a climate where both men and women feel able to share these things just as they would any other business issue.*

9. The decision of whether or how to apply this knowledge will be very individual and different for every woman

This research and this book are, above all, intended to be a helpful tool for your life and work. Knowledge is power, but to be truly empowering it must be applied in a way that is most helpful to *you*.

It would be easy to misconstrue my comments about understanding men to imply that we must always adapt ourselves to male attitudes and compromise ourselves in the process. Throughout this book I try to make it clear that that is *not* what I'm saying, nor would I ever want to imply it.

We have unique and valuable perspectives and specific strengths to offer as women—perspectives that men, for their part, also need to understand. It would be foolish, for example, for us to stifle those strengths just because they are misunderstood by men. As noted earlier, just because men have common rules and expectations doesn't mean we have to meet them.

For example, in chapter 8 you will see that one common value held by many men is to "suck it up." For many men, this involves pushing through the pain and enduring whatever they need to endure to get the job done. In the workplace, that sometimes translates into expecting long hours from themselves and everyone around them, and setting aside family obligations.

As all of us know, juggling our professional and personal lives isn't easy—especially in the face of intense expectations at work. If we have earned some hard-won victories in work-life balance, should we give them up simply because men may be privately frustrated that we are sticking to our boundaries? Not necessarily.

In this or any other example, I would argue that the key is to know how particular words, actions, and choices are likely to be perceived—and then make the informed decisions that are right for us.

10. This is a great time to be a woman in business

Finally, despite the very real hurdles and balancing acts many women still face in business; despite the stubborn persistence of some deeply held prejudices and hard-to-crack good ol' boy networks; despite the unique challenges that most men never have to confront and don't understand, I would argue that this is a great time to be a woman in business.

After conducting these interviews, I'm aware as never before of the opportunities that I have enjoyed and would never have experienced in another country or century. If I had been stopping men on the subway thirty years ago to ask them questions about their perceptions of women in the workplace, the answers would have been quite different. If I had asked men on airplanes to take a test survey about women in the workplace, would they have taken it seriously? If I had been born into my mother's generation, would half of my graduate school classmates have been women? Would I even have been *admitted* to graduate school? Today, the enrollment at American universities is an astonishing 56 percent female to 44 percent male.

Tragically, even today, women in many other countries have few rights and fewer personal and professional dreams. How different would our life and prospects look if we had been born and were working in other corners of the planet?

The man who probably had the most comprehensive résumé of anyone I interviewed gave me a great perspective on this. He is someone who ran one of the most successful franchises of an internationally known company, later rose to one of the top executive spots inside the company, and then started several other business that are now household names both in the United States and overseas.

Here is what he said:

In the U.S. we have certain foundational ideas that make us unique in the world. For example, how we approach failure in the marketplace, or how our Constitution was created. There are parts of our infrastructure that are so basic to our country that we don't even see or talk about them because it's like trying to talk to a fish about water. It's there everywhere.

One of those things, in the United States and a few other countries, is our investment in women. It is very, very unique given where the rest of the world is.

We lived in Mexico for a while, and also in China. China has 1.2 billion people, but from a human capital standpoint they actually have probably only the equivalent of 700 million: They invest in women so little that they will only get one-fifth of a person's worth of productivity from each woman.

America's investment in women is something that makes us much more competitive from a long-term standpoint. Look at what Title 9 has meant for this country; our investment in supporting girls from the youngest ages is simply enormous, and it is just beautiful in terms of the opportunities it creates and the implications for those girls as they have become women. People don't talk about it much, but it is spectacular. It creates an environment for this book that is very relevant.

> *"America's investment in women is something that makes us much more competitive from a long-term standpoint."*

I would like to suggest to your female readers that this is a point of hope for them. As much as they think there is a guy's club—and there is, sometimes—they are in an environment that is truly unique in its willingness to invest in women. We celebrate and embrace diversity better than almost anywhere else in the world. There are only a few countries in the world with similar attitudes. In the American workplace today, people understand that diversity is a good business idea, and that they will make more money if they can embrace diversity. This is a unique environment, a fertile environment, for women to succeed.

As I write this, I am well aware of my ability to take that investment in women for granted.

Yet the process of talking with so many men has highlighted the encouraging truth that it truly is a great time and place to be a woman in the workplace. We stand on the shoulders of those who have come before us, and despite the challenges that still exist and the distance we have yet to travel, that is worth being grateful for.

CHAPTER 3

"It's Not Personal; It's Business"

Two Different Worlds, Two Different Laws of Gravity

One theme running through the romantic comedy *You've Got Mail* is just how differently men and women view the concept "It's not personal; it's business." In the movie, Joe Fox (played by Tom Hanks) owns a massive Barnes & Noble–like bookstore chain that opens an outlet near a beloved children's bookshop run by Kathleen Kelly (Meg Ryan). Kathleen is unable to match their discount prices and tries valiantly to hang on, but eventually goes out of business. Joe discovers that the woman he's been ruthlessly competing with in business is also the anonymous woman he's fallen in love with online—the woman to whom he had been giving business advice such as "Fight to the death," and "You're at war. It's not personal; it's business."

Later, he starts to apologize for putting her out of business, saying, "It wasn't personal—"

Kathleen interrupts. "What is that supposed to mean? I'm so sick of that. All that means is that it wasn't personal to *you*. But it was personal to me. It's personal to a lot of people. What is so wrong with being personal anyway?"

That short exchange captures a common source of friction that I heard many times, in one way or another, as I interviewed men and women about how each views their working life.

ONE WORLD OR TWO?

Many women tend to have a holistic view of the world, one that takes work matters, professional relationships, personal activities, family, and so on, and views them all as part of the big picture called "life." Work, providing for one's family, and advancing professionally are all viewed as part of our overall life.

As a result, women tend to have the same feelings and perspectives in different areas of our life. When we are feeling attacked, underappreciated, or disappointed at work and someone says, "It's not personal," it doesn't ring true to us. *Well, it's sure personal to me.*

Men, on the other hand, tend to have much clearer boundaries. It is as if there are two different worlds: "Work World" and "Personal World." In a man's mind, the two are utterly distinct from one another, and they function by very different rules. Every morning when he heads to work, a man feels as if he physically leaves one world with one set of rules behind, crosses an emotional bridge, and enters a totally different world with a different set of rules and expectations.

> *In a man's mind, it is as if there are two different worlds: "Work World" and "Personal World."*

A comment from Richard, the president of a financial advisory group, captures that distinction:

> Business becomes its own box. The man presses the button for the tenth floor and when he walks off the elevator he's now in "Business." Everything about the rest of the world gets suspended. It's not personal, not relational, not religious, not civic: It's business.

When he says, "It's not personal; it's business," he actually means that. It's like, "Don't you get it? I've crossed the bridge to the business world and until I cross the bridge back to home, this is where I am. And there are rules here—written and unwritten—that govern this world."

The idea of "the business world" is a construct that men have learned to embrace. It may be a fiction of their mind, but to them it's very real.

The graphic below is an attempt to capture this difference visually:

TWO DIFFERENT WORLDS:

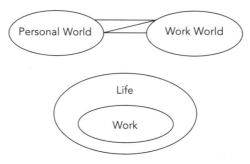

Because of these two very different ways of looking at the world, a phrase like "It's not personal; it's just business" tends to mean something different to a man than women might realize—or than women might mean when women say the same thing.

What women mean by that phrase can often be summarized as "I know this situation [a layoff, a missed promotion] is personally difficult, but please realize this is not about you. This was a decision that had to be made for purely business reasons, such as that we won't have the cash flow next quarter to pay your team."

What men mean by that phrase can be summarized as "You and I are not in Personal World now, we are in Work World. So this situation is *not* being handled by the rules one sees in Personal World.

Instead, we are handling this by the rules of Work World, and *that is how you should perceive it*. You shouldn't even *have* the same feelings as you would in Personal World."

In the initial survey question, roughly six out of ten men stated that the two worlds function very differently. I was surprised that the number wasn't even higher, given men's overwhelming agreement with the question in my interviews. So I cross-tabbed this "theoretical" question with several that provided actual workplace examples—and discovered that once they were confronted with real-life scenarios, every single man who took the survey actually did expect the working world to operate very differently from the personal world.[1]

Stop and think for a moment about your view of working life and personal life. Which statement best describes your view?*
(Choose one answer.)

a. Things operate differently at work than they do in your personal life. You can adhere to the same values or personality in each place (for example, being honest, or compassionate), but the expectations and culture of each are simply different, so you adjust to each.

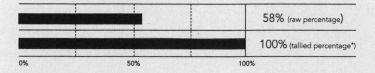

58% (raw percentage)

100% (tallied percentage*)

0%   50%   100%

b. The way work life and personal life operate are not that different, so you can operate pretty much the same in both arenas.

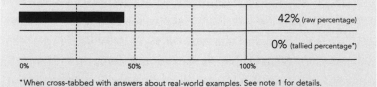

42% (raw percentage)

0% (tallied percentage*)

0%   50%   100%

*When cross-tabbed with answers about real-world examples. See note 1 for details.

The men were clear that it is the operating rules of the environment that change, not a person's personality or values. In their minds, they are the same individual with the same temperament, the same beliefs, the same values. But the environment has changed around them and so they adapt to the rules governing that environment.

A good analogy would be as if one world is playing the game of paintball, and one world is playing the game of poker. You as the player are the same person, with the same values—for example, "One should never cheat"—but (in the man's mind) there are two completely different games with different rules.

Before women can figure out ways to be more effective at working with our male colleagues, employees, and bosses, *or* confront assumptions that we believe are incorrect, we need to know what they think those rules are and just how deeply they are embedded in the male psyche. In the next chapter, I will provide a list of the perceived rules or "natural laws" (such as "You just don't take things personally at work"), as well as dive into several in more detail. Several of the others are so important that they will be covered much more extensively in their own chapters.

THE REASON BEHIND THE RULES OF THE WORKPLACE

Several highly skilled female associates have told me, in exasperation, that they feel stymied at work because they can't get an entrée into what seems like a murky world of good ol' boy passwords and secret handshakes. As one friend put it, "I feel like there is some sort of secret code to which all my male colleagues are privy, and I am not."

What these women are picking up on is very real. But it is not secret and it is not a code: Rather, it is a deeply rooted set of male expectations that can be uncovered and understood once women know what to look for.

> *It is not a secret code: is a deeply rooted set of male expectations that can be uncovered and understood once women know what to look for.*

Simply put, men have built up certain expectations and knowledge about how to relate to each other at work—and how not to. From the time that boys are told "Don't be a sissy" for crying on the playground, they learn how to approach and interact with each other. And they know how they will be viewed if they don't. They grow into adult men with a set of expectations on how to relate to one another at work. And subconsciously, they expect women in the workplace to relate in those same ways, and sometimes view them poorly if they don't.

The executive consultant on the airplane whom I described at the beginning of the book told me that he sees some women "sabotage their careers because they will treat the men they work with *in a way that no man would treat another man*" (emphasis mine).

Since the working world was almost entirely led by men until just a few decades ago, the expectations and the knowledge that men have of how to approach one another led to the expectations or "rules" that they believe govern the working world. As one software executive put it:

Remember, I didn't come up with this. I found the workplace this way. And I just fit into rules that already existed. It is as if someone came up with it hundreds of years ago.

Someone somewhere decided that, for example, emotions will negatively affect productivity.

"It's not personal; it's business" is like gravity. It's just the way it is. It is the way the world operates. I mean, I don't like gravity when I'm falling out of an airplane, but you can count on it operating that way.

And because men view the personal world and working world as different, the natural laws of one world don't necessarily apply to the other. It is as if, for example, one world has regular gravity (you drop a pen and it falls to the ground), where the other world doesn't—so you drop a pen and it floats.

Men's perceptions of the natural laws of the working world and the personal world are just as distinct, and seemingly just as enduring. As Richard, the financial advisory group president, pointed out, "If you understand the rules and follow them, all the moving parts work. There's no incentive to stop doing this."

There's also, in a man's mind, a strong incentive to *keep* doing this: He knows the perception he'll encounter if he doesn't. But when women bump up against these perceptions, they are often surprised by men's negative reactions.

Two-thirds of men on the national survey believe that talented professional women sometimes do things to damage their perception among men. Some of the most common examples shared were words and actions that probably seemed harmless, but led to reactions like these (you can see all the reactions at TheMaleFactor Book.com):

- "In talking about her personal life, she means well—she's trying to connect with the team. But she doesn't realize she's actually coming across as unprofessional."

- "[Veering from working world rules] from time to time is one thing, but when they are characterized by it, it may hurt their perception of being considered strong and confident."

- "The other department managers are also male, except for the HR manager. We see [how she handles certain things] and it drives us crazy."

- "It completely undermines what she is trying to do."

By contrast, the men seemed to really appreciate the women who *did* understand the perceived rules, and followed them. As one survey-taker put it, "Keep up the good work. My female peers 'get it,' and I enjoy working with them."

I'm not suggesting that a man's expectations and perceptions are right or wrong, or that women need to change the way they work to adapt to them. But it is in our best interest to understand what they are. I also think it is important to understand the inner wiring in a man that leads to those expectations in the first place.

A MAN'S INNER WIRING

Men's beliefs about how the working world should operate seem to arise from three facts about how men's brains are wired, and how they relate to other males from childhood.

1) The Male Brain Naturally "Compartmentalizes"

As I'll discuss more in chapter 5, the male brain finds mental multitasking difficult, and is set up to naturally compartmentalize emotions, thoughts, and sensory inputs—whereas the female brain is the other way around. That is a simple summary of what is actually a complex truth.

In our book *For Men Only*, my husband and I compared a woman's thought life to a personal computer with multiple windows open at a time. Most women know what it is like to be aware of, thinking about, or actually doing many things at once, and can transition seamlessly back and forth between personal and work tasks. Neuroscientists have discovered that anyone's ability to multitask like this depends in large part on the amount and type of connectivity along the corpus callosum, the main superhighway between the left and right hemispheres of the brain. A 1999 *Journal of Neuroscience* study demonstrated that the influence of estrogen gives women far more of that connectivity, and thus a superior ability and predisposition toward thinking about and doing many things at once.[2] The downside to being able to manage all those open windows, however, is that most women (81 percent according to my survey) have a hard time "closing out" thoughts that are nagging them.

Most men, by contrast, find all those multiple windows exhausting just to think about. A man's thought life is more like a computer with one window open at a time—he works on it, closes it out, and then opens another. And he usually has no trouble "closing out" thoughts that are bothering him. (Hence the tendency for a man to tell his wife, "Just don't think about it"—advice that may seem easy to him but feels impossible for her.) In other words, he is far more predisposed to compartmentalize—and better at it.

Brain scientists have discovered that a person's tendency to compartmentalize stems largely from fewer connections within their corpus callosum superhighway, as well as its unique makeup. According to researcher Rita Carter and neuropsychologist Christopher Frith in *Mapping the Mind*, the corpus callosum is 25 percent smaller in men than in women.[3] Further, a team of Israeli fetal researchers found that the in-utero influence of testosterone decreases the growth of nerve connections between the hemispheres, making mental multitasking much more difficult.[4] But what men gain from their brain structure is a superior ability to compartmentalize and deeply process various functions and thoughts without being distracted.

Neuropsychiatrists at the University of Pennsylvania have found that within the corpus callosum, men have far more gray matter (where thinking and functioning occurs) than women, where women have far more of the connecting white matter used to send those thoughts from one area of gray matter to the next. As a result, men's thoughts are more isolated—less interconnected and more compartmentalized. As Dr. Raquel E. Gur explained in the 1999 study, this promotes an extreme ability to concentrate within any one mode of thinking or functioning, without being distracted by a connection to another type of thought.[5]

In other words, men's tendency to segregate "personal" and "work" is something they do automatically without thinking about it—both because their brains are structured for it, and because their brains *aren't* structured to bounce thoughts back and forth easily. And as you'll see, that affects almost everything about how men think, feel, and process information. I have seen two different *ways* that they compartmentalize personal and work thoughts.

> *Men's tendency to segregate "personal" and "work" is something they do automatically without thinking about it, in part due to their brain structure.*

MEN TEND TO SEPARATE THEMSELVES AND THEIR PERSONAL FEELINGS FROM THE JOB

One executive brought up a perfect illustration of how completely men separate themselves and their personal feelings from the job (or at least try to), by drawing on his memory of the old Looney Tunes short cartoons. In the cartoons, Ralph Wolf and Sam Sheepdog walk to work, chatting personably ("Morning, Ralph!" "Morning, Sam!"), clock in, and take up their positions. When the work whistle blows, Ralph and Sam clash and fight each other intensely—Ralph's job is to try to steal and eat the sheep, and Sam's is to protect them. They try to blow each other up, bash each other on the head, and so on. But when the lunch whistle blows, they stop in mid-bash, go companionably to share a meal, and then, stretching and yawning, return to their positions with Sam's hand clenched around Ralph's throat.

The executive I spoke with pointed out that this is precisely how men view life: They completely distinguish between personal and business; one has little or no effect on the other.

One man in the broadcasting industry gave me a real-world version of Ralph and Sam—a story that I have heard, in essence, from many other men.

> There's a guy, Bob, that I used to work with. He was at Network A and when one of the key players there moved on to the CEO position at Network B, he brought Bob along to see if he could take a crack at transitioning to a new type of sales. He and Bob had worked together for several years and were good friends.
>
> A year later, he fired Bob because he just wasn't measuring up to expectations. Bob wasn't selling enough; he'd come from the cable world and the new network was in broadcast television, and he just couldn't make the transition. Now, the thing is: Bob and the CEO continue to be the closest friends. They go on vacations together. I just saw Bob recently and he and his wife had just come back from a visit to the CEO's beach house in Florida.

I met the man who told me this at a restaurant with his wife. She owns a thriving retail store herself. She told me, "I've had to fire people several times, and have been fired myself . . . and I can't imagine still wanting to be close friends afterward. I don't know how he does it."

Her husband just shrugged. "Obviously, Bob didn't take it personally. He may have disagreed that he wasn't measuring up to expectations, but reasonable people can disagree. A lot of this has to do with an ability to compartmentalize. And that comes with experience. When Carly Fiorina was fired from HP, I don't think it was because the board didn't like her. And I'm sure she didn't take it personally. When you get higher up, you understand the mentality and understand the whole business process. How things work and how executive management works and thinks. The more experienced you are, the more you compartmentalize."

In other words, this executive assumed that the more experienced and astute you were in business, the more you would compartmentalize this way. And that the less you did so, the less "businesslike" you were. As I listened, I couldn't help but think to myself, *I wonder what he would say if I told him compartmentalization has more to do with brain structure than with experience.*

AT WORK, THE PERSONAL WORLD GOES AWAY

To many men, once they have crossed the bridge into Work World, it is as if Personal World has vanished into the mist during the workday. Here is how Ben, an experienced headhunter, put it:

> When a working mom is at work she knows where her kids are, knows what the kids are doing, knows that they are OK and continues to operate just fine with these multiple tracks going inside her head simultaneously. And it is one of the

same things that makes women such extraordinarily good multitaskers in their jobs.

Men, on the other hand . . . well, let me just say that while I'm sitting here at work, I have to almost go into a different world in my mind, even to tell you my daughters' names. There is this whole other world that I am in. There are pieces of that that are healthy, because that's how we as men can get stuff done. But there are other pieces of that that obviously aren't so good, and that we know can cause us lots of trouble.

2) The Male Brain Becomes Ultrafocused

In addition to completely removing or compartmentalizing his personal world and personal feelings, a man also has a greater ability to become hyperfocused on whatever project he's working on. This is also due to his brain structure and hormone mix, and it has two relevant effects.

EVERYTHING ELSE GETS SCREENED OUT—AND THAT FEELS GREAT

Neurologists speculate that being able to function in a hyperfocused state was necessary for men to survive as ancient hunters. Most men I spoke with described the ability to go into this focused state as important for their productivity. And that is understandable, given their relative inability to multitask effectively. They go into "the zone," where they are intensely focused on one thing at a time; everything else gets screened out. That sense of intense focus feels good to them. In a minor way, it can provide the same sort of high that men would get from a postexercise endorphin rush.

However, the downside is that a man can also miss or screen out things that shouldn't be overlooked, things that may be important for good management in the working world. It may be an actual decision to screen out something the man thinks of as "personal feelings" or "extraneous," or it may be that he's so focused on Project A that he's missing the impact of that on Project B (or on Person B).

The chief financial officer (CFO) of a Fortune 500 manufacturer put it this way:

> Men tend to look back and say, "Oh, shoot, there were victims along the way." Honestly, we can be oblivious to all the other things going on. But it's not a lack of care. Not at all. You're trained as a kid that winning is everything. You get your competitive juices flowing and you hurt the other guy—or yourself—and you literally don't even notice.

That sort of miss-everything-else focus is not at all unusual for men. Thus, at times, what may look like insensitivity or even callousness may actually be a simple function of brain anatomy.

ANYTHING THAT INTERRUPTS A MAN'S NATURAL FOCUS IS DISPROPORTIONATELY DISRUPTIVE TO HIM

While being intensely focused feels great to a man, and allows him to be productive, *not* being able to intensely focus feels not only unproductive, but disruptive and disconcerting. Uninvited interruptions or a switching of direction—whether personal or work-related—can be incredibly frustrating.

It was telling that when I showed two software executives—David and Gregg—the "Personal/Work World" graphic on page 38, they immediately seized on this interruption issue:

DAVID: I love my wife and daughter. But if either of them call me during the day, it is a real distraction. I will have to expend extra effort to get back into work mode. And I will expend extra effort that I wouldn't otherwise have to spend. Men have limited capacity to deal with uninvited distractions, and I just lost some of my capacity right there.

GREGG: It's not that with this intrusion you've lost the connection to the work world. That's not it at all.

DAVID: It's that there's this other thought open in your mind that prevents you from being 100 percent efficient.

GREGG: Yesterday was a good example of this. In the morning, my wife asked if I could go run by the house over lunch and drop the dog at the vet. She didn't think it was a big deal; it is over lunch, after all. But now until that's resolved—such as "I got the dog and I'm back"—somewhere out there when I start the day, I know that at noon I'm going to have to take an hour and go get the dog. Just having that open thought in the back of my mind is disruptive. A guy wants to work at 100 percent productivity for 100 percent of the time. And that distraction, that open thought, means that there exists in his day a portion where he is working at 70 percent of capacity. Or 30 percent or 0 percent. It's suboptimal.

3) Men Strive to Protect Themselves from Emotional Pain

Men are far more sensitive to being hurt than most women realize. In many ways, a man's tough or unemotional façade exists to cover a vulnerable interior that he feels a strong need to protect. And as we'll explore in later chapters, most men don't feel as natural or adept at handling their emotions as women do.

Men's business-world rules flow naturally from their stark compartmentalization of the working world and personal world. But they are not just compartmentalizing because they can—they instinctively compartmentalize because they also feel a need to do so, to protect themselves.

One man I know, Eddie, had a tough time, emotionally, when his consulting contract with a good friend was unexpectedly terminated. He was a complete contrast to the story I told earlier about the broadcast salesman who continued to vacation with the boss who had fired him. A mutual friend explained why Eddie was so deeply affected:

Eddie really pours himself into things. He puts his heart out there. That is why most other guys set up this idea of these two different worlds, business and personal. What wounded Eddie was his level of expectation. His boss was a close friend before and during the whole contract. I'm guessing Eddie allowed himself to feel like it *wasn't* just business. It *was* personal. And that's when it hurts. If Eddie had been just an arm's-length consultant, when they terminated his contract he would have said, "It's business," and moved on.

From a guy's perspective, it is totally self-protective to have these "It's business" rules, because once you make it personal it hurts so much. Guys know we don't do personal things as well as we want to; we know that with our families when personal issues come up, it's complex and confusing. So business is almost a sanctuary or oasis away from those jumbled emotions. And when we let the two worlds intersect we are in grave danger of not only impacting the efficiency of the business, but our ability to do it well, and to *survive* business emotionally. If you lay your heart out there you'll get crushed. Business is cold and hard and people don't usually have your personal interests at heart—they *can't* have your personal interests at heart! So when you allow yourself to get personal, you put yourself in grave danger.

"From a guy's perspective, it is totally self-protective to have these 'It's business' rules, because once you make it personal it hurts."

Men didn't formulate or subscribe to the "It's not personal" rules of the business world because they as men have no emotion. They created them, in part, because emotion is so hard for them to handle.

TWO POSSIBLE PATHS; TWO POSSIBLE PERCEPTIONS

In my interviews, it seemed as if men in the workplace look at everyone they work with and mentally place everyone in one of two camps:

- Those who remember which world they are in and operate accordingly

- Those who don't appear to remember that they are in Work World, and at times operate as if they are in Personal World

If they see someone operating within the rules of the working world, they view that person one way; if they see them as bringing in the rules that govern personal life in the personal world, they view them another, more negative way.

If You Are Perceived as Operating by Personal World Rules at Work . . .

Anyone who is seen as not remembering what world they are in—man or woman—will be viewed negatively. But a cold hard fact is that the vast majority of the men I spoke with felt that men rarely mixed up their worlds, where women did so regularly. Not that *most* women did so, but that most of those who did so were women.

In fact, it is worth noting that the rare man who was seen as taking things personally or getting emotional at work, for example, was viewed more harshly than a woman doing the same thing. One man grimaced and said, "If men see a man take something really personally, we might not say anything, but we'll think, *There's something really wrong with that guy.* We might get frustrated with a woman who does it, but we won't think she's a bit 'off.'"

That said, the men tended to view someone operating at work by Personal World rules in one or more of the following ways.

"THAT PERSON LACKS SELF-CONFIDENCE AND SELF-ESTEEM"
Look at this telling quote from Norm, a finance executive:

> It's not just women who take things too personally. I have seen it in men every now and then too, and it sabotages their careers. It shows they lack self-confidence and self-esteem. The women who are successful have self-confidence enough to say "This isn't about me; it's about the task we have to perform." They realize it's actually about the *other* person and that person's perception: "So Bob didn't like this particular proposal; well, a hundred other people might like it. But Bob is the boss, so I accept it and move on."

"THAT PERSON IS DEFENSIVE AND INSECURE"

Look at this representative comment from one of the men I interviewed: "Women take things more personally and that drives their actions and reactions. To me, it looks like this constant, 'I've got something to prove; I've got to show you I'm in charge,' thing. It makes them look like it's not about taking actions to get their work done, but more about showing 'I'm in charge and I've got the power!'"

"THAT PERSON IS MORE EMOTIONAL, LESS STABLE, AND LACKS SELF-CONTROL"

Men frequently associated those who took things personally and broke other Work World rules with "being emotional." And that has a host of negative repercussions in terms of how they view someone, as I'll discuss in more detail in chapter 5.

> *Men frequently associated those who took things personally and broke other Work World rules with "being emotional."*

"THAT PERSON IS NOT A TEAM PLAYER"

Here is how Norm, the finance executive, put it:

> Business is like the military. If you can get with the mission, and take the hill and convince people to follow you, you'll be successful. But to do that, you have to take your whole personal self out of it. That is what boot camp does—it takes yourself out of the equation. Like the military, business needs to be a *team* sport to succeed.

Over and over again, I heard men carefully suggest that women frequently did not come across as team players—which puzzled me since, empirically, women tend to be more collaborative than independent. It took me forever to realize that the "not a team player" perception was arising from something as innocuous as not "taking your whole personal self out of it."

"THAT PERSON IS NOT MATURE, SOPHISTICATED, OR BUSINESS-SAVVY"

Fundamentally, someone who doesn't adhere to the perceived natural laws of the working world isn't seen as "businesslike." Here, for example, is what one senior partner at a worldwide accounting and consulting firm said about gossiping:

> Among men, there's a bit of an unwritten rule. If a man passes on unsubstantiated information he says, "I don't know if this is true, but you might want to look at it." Or the man would be more likely to go to the source and deal with something directly. Whereas some women will talk around the office. But it is not very business savvy to do that. It is human nature to think, *If I've got goodies, I want to share them*, but it is a sign of maturity when you don't have to share.

THE CONSEQUENCES OF BEING SEEN AS LESS SECURE, MORE EMOTIONAL, AND NAIVE

Not surprisingly, any or all of those negative perceptions of an employee could undermine or sidetrack his or her career. Geoff, the Fortune 500 CMO, offered a useful perspective on this.

> A woman who doesn't understand how men think won't necessarily get herself into a fix—but she'll get herself into

the neutral zone. She won't get into the club. Men are inherently defensive about things by nature. So they put certain people in the neutral zone, and are always defensive around them, and that's not a good place to be.

If you're thought to be high maintenance, if your behavior is not predictable, if someone's not sure where you'll come out, or thinks you could cause a fuss; if you don't get the silent code, if you're not a team player . . . it all gets you into the neutral zone. You will not be sought out or you'll be marginalized, even if you're smart. This happens to women much more than men, simply because men tend to instinctively understand what they did that caused that perception, and then they either self-correct, or know they have to get out.

The thing is, the woman may still get good reviews—her reviews will be neutral or even positive. She reads this as mixed signals and a guy wouldn't. He would *know* he has to move.

But actually . . . since women have better sensitivity, they can read the danger signals even better than men *if* they know what to look for.

I asked Geoff what he thought women should look for. What are those danger signals?

It depends on the type of man who is giving the signals. It could be anything from a lack of warmth to never seeking your opinion, to belittling you. I saw one man solicit an opinion on a new advertisement. He asked several members of his team . . . Bob? . . . Julie? . . . Penny? Penny said, "Use full color." And the man totally ignored her, and said, "Bob, coming back to you . . ." He is sending a clear signal, and anyone who knows what's good for them will begin to avoid her. It's a very Asian custom.

If he sends even stronger signals, he could be subtly belittling her, saying, "When we want to get to that we will." He's hoping she'll get the hint and leave. The problem comes when she doesn't. If she sees the signal, she should go to him and say, "You know, I'm interested in this other opportunity in the sales department. Can you help?" If he says, "Sure!" that's her next signal.

When you get the first signals that your opinion isn't valued, there's time to repair the damage, or at least to switch to a different position. Once you feel belittled, it's time to leave the company.

We had to coach one woman on my team because she's brilliant, fast, and highly effective, but she scared the hell out of people. But she read "the signals" early and was open to coaching and totally changed. And her new rankings shot through the roof, from below average to the top 1 percent.

WHEN PEOPLE STAY IN WORK WORLD . . .

Despite the many examples of women mixing the rules of the personal and business worlds, it was encouraging to hear the many examples men told me of female colleagues who were perfectly in tune with the expectations of the working world. It was also interesting to see the high degree of gratitude and respect that those women engendered.

As a national sales director named Louis put it:

I have ten very talented women working for me, and two of the ten do not let these things [such as taking things personally] become an issue. As a result, they are extraordinarily valuable to me. I always know what I'm going to get, and

I can trust them completely. When women can both bring their skills to the table *and* eliminate the subconscious unknowns or discomfort that many men have when working with women—just from the unpredictability of it—they are viewed as among the most valuable employees in any business.

> "The women who do not let these things become an issue are extraordinarily valuable to me. I always know what I'm going to get, and I can trust them completely."

One very successful and wealthy businessman put it this way:

Some women have a tendency to make it about *them*, rather than recognizing it is about business. But when women look at [a problem or issue] as "What's the essence of this and how does it impact the business," rather than "How does it impact me," they rise to the top.

CHAPTER 4

The "Natural Laws" of the Working World

As we saw in the last chapter, the mental construct of Work World comes with its own set of "natural laws"—expectations of how that world functions. These are not "tried and true tips for how business works best," as much as they are part of a deep, instinctive belief that "this is just how it *is*," and that ignoring the natural laws of the business world would be as foolish as expecting the physical law of gravity to be suspended when you step off your roof.

Although I am focusing on the fact that these expectations are instinctively shared by most men, many female readers will recognize that experienced businesswomen frequently share many of them as well.

So what are these specific expectations of the working world?

The rules that men view as the inescapable laws of gravity in the working world are based on one overriding principle: Everything that happens at work must advance the business and one's role and tasks within it as effectively as possible. As one executive put it:

> In one's personal life, if your wife or girlfriend or child is upset, you listen as long as they need. At work, efficiency and effectiveness dominate. In my personal life, those don't necessarily

dominate—it's not about what I can get accomplished, and how quickly and how well. I'm willing to listen and spend time on things that don't produce something—although you could say that they produce a happy wife and thus a happy home life. But at work, I've got to get these certain things done. Period.

Again, most men don't expect employees or colleagues to change their core values or personality to fit the working world (although, to be honest, some do). They simply expect that they and everyone else at work will behave consistent with the rules of the working world, *not* those of their personal world.

And even when a man shows friendly, caring behavior at work that might otherwise be seen as Personal World behavior, that isn't necessarily the case. Often, the man has simply decided to apply personable behavior for a business purpose.

One business owner, who I'll call Jim, explained how this works. I've known Jim personally and professionally for years. One of my close friends—a single mom—is his "right hand" person and loves working for him. Here is what he said about how "personable" behavior doesn't mean "personal rules" are in play:

JIM: It's not that men are brutal and everything's business and you steamroll over people. But when you're at work, you're in a different world. And the rules are different.

ME: But you are nice at work, right? I've done projects with you, and you're very pleasant and caring. I'd say that was being personal. For example, I heard that Sara just missed a big deadline because her son was sick. You didn't yell at her, did you? You treated her kindly and with concern even though her missed deadline is bad for business. Isn't that being personal?

JIM: I'd say it's being sensitive. When I treat Sara nicely am I being personal? No, I'm not. Being personal would mean taking time with her to sympathize and find out what went wrong with her little boy, and checking back on how it's going with the family. And generally showing interest in her problem that is non-work-related.

I didn't do that. What I did do was use a strategy that I believe to be sound business to keep her happy, motivated, and productive, so that our shared business goals can be achieved. I do care about her as a person, but my interest at work is in not impeding her productivity or contribution to the business. She's valuable and I need to keep her productive, so I'm "nice" to her—that's just good business.

The guy who screams at her has similarly made a business decision to engage her with a strategy that he believes will serve the purposes of the business. In my opinion, he has a flawed strategy that is likely to be counterproductive. But he apparently thinks that it will whip her into shape.

Neither approach is personal. It's all about business, executed with different strategies.

ME: I just don't believe the screamer is thinking about it as a good business strategy at that point in time. I think he's just furious.

JIM: I agree, sort of. It is a strategy or a style that he's developed for better or worse over the years. It's not necessarily thought out or the subject of careful reflection at that moment. But it is still manifested for reasons that he ultimately thinks will advance the business. Otherwise, he wouldn't have developed and continued with that style.

ME: But would you ever treat someone unkindly for business reasons?

JIM: If I ever did, it would be because I was having a bad day; not because it was a business decision. And then it *would* be personal, it *would* be operating according to the rules of the personal world, where you let your emotions get the better of you. It would be wrong and regrettable not just because it goes against a value I have of treating people well, but also *because* it was letting personal circumstances impact what was best for business.

THE LAWS OF GRAVITY

So what are the "laws of gravity" that men believe govern the working world? I do not present them in any particular order of importance—because men believe they all exist and are all equally inescapable. Also, just because men believe these are "the rules" of business doesn't mean that they always follow them perfectly themselves! But these *are* the standards they believe they and everyone else should live up to.

1. One Can Never Take Things Personally

In your personal world, you can take things personally. In Work World, men believe, you don't take things personally—because whatever is going on with you is not about *you*. It's about the business.

> *In Work World, men believe, you don't take things personally—because whatever is going on with you is not about you. It's about the business.*

My "core question" in all my interviews and on the survey was, essentially, "Is there anything that you've seen talented women do that undermines their effectiveness with men, simply because the women don't realize how it is being perceived?" If the answer was yes, I would ask the man to elaborate. And one of the five most common things I heard in my research was: "Women sometimes take things too personally."

The CEO and COO of a well-known $5.5 billion organization, leading thousands of employees and a massive external distribution network, had a unique perspective on this. For years, the organization had rolled along without well-defined performance measures or a modernized system for employee evaluations. Marty, the CEO, had brought in a new chief operating officer (COO) to change that. The COO, Ronald, had come from another household-name company with an excellent system of performance measurement and review, and had spent the previous year applying it to the new environment.

I interviewed Marty and Ronald together. When I asked them if there was anything women might do that undermines their effectiveness, they glanced at each other with raised eyebrows.

MARTY: It's probably most apparent to me in performance reviews. This has been a real struggle for us, because we're trying to be nice, but we are putting some pretty strict performance metrics in place, to be able to measure what we do from an organizational perspective. It's a tool that enables me to do a performance evaluation with you and quantify why I am rating you a certain way.

RONALD: In this past year when we have gone to the updated performance review process, the men have been a piece of cake. But I have struggled with the women. Marty works with several senior women on the executive team, and he struggles too. When we tell employees what they need to improve, the men just hear, "You did not do what we needed you to do. What will you do to get better?" When we work with the women, we can have the same data in front of us, but all the women seem to be hearing is, "We do not like you."

MARTY: The men may say, "Well, I disagree with you about that." Or, "That's fine." Then they walk away and it's over. It's not really that way with the women, even the senior women.

RONALD: This carries over beyond performance reviews, too. The men have a tendency to take things less personally. It's all about the business. We can disagree, we can argue and fight, but when we walk out of the room it is over. I have seen that dealing with the women, there is a lot of carryover. It is more personal. Even when we are discussing business, I see women carrying it over a lot more than the guys.

TAKING THINGS "TOO PERSONALLY" IS BAD FOR BUSINESS
The men I spoke with were very direct about their belief that anyone taking things "too personally" was bad for business—and that, unfortunately, most of those who did so were women. Here are just two of the dozens of examples that I heard:

THE OWNER OF AN ADVERTISING COMPANY

This week, I told one of my midlevel staff that she had to speed up. I should explain that a lot of our deadlines are like dominoes, with everyone depending on everyone else meeting deadlines so all the moving parts mesh. All our staff know they are measured by three things: how well they do on client visits, on the content of their projects, and turning things in on time. She was doing two of these three really well for how experienced she was.

I had to tell her that one of the three was below standard and

we'd missed a client deadline; and in the past that client had specifically told us their deadlines were not negotiable. I had to tell her
that she had made us miss a deadline with that particular client. So
when I spoke to her, I told her we had a single problem: You have
to speed up.

But I could just sort of tell that she was not hearing "You need
to speed up." She was hearing "You've failed, you've let me down,
this isn't working, I'm disappointed in you." I'd said: "You need to
speed up."

Now, I could see this happening and so I had to circle back
around and tell her, "I need to be sure you know I'm only saying
this one particular thing." But I could tell she was wounded and I
couldn't get her to focus and hear exactly what I was saying.

The moment she took it all personally the meeting went out the
window. I was trying to move to ongoing strategy and I never got
there. I was *trying* to get to the next step of saying, "Here are some
ideas on speeding up," but I never got there because in my view
she took the whole thing personally.

She apparently cried after I left the room. And I had to tell the
other partners, "I met with her, but she wasn't able to hear what I was
saying, and I don't think it's going to make any real difference."

"*I* was trying to get to the next step of saying
'Here are some ideas for improvement,' but
I never got there because in my view she took
the whole thing personally."

A SENIOR PARTNER AT A WORLDWIDE CONSULTING COMPANY

On our team this year we had two women who had not been working together particularly well. One of the women, a specialist we really needed, gave notice that she was resigning, and the other senior woman on the team assumed the resignation was because of her and jumped to the conclusion that she would be held accountable.

But the consequence of that was that she began a big defense campaign that she wasn't responsible. And she was so annoyed with the woman for leaving and interpreted it as a slight against her, that she didn't talk to her for three weeks.

It looked so bad for her that she made a mountain out of a molehill. Even worse, it turns out that we had had a chance to convince the specialist to stay on, but we lost it because the other woman wouldn't return her phone calls. So of course the specialist drew huge conclusions about that and was extremely annoyed by it.

Why couldn't the senior woman have just said what a guy would have said? Something like, "These things happen, and I think you're making a mistake, but we wish you well." But the senior woman made it about *her.*

A banking executive, Niles, had just had to fire a key female manager the day before I spoke with him. When he told me that she had a hard time not taking it personally, I asked, "How can someone *not* take it personally?"

Niles answered, "Because it is about your work, not about who you are. It is not that I dislike you as a person. You may be a wonderful person, have a great sense of humor, and be great to work with. But you have to recognize that for the assignments that you were given, they were not up to the standards that have been set for you and for your organization."

Having spent years hearing how much a man's identity is tied up in what he does, and in his ability to provide for his family, I told Niles I would have expected men to take it *more* personally if they were fired. He responded, "There is an element of taking it personally even for men. A little bit. Because you are what your work is. But I *have* been fired, and I would then tell myself, well, I may not have given it my best effort. Or I did, but I was a square peg in a round hole, and just wasn't able to deliver up to expectations. After all, if I was hired by NASA to launch a rocket, regardless of how hard I tried I wouldn't be able to do it, because I didn't have the skill set or experience. There are any number of reasons why someone might receive a poor evaluation. It's got to do with that person's skills, abilities, interests, and their desire to do a good job. But for whatever reason that person may just be in over their head, for lack of a better term. And as long as his boss doesn't get personal and critical and mean, a man generally won't take it personally. He might go home and get upset and talk to his wife, but he won't take it personally at work."

Niles's comment points out a common (and eye-opening) distinction: In a man's mind, you can be quite upset about the situation itself, and yet still not take it personally.

All this said, despite the men's overwhelming unanimity on this point, I believe that men's assurance that they "never take things personally" sounds better in theory than it sometimes works in practice. As I'll describe in a later chapter, I have found that there are certain things that men are *more* likely to take personally than women. Yet that doesn't negate the primary point that they expect people in the workplace to take nothing personally, and look askance at those who do.

2. You Essentially Become Your Position

Another of the perceived natural laws of the business world is that a job-holder is essentially seen as a temporary holder and custodian of his or her position—a position that, in most cases, exists independent of the person, and will be there after they leave. What that is supposed to mean can be outlined as follows:

- As cold as it sounds, it is the position that is critical to the company, even more than the individual person.

- The position-holder is supposed to do what is best for that position and the company, not necessarily what is best for the individual as a person.

- The position-holder is supposed to live up to the responsibilities of that position even when the individual doesn't like those responsibilities very much.

Most companies claim (and usually believe) that their greatest strength is their people—the individual people who fill all those boxes on the org chart and pour themselves and their personal passion or interest or talents into their work. However, the fact remains that when Company ABC needs a salesperson, or a vice president of marketing, or a programmer in the IT department, they are trying to find the best person to fit a particular position or role. The position usually *does* exist independent of the person.

As a result, in the eyes of the working world, when you get off the elevator in the morning or walk through the gate or company doors, you are, essentially, seen as a particular role as much as you are seen as an individual. Because of men's ability to compartmentalize, it is as if they see you as *two* entities: you, and the position you fill, and they are two different things.

YOU ARE EXPECTED TO DISTINGUISH BETWEEN YOURSELF AND YOUR ROLE

There are many cases in which applying your personal passion, knowledge, and skills will make your position stronger, add value, and make the company more effective and productive. But there will also be cases where you do not find yourself in alignment with the needs of your position within the company. In those cases, in accordance with the rules of the working world, you either do what the position demands or you leave and find another position. In other words, you must do what is best for the company according to your title or position, even when that isn't pleasant.

One man I interviewed is the founder and owner of a well-respected executive search firm that places C-level executives with Fortune 500 companies. Let me call him Cole. I've drawn on his insights in several of the following chapters, as his three decades in the executive search industry provided some unique insights. Here is the distinction he makes between himself and his job:

> I have fired a lot of people over the years. I am not particularly proud of that. I'm a very empathetic person, and it is, in some ways, always emotionally disconcerting to me. But it's one of the things that I have to do. I actually often picture myself sitting in another chair as a third party, directing a play. It is not Cole firing Shaunti. It is the president firing a vice president. It is the director firing a manager. If you've got a role, you've got to play the role, like a doctor has to remove a tumor or a dentist has to dig in the back of a mouth and pull the tooth. They've got bad jobs today. My job today is a bad job. I have to terminate somebody and I am not going to enjoy it. But that is my job today.
>
> So when I say it is "just business," it does not mean that I

do not care about you. The dentist undoubtedly cares about the person whose tooth is failing. And the doctor cares about the person whose tumor needs to be removed. But they have got a job to do and I do not let their concern for that person overshadow their responsibility.

If you are failing in your role, I have got a job to do too. And the job is to confront you in a way that either beneficially resolves your failure to perform, or that removes you from the organization so that your failure to perform does not create a broad spread failure of the entire organization.

*"So when I say it is 'just business,'
it does not mean that I do not care about you.
But I have got a job to do and I do not
let my concern for that person overshadow
my responsibility."*

As we continued this conversation, it became clear that this ability men have to set themselves outside or separate from their work role is another reason why men are able to take things less personally at work. While their personal identity is often closely tied up in their job; they can still choose to see challenges or criticism as being more about the *job* or the position, and less about them.

IF YOU HAVE TO CHOOSE, YOU SUBORDINATE YOUR
PREFERENCES TO THAT OF THE POSITION AND YOUR BOSS
There are times when a person's expectations and those for his or her position collide. And in such cases, the expectation of the working world is that employees fill the *role* to the best of their ability, rather than to do what *they*, personally, prefer or even think is best.

Let me give you an example from my own experience. At the Federal Reserve Bank of New York my job involved detailed analysis into the facts—as far as I needed to go to get the truth. Working with Japanese banks that (like many international institutions) didn't have the same standards for disclosure often put me in the position of being a kind of financial detective, trying to uncover and fit together facts that others would prefer to stay hidden. I often had short deadlines, and would work around the clock if necessary to do as much analysis as I felt was needed to understand what was going on and properly brief senior officials.

Later, however, when I moved to Atlanta and began working as an independent analyst for a consulting company, I found myself clashing with my employer. I was doing the same sort of work, but now I was billing my hours on projects that would earn my employer a fixed fee. My boss kept asking me to cut down my hours for a certain type of report. And I would respond, "If I'm going to do it right, it will take at least twenty-five hours to do this type of analysis."

He finally said, "You're not hearing me. I've bid a certain amount for this project. That is what the client will pay me, no matter how much time you take. If you keep billing me twenty-five hours for these reports, I'm going to *lose* money employing you. I need you to do the seventeen-hour version of this analysis. You may think what you're doing can't be done in under twenty-five hours, but I'm asking you to do a different type of analysis: the seventeen-hour version."

That's an example of how what I thought best as an experienced specialist clashed with my position, which was, when it came right down to it, to make money for the company, not lose it.

In my interviews with men, I heard dozens of examples of men becoming exasperated with an employee—almost always a female employee—who wouldn't stop arguing over something she found to be important. The men were puzzled and frustrated as to why these employees couldn't simply present their reasons for disagreement, register their opinion why it should be otherwise, and then accept and faithfully implement their boss's decision, even if it differed from their preferences.

Kevin, a national human resources director for a major consulting firm, told me that many of the people directly reporting to him were women. And many of those women were skilled and talented and had "strong personalities." Their personalities often served them well, but sometimes they drove the men they worked with crazy because they didn't see that by pushing back constantly they were breaking one of the cardinal laws of the business world:

> Men have these issues and concerns too, obviously, but they tend to be able to overlook them when they need to, or not let them affect the workplace as much. Women tend to have more difficulty looking past small issues. I've seen it many times; it is as if women have a harder time seeing gray; they want to see more black and white in every situation. They seem less likely to see ways of compromising. If they are working on a project team and their point of view is not the one that the team decides to pursue they may have a harder time accepting that and moving on and looking at the bigger issue. They tend to let smaller issues bother them and get in the way of accomplishing the bigger goal.

Now, what Kevin sees as a "difficulty in looking past small issues" may actually be a result of a woman's relative difficulty in closing out mental windows that are bothering her. And they are probably bothering her because she sees an unresolved issue that could come back to haunt the group or company later. When I asked the men how a woman should handle such a situation, the most common answer was to put her concerns in a short, clear e-mail so she can be sure her boss has heard her accurately and it is documented. But as one representative man put it, "Then you need to explicitly say 'but you're the boss,' and let it go. He has heard you, considered your point of view, and has made a different judgment call. You may disagree with it, but if he's the boss it is his call to make and you'll only hurt yourself by implying he's being stupid."

3. One Doesn't Make Business Decisions Based on Personal Factors

One rule that men feel governs the business world is widely known, but isn't always perfectly followed by either gender. It is, basically, that when you are at work you do not make business decisions based on factors that are considered "personal"—such as how you feel about someone as a person, circumstances outside the work world, or your emotional response to a particular person or situation.

Jackson, who ran a start-up company, described the basic premise this way:

> When I'm in business mode, I'm not operating out of the emotional sensibilities that I would be operating from in my personal life. I may be ticked off at you, but I can separate that out when I'm in business mode, for the good of the enterprise. Or I may think you're the best person around, but I can't let that feeling—which belongs on the personal side—dictate what I deem to be best for the business. In personal life, personal feelings matter. In business life, personal feelings shouldn't be a consideration, except to the degree that they are going to affect the business.
>
> My employees are very loyal and people seem to like working for me. So I hope I'm not an ogre. But still, I've got a family to provide for, so I'm not here to win a popularity contest. If anyone's feelings are going to get hurt, it's not going to be my wife's feelings because we're on food stamps.

Now, if being liked *helps* my job, I'm all for it. But otherwise, if by trying to be everyone's best friend it hurts my job or my business, that's gotta change.

> ▪ *"In business life, personal feelings shouldn't be a consideration, except to the degree that they are going to affect the business."*

Now, I have viewed many men as breaking this rule. I've seen the good ol' boy network at work, and have been frustrated by being left out of ostensibly personal outings at which work was discussed. I've seen business contracts awarded and decisions made based on what looked like outside personal relationships. And many of the men I interviewed talked about the importance of considering an employee's feelings and morale in the workplace.

To help me understand this apparent contradiction (and others), I set up a focus group of six experienced businessmen and two high-level women to talk through these issues. These individuals generously gave me a full workday to help me clarify a few concerns that had stymied me. On this particular subject, all the men were unanimous in saying that what I perceived as inconsistencies in men's actions and behaviors, weren't. Here is how they clarified this "rule":

- Factors that seem personal are usually deemed best for the business.

- You cannot change a decision based on purely personal factors—such as someone's feelings. You can, however, consider their effect when implementing your decision.

FACTORS THAT SEEM PERSONAL ARE USUALLY DEEMED BEST FOR THE BUSINESS

People who have been in business for any length of time have seen cases where they or others make business decisions based on personal affinity. For example, giving business to a subcontractor who is in your regular golf foursome, instead of conducting an open bid. Or moving Jackie into your department instead of Bob because you get along with her better. Or making a decision to cut back on benefits and expenses and trim everyone's salaries when losing a big client, instead of terminating multiple employees they've known for years.

When I raised those examples and others, the men pointed out that this "rule" of business—that you don't make decisions based on personal factors—*doesn't* mean "you always do a systematic study of every conceivable option to choose the best one." Each example that looked "personal" was still based on the ultimate principle of doing what the men thought would be best for the business, rather than what wouldn't be—even if it included going with the "easy" option (like employing someone you know and trust) instead of conducting a systematic search. In fact, sometimes what was "easiest" was viewed as what was best for business, because it allowed the person to devote limited time and resources to other decisions.

As the men saw it, a male boss wouldn't toss the subcontract to his golf buddy if he didn't feel the buddy would do a great job. Nor would he choose an employee just *because* she was easy to get along with, if she wasn't also extremely qualified. (The "getting along" part was deemed a business asset, because it would free up the boss's mental and emotional resources for other aspects of the business.) Similarly, the small company that refuses to lay off some of their employees when they lose a big client does so not because they personally like the people but because they believe business will turn around and there is a quantifiable business benefit to not having to rehire and train people.

Each factor that could be seen as "personal" still didn't trump—and in some cases actually advanced—the primacy of the business purpose in the men's eyes. And the men agreed that *if* anyone did allow a personal factor to trump a business purpose, they would definitely be viewed as non-businesslike, and would be breaking a core business expectation.

YOU CANNOT CHANGE A DECISION BASED ON PURELY PERSONAL FACTORS—SUCH AS SOMEONE'S FEELINGS. YOU CAN, HOWEVER, CONSIDER THEIR EFFECT WHEN IMPLEMENTING YOUR DECISION

Two-thirds of the men on my survey (and 71 percent of the male executives) believed that you cannot allow personal factors such as hurt feelings to *change* a business decision that you would have otherwise made. You can, however—and many guys said you should—consider personal factors when deciding how to *implement* the decision after it is made.

For example, if the best thing for the business is deemed to be shutting down a programming department and outsourcing to Asia, the men said one should not change that decision out of concern for the employees who will lose their jobs. But you can and should deal with the reality of how the news will *affect* employees, both out of a personal care for your people and due to other employees' morale, which is a very real component of business productivity.

4. You Get Business Done Despite Personal Factors

I'll go into this (and the next two rules) in more detail in later chapters. But another consequence of the way men compartmentalize the business world is that many men feel that personal issues aren't "allowed" to impact business. Obviously, in real life, it doesn't always work that way. A flu bug, for example, is unlikely to politely wait until your big sales conference is over. But the "natural law" expectation is there, regardless, and it has a host of implications, including the expectation that people will get the job done despite Personal World factors (divorce, family needs, depression, the storm putting a tree through your living room . . .).

> *Many men feel that personal issues aren't "allowed" to impact business. Obviously, in real life, it doesn't always work that way.*

5. Emotions in the Workplace Have to Be Related to the Business

Men brought up the subject of emotions in nearly every interview. It is so central that I've devoted an entire chapter to it (chapter 5).

In men's perceived "rules of the workplace" it is expected that people show emotions only when they are related to the business (and only infrequently then).

A man on my advisory team, Douglass, is in charge of an internationally known corporate-sponsorship group. Even though he seemed to be an exception in not minding certain emotions, he made an interesting comment about what emotions will *always* be viewed as inappropriate in the workplace:

> Even in a tough environment, I have seen women tear up and even some cry, and it has been totally fine. But it's been fine because it has been appropriate. In fact, if anything, in a right setting it can cause a man to think, "Oh man, what have I done?" and wake up a guy to the fact that he's not handling something right. Or like a time we had to fire a

woman here, and when we told her she teared up and had a rough time with it. But that was totally appropriate—she's losing her job; I don't expect her to be a robot.

When it is *not* appropriate, ever, is when a woman cries in the workplace over something that does not have anything to do with what is going on. Like when we are working on a deal, and the deal is falling apart and it has nothing to do with us and then somebody gets teary about that. Because honestly, some women tend to take things personally that should not be taken personally.

6. Conflicts Are Task-Specific and Should Never Carry Over and Become Grudges

Because people are filling a role or a position that is separate from them personally, even intense conflicts never carry over beyond the issue at hand. Think Ralph Wolf and Sam Sheepdog.

A majority of the men I spoke with brought up this issue as something they perceived that women handled very differently from men. One finance manager pointed to my diagram about "Personal World" and "Work World" and said something that I've heard, in essence, dozens of times:

I've been in meetings where I had heated disagreements with guys, and later that day, we're having a beer and talking about the game. The men went back to the personal side of the bridge. If a woman was heated, it would be much more difficult to go bowling later.

SENDING THE RIGHT SIGNALS

For better or for worse (probably for worse!), one of the most common denominators in the business arena is how easily men perceive someone as violating the rules of the working world—and thus being seen as "un-businesslike." And that perception is much more likely to apply to women, simply because women may not see the world and their actions in the same way that men do. We may add great value and yet inadvertently be doing things that leave a male colleague, boss, or client uncomfortable or frustrated.

So how do we avoid sending the wrong signals, and send the right ones instead? We may not necessarily agree with the men's advice, below, but if we know what it is we can make an informed decision. Here's what they suggested:

If Something Might Evoke Personal World, Don't Let a Man See It

One of the simplest tools for managing men's perceptions is to ask yourself: "Is this what a man would expect to encounter in Work World?" If the answer is no, the men I spoke with suggested, don't let men hear it or see it.

> *Ask yourself: "Is this what a man would expect to encounter in Work World?"*

Some of the best advice I received early on in my career was from an older, wiser female friend who had left a big company and had begun her own consulting practice. I was at her office late one Thursday afternoon, as we were getting ready to knock off work and head to a community theater rehearsal scheduled for that night, and all the next day. A fellow consultant called her to ask for input on a proposal. She told him, "Frank, I'm heading out to a meeting now and I'm in meetings all day tomorrow. I'll look at this over the weekend, and get back to you Monday."

As she put down the phone, she looked at me, and said, "Just so you know: Don't ever tell a man in business that you can't do something because of personal commitments. You're 'in a meeting.' He doesn't need to know that it is with your kids' dentist. If he does, he starts to think this irrational thing that you allow personal life to interfere with work. Don't even give him the opportunity to go there."

Every office has its own culture. But whenever you have a choice, it rarely hurts to err on the side of caution. When something as simple as seeing a woman apply lipstick at her desk can yank a man back into Personal World, it is worth being aware of it.

Force Yourself to Not Take Things Personally at Work

Women's brain structure may make compartmentalizing emotions and feelings less natural, but we can do it. The men suggested making whatever effort was necessary to take personal feelings entirely out of the equation. Try to mentally separate yourself from your position, or force yourself to respond calmly when you feel yourself getting upset. Remind yourself, "It's not about me; it's about the other person and their perception." Most of us need a place to vent at times. We can do that off-site, back in Personal World.

Don't Be Afraid to Apply the "Rules of the Working World" in Your Own Way

Men don't expect women to be exactly like them. If we are going to adapt to the perceived natural laws of the working world, we need to do so in a way that works for us, can be sustained over the long term, and allows us to respect ourselves in the process.

Geoff, the Fortune 500 CMO, gave this valuable piece of advice:

It is so important for women to understand how men communicate and think: how they tend to form clubs, and have their own language and expectations. For example, men are hunters. But don't try to break into their clubs and go hunting. *Don't try to look like them, but try to be perceived as compatible to them.* [Emphasis mine.] If five guys go to Bernie's Bar and you show up, it will look like you're trying too hard. If you happen to see them there, that's OK. But don't jump in with "How about those Packers?" Say "I notice the *Wall Street Journal* said such-and-such." It's a good icebreaker.

If you really want to play golf, don't insert yourself into their weekend game. Instead plan a golf tournament and invite them. And don't put yourself in their foursome. Give them a chance to see how good you are.

PERCEIVED AS EQUAL

It is important to emphasize *why* most men expect everyone—men and women—to function according to the same rules: It is because they view men and women equally. Their frustration with women who (they think) don't function according to the natural laws of Work World stems in large part from an egalitarian view. They expect women to approach the working world in ways that are no different than a man would.

Here is what Cole, the executive search founder, said:

There was a time, even fifteen or twenty years ago, when men expected women to approach them differently than other men would approach them. There was this expectation that if a man was going to say something, he would say it one way and a woman would say it in another way. There was kind of an old school viewpoint about it.

Today, I do not expect a woman to treat me any differently than I expect a man to treat me. I do not expect to be paternalistic toward a woman and I do not expect her to defer to me. That is what men expect; and that's a good thing.

> *"Today, I do not expect a woman to treat me any differently than I expect a man to treat me."*

You may or may not view men's working world expectations as correct or useful. But if you can recognize and use them as stepping stones to get to the top, you can be part of changing the culture in any way that you think it needs to be changed.

Once men see that their understanding of business isn't, in fact, the only way of seeing the business world, they, too, may become more adaptable—because they'll see it works. One of the most telling studies I've seen in recent years is the 2008 Catalyst study showing that companies with female board members were far more likely to see female employees rising through the ranks. While much of this is probably due to companies paying more attention to women's advancement, I'm sure that some of it is the cultural shift that takes place when women rise to the top, and demonstrate the business value and viability of their different perspectives.

CHAPTER 5

"She's Crying—What Do I Do?"

How Men View Emotions in the Workplace

After a meeting with a high-level female consultant about the topics addressed in this book, she sent me a small gift wrapped in funky paper. Inside was a notepad by cartoonist Leslie Murray with a snappy female character saying, "Laugh and the world laughs with you. Cry and men have no idea what to do."

I had to chuckle, because that observation has come across as all too true in my interviews and surveys of men in the workplace. And like many women, I have seen that reality in my own professional life—including in an unexpectedly difficult and emotional meeting I experienced a few years ago.

After *For Women Only* came out, I developed close working relationships with many national and international organizations that help families on the subject of marriage, speaking at their retreats or corporate meetings, appearing on television or radio broadcasts, and passing research back and forth. Early on, when a few female readers inaccurately spread the rumor that I was "laying all the blame for bad relationships on women" (instead of recognizing that I was simply explaining how men think, and had written the other side of the story in the men's book), one organization was particularly helpful in using its influence to distribute my research and correct that misunderstanding.

So when I was in their area some time back and several members of a small counseling working group wanted to meet with me, I willingly agreed. I was totally unprepared to be blindsided. In disbelief, I listened as several people I respected laid out a list of about twenty inaccurate accusations against my message, concluding, essentially, "You are laying all the blame for bad relationships on women." At the time, all I saw was people I respected accusing me of the same damaging misperceptions their organization had helped me correct.

It was a long and emotionally exhausting meeting, and I ended up angrily trying to defend myself, shedding tears—and then getting angrier that I was presenting myself so poorly.

Thankfully, in the months following the meeting we were able to trace the cause of the problem, correct those misperceptions, and restore the relationship. But for the next year, every time a man in one of my interviews brought up their private perceptions about a woman becoming "emotional," my mind would bounce uncomfortably back to that meeting. I now *knew* how it must have been perceived. In fact, several times I described that scenario to the men I interviewed, to get their perspectives—thoughts and advice I'll share later in this chapter.

I would guess that almost every woman has been in the mortifying situation of becoming "emotional" in a professional setting—and wishing that she could turn back time and do it differently. Or vanish into the floorboards.

In one interview, I was speaking with the vice president of human resources of a large technology company. When I asked him what women might unintentionally do that hurts their effectiveness with men, he laughed, and in one smooth move rolled his chair to the corner of his L-shaped desk, picked up a large box of Kleenex, rolled his chair back, and plonked the box down in front of me. "Do you see this box of Kleenex?" he asked, raising his eyebrows.

"If I only worked with men, there would be no box of Kleenex on my desk."

It is no surprise to women that men view emotion as inappropriate in a work setting. But most women don't realize just *what* men view as "getting emotional" in the first place (it's more than just crying), how negatively most men view it—or how positively they view a man or a woman who handles emotion and other interpersonal issues in ways they see as valid and constructive.

> Most women don't realize
> just what men view as "getting
> emotional" in the first place.

This issue of managing emotion was one of the top topics that came up in my interviews; men clearly thought that an inability to manage emotion well was a way talented women sometimes shot themselves in the foot. Yet these same men often commended women for their superior empathetic, listening, and interpersonal skills. In short, many men clearly saw the benefits of someone who was "relational" but not "emotional."

Are men really that uncomfortable with handling emotion and interpersonal issues at work and if so, why? How negatively do they view emotions in the workplace? What does "getting emotional" mean to men in the first place? How do men think emotions should be handled—and how can we manage perceptions of ourselves in this area?

"MEN HAVE DIFFICULTY COPING WITH WOMEN'S EMOTIONS AT WORK"

A male friend of mine gave me some context for this discussion. He told me, "Men have spent a lifetime mastering their own emotions—seeing them as inconvenient and counterproductive. We often even see them as capitulating to a side of ourselves that gets in the way of the logical side."

Some of the most fascinating interviews I conducted were with entrepreneurs who had hired a woman to run their business for them: essentially, a man hiring a woman to be his own boss. I came across a surprising number of these situations. One such entrepreneur, Paul, had hired a strong, no-nonsense woman, Jennifer, as his new president when his wireless telecom company hit a wall in its growth. He spent a large portion of our interview talking about her strengths. But when I asked him if there had been any bumps in the road that he viewed as being gender related, he brought up something that I heard over and over in many of my interviews—her "emotional side."

> At work, men have difficulty dealing with that emotional side from women. I think that is multiplied in a work environment even more than in a personal one, because when women show their emotions in a work environment, men perceive weakness. From our company's standpoint, with Jennifer being a strong-willed, emotional person, it is so easy for a man to view those emotions as negative, as weakness. When we see emotion, we automatically see it as, "You are not thinking."

I found that the assumption that "emotion" means "you are not thinking" is nearly universal among men, and often lends itself to a fear of emotion getting involved. In the interview above, Paul respected Jennifer enough to hire her as his superior in his company. So I asked him how he worked through his concern about her being "emotional." Did it ever make him wonder how she would handle his business? His reply:

Whenever I encounter that situation [emotion] I have to get into my logical side and try to keep in mind why I hired her; I mentally review her qualifications. I know she is extremely smart. And I know she is capable, despite the emotional side of things. I also force myself to recognize that her emotional capacity can be very positive, but it can also be a problem if it gets too far out. Which it has with Jennifer from time to time.

> I found that the assumption that "emotion" means "you are not thinking" is nearly universal among men.

WHY EMOTIONS AND INTERPERSONAL DYNAMICS ARE DIFFICULT FOR MEN

When faced with significant emotion, men often get a "deer in the headlights" look. With lesser interpersonal or emotional issues, they also have a tendency not so much to avoid them as to not notice them in the first place.

Why is that? Part of it has to do with the hardwiring of the brain.

The Shorthand Summary: Emotion Furs Up the Gears

As explained in the chapter 3, women are more hardwired for mental multitasking than men, whose mental default is to compartmentalize things. And nowhere is that more evident than in how men and women handle emotions. The multitasking female brain is wired to be able to process strong emotions and (up to a point) think clearly at the same time. But since the male brain is not wired to simultaneously process thoughts and feelings quite as easily, the presence of strong emotions makes it much more difficult for him to think clearly. And because men can't think as clearly when they are experiencing strong emotion, they assume women can't, either.

Let's look at the reasons for this in more detail.

THE MALE BRAIN HAS LESS INFRASTRUCTURE
TO HANDLE EMOTION

Being able to assimilate, understand, and talk about emotion requires an enormous degree of multitasking communication between different parts of the brain—especially between the left and right hemispheres, across the corpus callosum superhighway. And as noted in chapter 3, that structure is 25 percent smaller in a man than in a woman, with much less connecting white matter available to simultaneously process thoughts and other inputs—such as a surge of emotion.[1] Both factors limit the neural connections available for a man to process emotions quickly, and make the process slower. Instead, as noted earlier, men's larger amount of gray matter within the corpus callosum makes their brains ideal to process information in a more deliberate, sequential fashion.[2]

In a woman's brain, then, communication across hemispheres is a bit like an eight-lane superhighway; a woman has a lot of capacity to absorb and process an extra volume of "traffic" or input—both thoughts and emotions. Traffic moves quickly, and it takes a lot of traffic to clog things up, so in most cases she can process a relatively high degree of emotion and think clearly at the same time. In a man, however, the infrastructure is more like a major parkway with multiple built-in traffic stops to allow for extra thinking time. With either type of infrastructure, all the thoughts and emotions will eventually be processed, but a man's system can't handle the same amount of volume as quickly. As a result, a surge of emotions can fairly easily overwhelm a man's ability to think clearly, which is why men tend to instinctively shut down or set aside that emotional traffic to deal with later.

> *Because men can't think as clearly when they are experiencing strong emotion, they assume women can't, either.*

While this infrastructure puts men at a disadvantage when trying to process many thoughts and emotions at once, its deliberate pace gives male brains the advantage of processing everything more deeply, so that nothing is missed due to neurological distractions. Just as getting slowed down by rush-hour traffic gives you extra time to figure out the best way to handle that tricky nine a.m. client meeting.

EMOTION TRIGGERS THE NONTHINKING PART OF THE MALE BRAIN

When confronted with strong emotion, a man's brain, unlike a woman's, is predisposed to rely on an instinctive, nonthinking area of the brain. As Michael Gurian explains in his book *What Could He Be Thinking?*, "The male brain relies more heavily on brain-stem activity than does the female brain, especially during emotive experience."[3] Translated, that means that when a man is confronted with strong emotions in others or begins to experience them him-self, his brain activity often reverts back to the more primitive "nonthinking" area, the brain stem. The brain stem regulates ac-tivities that don't require thinking to function (like digestion) and is often called the "fight or flight" center that we all revert to in a crisis. But what is less recognized is that, according to a study by University of California psychologists, the male brain experiences a flood of strong emotions (like a crying woman) as a crisis—and thus jumps to the fight or flight center.[4]

This is another reason why the presence of emotion makes it difficult for a man to think clearly, and why they often feel a need to filter out emotion in order to think things through, make deci-sions, and get things done. (It is also one of the reasons why in relationships a woman can feel that a man goes into a sort of "fix-it mode" when she's describing an emotional problem. She wants her feelings to be heard. He, on the other hand, instinctively recognizes that her feelings will impair his ability to help her deal with the problem [which is what he thinks she wants], so he automatically compartmentalizes them to remove them from the equation.)

When a man (at work or home) must deal with emotions di-rectly, his adrenal system kicks his brain into a higher gear to handle the instinctive demands and anxiety of experiencing, thinking, and talking about those emotions and the reason for them. But as with any activity requiring an adrenaline surge, the completion of that task and the letdown of adrenaline often bring a disproportionate sense of weariness. Which is presumably why so many men describe emotions as "exhausting."

In my interview with Cole, the executive search leader I men-tioned in chapter 4, he focused most of his comments on this issue of men's perceptions of emotion and interpersonal interactions in the workplace. (Cole was unusual for a man in having a high ca-pacity to process emotions, and I quote him several times in this chapter.) At one point, while discussing the large number of men who feel emotions are a "waste of time," he added:

> It's not just the time, it's not the minutes, it's the energy. I am not a typical guy in some ways—I have high "feminine" scores for qualities like empathy. But even for me, emotions take a *lot* of energy. There is only so much energy that a person has during the day. For men there is nothing more draining than being in a spontaneous, unexpected emotional situation. A man's adrenaline has to kick into high gear to handle it. And so if it's a big emotional thing, we go from being very, very energized to being just exhausted when the adrenaline wears off. To a lesser degree, every single emotional encounter during the day creates a little of that exhaustion. It taps whatever energy resources we've got. And this is coming from a guy who tries to get other guys to realize that emotions can be a good thing.

MEN'S NEURAL PATHWAYS ARE MORE LIKELY TO BYPASS EMOTIONAL CENTERS

Women who feel themselves getting emotional at work or in a meeting may wonder how the men in the room are able to *not* get emotional, to stay emotionally detached. Much of the reason has to do with an area in the middle brain called the cingulate gyrus, studied by a team of neuroscientists from the Brain-Body Institute in Ontario, Canada. As Michael Gurian describes it in layman's terms, "The cingulate gyrus is a very powerful emotion-processing element of the limbic system. The female brain processes more life experience through the cingulate gyrus than does the male. With more neural pathways to and from this gyrus in the female brain than in the male, the female brain is more emotion laden."[5]

In other words, one reason men don't experience as much

emotion isn't just because they compartmentalize it out, but because their thoughts and senses often bypass the emotional centers that would have added on emotion in the first place.[6]

MEN ARE LESS LIKELY TO PICK UP ON SUBTLE INTERPERSONAL AND EMOTIONAL SIGNALS

I enjoy those "shoot the target" games at fairgrounds and amusement parks, and can do a pretty decent job when the target is stationary. But as soon as the little metal ducks or bunny rabbits begin to move, I'm done for. I try to track with them, but become more and more off-balance, and eventually end up shooting wildly, frustrated, unable to keep up, and unable to hit a thing.

Interestingly, one commercial real estate developer I talked to compared men's attempts to read and handle interpersonal issues to "trying to hit a moving target." Up to a point, they are fine. But after that point they are overwhelmed, and don't feel as well equipped to handle it. According to research published in the professional journal *Neuroimage,* men's brains have far fewer of the hormones such as oxytocin (the "tend-and-befriend" hormone) that allow people to recognize and empathize with each other.[7] In addition, neurobiologists at the University of California explain that the male brain's structural focus on its "action center" (the amygdala) leads to men being less likely to pick up on the "soft" signals in the first place.[8] So handling interpersonal issues can feel uncomfortable to them; they feel much less natural at it. They aren't as instinctively good at reading faces or body language as women are, so in some cases they end up misreading interpersonal cues or missing them altogether. And the inadequate feeling they experience as a result is terribly frustrating—in fact, the men I spoke with describe it as one of the worst feelings a man can have.

As the real estate developer said:

I value the typical "guy way" of handling relationships at work because it's predictable. I can see something coming or feel it coming. Whereas, if you have the unknown, it's uncomfortable not knowing if someone's going to fly off the handle. There is comfort in knowing what the rules are and what the process is going to be. There is a lot more stress with uncertainty.

HOW MEN HANDLE EMOTIONAL AND INTERPERSONAL ISSUES

We have seen how men *feel* about emotional and interpersonal issues with women; but how men actually *handle* them is complicated not only by their innate predisposition and discomfort with emotion, but by the very fact that the other party is a woman.

Tyler, the executive vice president (EVP) of a well-known entertainment company, put it this way:

> The majority of those in my group are women—but like a lot of places, the senior levels of the company are mostly men. Our CEO is a guy with a temper at the drop of a hat. I'll tell him to cut it out—but I can't do that when a woman gets upset. I can deal differently with a guy than I can with a woman. I can easily be frank with other men, but it's just harder with women. I still do it, but it's more difficult. Especially when you don't know how they will react. You know how men will react. You don't always know that with women.

How *do* men handle difficult issues when the other party is a woman?

They Filter the "Soft" Issues Out, or Avoid Them Altogether

As you have seen, one of the most common ways men handle emotional and interpersonal issues is to filter them out or avoid them altogether—either purposefully, or because they miss them to begin with.

This issue came up in one long conversation I had with two executives in an airline club room. The first man said, "We're just not that great at the interpersonal stuff sometimes. So it's easier to just ignore it."

His colleague replied, "Let me be more blunt. We avoid it *because* we're bad at it! And we *know* that we are bad at it! You know how we were talking about the 'rules' of the business world that men came up with? And that one of those rules was to not be influenced by emotions? Well, we're really smart. One of the rules we created was to *not* take into account stuff that we're poor at doing!"

They Force Themselves to See the Person Logically

The reaction of Paul, the telecommunications entrepreneur I introduced earlier, to the female president he recruited is a good example of this. When she had an emotional reaction to something, he had to "get logical and keep in mind why he hired her"; he had to "mentally review her qualifications." Essentially, he was talking himself out of viewing her poorly—although that was where his brain automatically wanted to go.

They "Accommodate" Emotion in the Workplace, Telling Themselves "If You're Working with Women, You Just Have to Expect It Sometimes"

The most subtle way men handle emotional issues may be the most problematic from a woman's point of view: The men simply make mental accommodations for women, privately thinking, "That's just the way they are."

Some men are more generous about this than others. One senior analyst I've known for years told me, "It's true that women are the only ones who ever get teary-eyed at work. But I don't think most men mind. Nor do we look down on women for being women, especially if the tears aren't about intrusive personal stuff, or a regular drama, or meant to manipulate."

But a lot of other men *do* mind encountering emotions in the workplace—even if they mentally accommodate it. As Tyler, the entertainment company EVP, told me, "I've worked in this business for twenty-five years, and I've had many women in here, in my office, crying. That hasn't happened with a single man."

When I asked him how it made him feel when that happens, he replied, "I want to roll my eyes. Of course, I don't. I just have to deal with it. But privately, I don't have patience for it. It's counterproductive. In my mind, it's unprofessional. And all it does is create gossip, and fodder for everyone to talk about afterwards. It's pointless."

Many men told me emotion at work was "pointless," clearly not recognizing that it is not as if the woman *wants* to bring emotion into the equation, on purpose. I must confess that internally, I was often dying to say, "*It's pointless? Oh my goodness—I guess we'll stop doing it then.*"

Many men told me emotion at work was "pointless." Internally, I was often dying to say, "Oh my goodness—I guess we'll stop doing it then."

WHAT DO MEN PERCEIVE AS "EMOTIONAL" IN THE FIRST PLACE?

In a man's mind, becoming inappropriately "emotional" includes a great deal more than spilling or fighting back tears. I have been in each of the situations described below more than once myself. And I had no idea that some of the words or actions men brought up would have been perceived as overly emotional.

Let's start with the most obvious one.

Becoming Tearful

Here is what one very successful and high-level businessman said—but his comments reflected the feedback I got from a great many men.

Most women I've worked with at one point or another have cried. That really throws you off in a workplace environment. Our natural reaction is to give the woman a hug, you know? But that is not appropriate. At almost every level of the companies where I have worked, from an officer in the company, to my VP of marketing, down to a secretary, I would say 80 percent of the women I've worked with have—at one point or another—been fighting back tears or have actually cried.

Handling that is a challenge. What is the appropriate response? "Go get yourself together"? There's not a whole lot of compassion in that.

Privately, I feel exactly like Tom Hanks's character in the movie A *League of Their Own*, when he says, "There's no crying in baseball!" That's sort of the way any guy feels at the office: There's no crying in business!

■ "There's no crying in business!"

Getting Upset or Defensive Too Easily

A parallel to crying—in a man's mind—is getting visibly upset or getting defensive (which implies that one is upset and trying to cover for it).

Kevin, the human resources director for a major consulting firm, told me that he had a senior benefits manager working with him who was "fabulous," except that she tended to get upset or defensive too easily. He found it "very off-putting."

Here is how he described one particular situation to me:

Just recently, we were in a group meeting discussing benefits packages for our firm in the U.S. and abroad. The benefits manager gave her presentation, and then someone asked a question of whether the data included such-and-such, or whether we should do additional analysis about a particular factor. They were basically playing a "what-if" scenario— "what if we did this?" But in her mind she heard it as, "Why did you not think of this already?" And so she responded very defensively, saying, "I already tried to do the analysis you are talking about," and, "We do not have the data necessary to do that," and, "The resource I used only had this particular data source; I would have to find other data sources and I do not know where to find them in the time frame you need me to do this." She basically went into a long discussion of why she cannot do what we wanted her to do.

When I asked him what, specifically, made her response seem defensive instead of just an explanation, he replied, "She immediately jumped to a defensive tone of voice, and her face got beet red. Basically, the whole room is like 'OK, settle down.' We understand this is an issue, but don't get in a tizzy. This is not an accusation against you."

"And yet you describe her as a 'fabulous' benefits manager."

"Yes, she is. She is very, very bright. It's just that she also has this defensiveness about her. Finally one day I asked her about it, and she said, 'It is just because I have this desire to please everyone. So when I'm questioned like that, I feel like they are *not* pleased. So I feel like I must have done something wrong and then I get defensive.'"

When I asked him how she should have handled it, instead, and whether he thought it would have been handled any differently if the person had been a man, he replied, "In my experience, a man will *never* get mad and emotional like some women will. She almost seemed on the verge of saying 'fine' and storming out. A man would never do that. I would expect a man to say 'I hear your perspective and I respectfully disagree. We can agree to disagree on this but let me first give you my perspective.' And then I'd expect him to leave it there. But I've seen women give off this vibe of just getting so frustrated and emotional and like, 'I cannot deal with this anymore.'"

The men I spoke with universally described defensiveness as

unpleasant to deal with. It wasn't that other men didn't put up a businesslike defense if they felt their statements or actions were not being properly understood. Rather, the men said they rarely heard other men get "defensive"—or as Kevin put it, "frustrated and emotional."

Now, as you will see in chapter 9, there are indeed some very specific things that men *do* get defensive, frustrated, and emotional about. But those feelings tend to stay hidden. Men purposely compartmentalize those emotions, so their inner turmoil is not seen by others.

Overreacting, or "Making a Mountain Out of a Molehill"

Another commonly mentioned behavior was the perception that women were more likely to blow something out of proportion.

Here is what Cole, the executive search leader, said about one such situation. He comes across on the page as somewhat harsh, but his tone was actually a bit perplexed.

> I had a meeting yesterday with a client who is a female executive at a Fortune 500 company, and I had to give her some bad news about the project that we are working on. I told her that our top candidate for a CFO search just took himself out of consideration. And when I said that, my client went "Aaahh!!" Just like that.
>
> I said, "It isn't as though I just told you that your father had just suffered a heart attack, or your son was arrested. It's just business." And she said, "I know, but he was our top candidate," and she goes on a bit about her disappointment. And, I hear her, but I am thinking to myself, "This is just business! There's no point in spending a whole hour on the emotional side of things."

I found this example was worth nothing because even as a more empathetic man, he felt that making something a bigger deal than he thought it should be was equivalent to becoming emotional. Clearly, the conversation with his client did not take an hour "on the emotional side of things." But that is what her perceived over-reaction felt like to him.

Many men shared stories and examples like this. But most also said that since they already thought of the woman's reaction as irrational, they were reluctant to confront it like Cole did. As one man put it, "I couldn't believe she was reacting that way . . . but I couldn't tell *her* that!"

As one partner at a major professional services firm described it, "In that situation, the guy says to himself, 'This is so unimportant. But I can't *say* it is unimportant because it is clearly important to her—for whatever reason.' "

"Jumping to Conclusions"

A number of men expressed the viewpoint that women were more likely to express a knee-jerk reaction to things, or were more likely than men to jump to conclusions. And that assumption carries with it the belief that the woman's decision or conclusion must be emotion-driven, and therefore not driven by logic.

Now, in some situations, it may be that a woman's brain's extra "processing power" (all those white-matter superhighways) may have allowed her to do countless calculations at lightning-fast speed, assessing X, Y, and Z, realizing that Z won't work, and leading her to voice an opinion before her colleagues. And because she doesn't explain her rapid-fire line of reasoning, the men in the room assume that she is jumping to conclusions. So they start saying things like, "Well, hold on a moment, let's think this through . . ."

Further, because male brains aren't as hardwired to pick up on subtle interpersonal cues, they may not have noticed critical factors (such as a client's facial expression) that informed the woman's rapid response.

When asked what women do to undermine their standing with men, one survey-taker specifically brought up "Jumping to a conclusion about a person's motivation or intention based on a brief instant or, for example, a nonverbal motion or communication."

Obviously, I'm not saying that a woman's instantaneous read is always right. Nor is anyone—man or woman—immune from knee-jerk reactions. But it is critical for women to realize that even when they are accurate in their rapid-fire logic, their decision making can easily be misperceived by men as emotion-driven, and therefore suspect.

> *Rapid-fire logic can easily be misperceived by men as emotion-driven, and therefore suspect.*

Holding Strong Opinions/Refusing to Be Swayed

Another common theme I heard among men—with varying degrees of irritation—was that some women seemed to form stubbornly strong opinions and refused to be swayed. Such women are seen as going beyond the sort of "push back" that happens in business disagreements. They are seen as "unable to let it go," and unable to defer to the decision of the boss or the opinion of the group. Such a perception led the men to think of the person in question as irrational and emotional.

One survey-taker, when asked what would undermine a man's perception of a woman, said: "If she gets emotional about a project. Some women who are skilled will not listen to others' opinions.

They are right about everything and will not discuss or listen to other sides."

Now, most people that I know in business would view someone who was "not listening to others' opinions" as being unprofessional. It is telling that this man—like many others—labeled it as "getting emotional."

Here are a few of the quotes from the men I interviewed that show how a woman's tenaciousness on her point of view is perceived by men:

- "She just gets so mad because she is not getting her way."

- "Why can't she wrap her mind around this particular topic? Why can't she see it in another way? Why is she so dead set on being right?"

- "After we told her 'no,' what started happening was all these people started coming to me and saying, 'We're going to lose the farm over this.' They were all riled up. And we knew it was because of her. She became very emotional and refused to be rational and made an emotional play to others. And she seriously hurt herself with our CEO and others."

Personality Conflicts

Because many men are (as you have seen) uncomfortable with picking up on or managing interpersonal cues and emotions, they also tend to be very uncomfortable with personality conflicts in the workplace—and are far more likely to dismiss interpersonal problems as personality conflicts in the first place. They see them as emotion-driven, and feel that they have no place in the work world. They feel like they should have to spend no time on managing "personal" conflicts between staff members or dealing with their fallout, and they resent it when that is not the case.

One businesswoman, Grace, told me a story of a conflict she had with a new woman who was hired for an influential position in a parallel department. Grace had been in the business for years as the right hand to an extremely busy president. She highly valued the cooperative, family-like environment of the organization. The new woman had a very different style, which Grace felt was brusque and personally demeaning. She felt it impacted the morale of her own employees and the culture of the entire organization. She became concerned that her employees would leave—or she would have to. Yet when she raised her concerns with the president, she got the impression he was impatient that she would even bring the conflict up. Several times, he told her, "This is between the two of you. You just have to work it out."

Most of us have been in situations where a certain senior person—man or woman—is extremely difficult to work with, and is causing good people to leave . . . and yet the leadership of the organization seems to want to do nothing about it. At least some of those cases are due to the inherent assumptions of male leaders that this is an emotion-based personality conflict, that it has no place at work, and that the individuals involved simply need to "work it out" and get back to business.

Anything They Don't Understand

Finally, there is something that men view as "emotional" that I believe is one of the most insidious and damaging assumptions to women in the workplace, because it is so deeply embedded in the male psyche, and is so difficult to confront. It is the common, subconscious assumption by men that there is some part of a woman that is "random" or inscrutable.

From boyhood many men have come to believe that to one degree or another, women are mysterious, not entirely consistent, and thus will never be able to be completely understood. Thus, as adults, when confronted with a woman's words or actions that confuse them or seem illogical, they too easily chalk it up to "that random part of her" and look no further.

I have seen this to be a devastating factor in the demise of personal relationships (when, for example, a husband sees his wife's unhappiness, doesn't understand the reason for it, and therefore assumes that there isn't one and thus it can't be addressed— instead of assuming there *is* a reason, that maybe it has something to do with him, and that it *can* be addressed). But I have come to see that such an assumption can be damaging to women's careers, as well.

I was shocked and sobered at the number of times I asked a man for an example of something he viewed as "getting emotional"— and was told a story that had nothing to do with emotion that I could see. Instead, it essentially demonstrated that he simply didn't understand the reason for her words or actions. It wasn't that he actively thought she was emotional, but that he didn't understand why she had said or done something. So he chalked it up to, "Well, it must have been random emotion."

Here is a comment from one senior executive:

> With my [female] sales director, you never know what Mary you're going to get. You see this much more in women than you do in men. Men are just more consistent that way. If they are bastards, they're bastards. You know what sort of situations trigger it. If you do X you get that reaction.
>
> Here, you never knew why the marketing director or the sales director would get offended. It was always potluck.

Just as there is usually a reason for what men do and say, there is usually a reason for what women do and say. And if our feelings have changed, there's a reason for that, too. But when men don't immediately see what the reason is, they are powerfully predisposed to think there isn't one and chalk it up to random emotion or inconsistency.

And as we'll see next, once men see someone as emotional, it has a big impact on how they view that person in the future.

HOW MEN VIEW EMOTION IN THE WORKPLACE

Because men think emotion has little place at work, it's no surprise that they view the display of emotion as unprofessional or unbusinesslike. But we may not realize that they often hold other, equally damaging perceptions as well. Here are some of their common assumptions when they see someone "getting emotional":

"This Person Is Not Thinking"

As one man put it, "The moment I see someone tearing up, I think, 'There goes the logical part of this conversation. We can now abandon logic.' Men think if someone is crying, they've ceased to be logical."

While a particularly intense flood of emotion makes it difficult for anyone to think clearly, science shows that women's emotional threshold is, in essence, much higher than men's. As we have seen, women can usually experience strong feelings and still be able to think clearly. But because men usually can't, they think women can't, either. To men, emotion *is* irrational in many ways.

One of my first in-depth business interviews was with Aidan, a change management partner at a global consulting firm. He described two recent situations as examples of when men would expect someone to *not* get emotional, and how he or other men perceived it when someone did. The first example is below:

CASE STUDY 1

There's a woman, Kelly, on my team who is extremely talented but so sensitive. She and I went to a sixteen-person meeting last week. The client was a major airline that was going through massive change, and invited four competing consulting companies to sit in one room and lay out ideas for how to handle it. We all knew we were competing for the whole job or part of the job. And our role at the meeting was to run the meeting, make a first pass, and suggest a starting point.

Kelly was so angry that everyone else in the room was dinging our ideas and that we were being criticized, that she said nothing the whole meeting. She and I were the only ones there from our firm, and it was odd that she wouldn't chip in.

So I couldn't rely on her take on anything that happened in the meeting, because she was so emotional about it.

Notice Aidan's assumption path: The fact that she was angry that their firm and ideas were being criticized led to her becoming inappropriately silent. The fact that she was silent meant (in his mind) that she was being emotional. As a result, he assumed she wasn't thinking clearly and thus decided that he couldn't rely on her judgment about anything that happened in the meeting. I heard similar assumptions from many men. So I included that exact scenario on the survey I conducted, asking the survey participants what they would think if a female colleague became "emotional and upset" by criticism of a team project. I'll show you those results in a moment.

Then I asked them what their reaction would be as they reviewed the meeting—would they assume she probably wasn't thinking very clearly, and thus doubt her judgment in reviewing the meeting? Or would they assume that her ability to think clearly was unimpaired?

Now suppose that you are leaving the meeting in which your female colleague was emotional and upset. As you prepare to review the meeting, what thought is most likely to be your first reaction? (Choose one answer.)

a. She's emotional, so unfortunately she's probably not thinking very clearly right now; it casts a doubt over whether I can trust her judgment of this particular meeting.

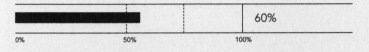

60%

b. She's emotional, but her ability to think clearly is not impaired by that; I can fully trust her judgment of this particular meeting.

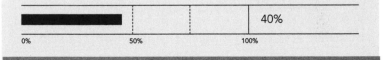

40%

Six men out of ten said that they would assume the emotional colleague wasn't thinking clearly, and that they couldn't trust her judgment of the meeting. And as the men's second assumption about emotion makes clear (below), I suspect the "real-life" percentage of men who might think that is even higher.

"This 'Not Thinking' Will Be Catching"

Because men find themselves starting to feel a bit out-of-balance when they encounter strong emotion, they assume everyone else in the room will be too. In other words, the moment an emotion that they perceive as out of place enters the proceedings, men fear it will cloud everyone's thinking and decision making.

As one marketing manager said:

I don't like the presence of emotion in me or others, in the work setting. On the squash court it's one thing—we can holler and get passionate, and it's infectious. And that is OK. But when emotion infects the meeting, it makes me feel really uncomfortable. Now I'm not 100 percent focused and I've got this jangling going on inside, and other people do too. I begin to fear that I'll have to have that same meeting on another day when people aren't getting emotional. Because what's getting done isn't getting done correctly.

Here is how one senior business leader put it:

When I see emotion in the room, my first feeling is truly empathy for that person because they are going through some trauma. But my second feeling is concern. It is the feeling you get when you're driving and realize that the car next to you is driving straight on and is not looking at the red light in front of them. It's a car wreck about to happen. To watch somebody conduct themselves in a way that could ultimately be destructive to their own best interests is just really a sad thing.

Here is how I asked the initial question on the survey.

Suppose you are in an important meeting that you know you and your team will need to evaluate afterward. One of your female colleagues contributes well to the discussion but also gets quite emotional and upset about some criticism of your team's project. Which of the following feelings are you most likely to have?
(Choose one answer.)

a. I fear that her emotion could draw others into it, and make it a more emotional, less productive meeting.

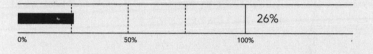

| 0% | 50% | 100% |

26%

b. I agree with (a), above, and as a result feel I would need to filter the emotional stuff out so I can think clearly.

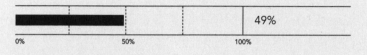

| 0% | 50% | 100% |

49%

c. I don't fear the meeting becoming more emotional; if it did, it wouldn't impact me at all.

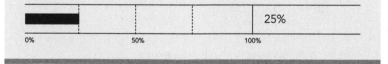

| 0% | 50% | 100% |

25%

In other words, three out of four of the men I surveyed were fearful that emotion would infect the meeting and make it unproductive. Most of those say they have to actively filter out the emotion in order to think clearly themselves. Given these numbers, it is likely that the response to the question we looked at earlier—whether women who became emotional in a meeting would or would not be able to think clearly—was artificially suppressed by concern over how the answer would be perceived.

"This Person Is Missing Things?"

A parallel to the "she's not thinking" assumption is the belief that if she's emotional, she's missing what's happening here and now.

Here is the second example Aidan, the change management partner, provided on this:

CASE STUDY 2

When you're a consultant at a client site, working with twenty of their people in a conference room, some of them won't like a consultant running things. That's their issue, not yours; get on with it. But I've seen that sometimes some women want so much to be liked that I really get the feeling that they are thinking to themselves, "These people wish I wasn't running the meeting" and get distracted by it.

These women are actually reading the situation very well, but are not able to just ignore that distraction and get on with the job. Their concern gets in the way of running the meeting, because they end up missing some of what is going on. They are not hearing what is being said. A few months ago, a senior member of my team and I had a key meeting with [a major soft drink company]. We ran the meeting and there were these tensions in the room, with some people who didn't think we, as outsiders, should be involved. Laurie was supposed to lead parts of the meeting, but she got so focused on those in the room who didn't like us. I could tell that she was getting defensive toward the people in the room for some reason. And it turned out later, they didn't even have an issue with *us*, but just with whether the project needed to be done in the first place.

She could have just addressed it and said, "It seems that you aren't in agreement here—let's talk about it." But because she was defensive about their questioning she kept pushing our point of view and our agenda really hard and didn't listen well to them at all.

And ironically, it was *because* she was emotionally intelligent and knew that their body language was bad that she picked up on their reservations at all! I honestly didn't see it at the time. But she assumed those reservations were because they didn't want us here. And instead it was that they had reservations about the project. And *those* would have been really important to hear!

We did go ahead with the project and unfortunately found out what the problems were as we went, but not through her. And that means we have reservations about her running a meeting again.

Men Believe That Negative Emotions Do Not Serve a Business Purpose

One reason women don't view emotion quite the same way men do is that women see that there can sometimes be value in it. In the previous chapter, Douglass pointed out that emotion in its right context can be a good signal of a specific employee need that has been mishandled and needs to be handled better. I think many women would agree with that. But such a conclusion appears to be the exception among men. Most of the men I interviewed didn't view the expression of emotion that way at all. In fact, some were completely perplexed by the idea that negative emotions could have some value.

Here is an exchange between me and senior software executives David and Gregg. They were in a jovial mood, and clearly joking around, but the content of what they said is telling:

"As a woman," I said, "I would argue that sometimes it can be helpful to study emotions within a business—that they can be used as a signal that something isn't right, that something needs to be improved—employee morale, and so on."

"My view," Gregg replied, "is that the probability of achieving that is so minimal that a better course is for the emotional people to quit being emotional!"

At this, both Gregg and David laughed.

Turning to Gregg, David said, "But Shaunti is raising an interesting point. She's saying there could be an actual business need for this; that emotions can be a signal of something that has to be addressed. Something that will be a net business negative if you don't deal with it."

"The idea that dealing with emotions in business could be positive," Gregg replied, "has literally never occurred to me before, ever, until you mentioned this."

Now, it is important to note that there were also many men in my interviews and on my surveys who were empathetic to those around them and recognized emotional and morale issues as critical to the success of business. The problem is that their willingness or capacity to deal with those issues sometimes seemed more robust in theory than in fact.

When a Man Gets Emotional, He's Seen by Other Men as "A Bit Abnormal"

Lest we think that men look down only on women for being emotional, it is worth explaining that men judge each other even more harshly. They are far less forgiving or willing to deal with a situation in which the person being emotional is another man. It doesn't seem to happen often, but when it does, it changes men's perception of that person significantly. Here is what Richard, the financial advisory group president, had to say:

The fact that men distrust emotions is just absolutely true. In the workplace, men basically are going to: (*a*), try hard not to be emotional themselves because they feel like no one will trust them or listen if they are emotional. And (*b*), they are going to hold suspect all people around them who get emotional. But men are especially hard on other men who get emotional. I think they think any guy who does that on any kind of regular basis is a little whacked out, and abnormal. I would feel like he's a bit suspect and would not want him working around me.

HOW MEN THINK EMOTIONS SHOULD BE HANDLED

When I worked at the New York Fed, I always marveled at how calm my immediate boss was in the midst of even the most nerve-wracking situation. He was an assistant vice president at the time, managing more than a dozen stressed-out analysts on deadlines that were often measured in minutes. Early on, I would sometimes literally *run* into his office holding a draft memo for him to review and correct, knowing that his boss—the executive vice president—needed it to brief the president in twenty minutes. And even though there were often two or three other analysts hustling in and out on similar missions, my boss always projected an ultra-calm front. He would deliberately scan my paper, note his red pen corrections, hand it back and calmly reach for the next anxious analyst's paper as I ran back out.

After a while, I stopped running. I realized that the more strung-out we got, the more calm he got, and that it was an excellent strategy to reduce tension and keep things moving efficiently. I also realized that the more stressed I appeared, the longer he took to review my work. (Presumably, I now realize, because he assumed I was missing things.)

Eventually I (and others) started copying his calm demeanor. Today, my own staff members sometimes wonder aloud how I can be so calm when I'm on a tight deadline or thrown a curveball. (Although as the example at the beginning of this chapter shows, I'm still working on that. . . .)

One investment banker perfectly summarized my boss's behavior—and the advice I heard from many of the men I interviewed:

Men have emotions too, but they harness those emotions. I don't want to be manipulative. But you can generate the right emotion around the topic, in order to create value toward your goal instead of allowing an unproductive emotion to naturally flow from the circumstances.

> *"Men have emotions too, but they harness those emotions. You can generate the right emotion instead of allowing an unproductive emotion to naturally flow from the circumstances."*

He went on to give me an example:

If a client calls me and says, "We are going to give you this big project," my initial emotion is "Yippee!" But I don't say that to my client. None of us would, right? We'll say, "Excellent. We can be out there tomorrow." And we hang up the phone and *then* we high-five it with our colleagues. We restrain our emotions.

Well, it works with negative things too. And this is where women sometimes don't restrain their emotions as much. So when a key employee comes in and says, "I cannot handle it here anymore; I quit," an ineffective response is to show my upset emotions. If I say, "Quit! What do you mean, quit? Think of all the things that I have done for you!" that does not help solve the problem. In fact, it is almost always an ineffective solution—for either gender—to show those negative emotions. It will just solidify a decision that we don't want.

So the right response is to harness these emotions and say, "Steve, I understand that the job has just been killing you recently, and that you're feeling less than appreciated. I would feel the same way. For the last few years, I have tried to show you appreciation, but for the last three or four months, I have absolutely failed to do that. And, whether you go or whether you stay, I want to tell you right now how sorry I am." That approach restrains negative emotions and tries to create value instead.

Again, I'm sure men experience the same feelings as women, and just find it easier to compartmentalize them. But women can be equally effective (perhaps more) at restraining and redirecting emotions to create value. Based on my experience with my boss at the Fed, I think it is a matter of being aware of and purposeful about it.

WHAT DO WE DO ABOUT IT?

Addressing the negative way men view the expression of emotion in the workplace can be done in one of two ways: working to manage the emotions themselves, or managing men's perceptions of women and emotion.

Managing Emotion

One business owner was referred to as "unusually sensitive" and "empathetic" by a venture capitalist I know. When I interviewed the business owner himself, he offered a helpful perspective for empathetic women on managing emotion in the workplace.

> The men or women who cannot disassociate themselves from the emotional trauma of the business world end up leaving it or failing. It does not mean you do not feel and it does not mean that you do not care. It means that you do not let your actions stem from an emotional response, and you do not let any outward show of your emotions hinder the agenda that you were trying to accomplish.
>
> What is even more important than setting them aside, is changing what emotions you show. Most people are willing to edit their words—we learn that we should think before we talk, so we do not always say everything we are thinking. And in the business context that edit function is really an important thing. But some people don't have the same ability to generate an edit function around their emotions. So in some instances they show emotions that are not particularly advantageous to the agenda that they are trying to accomplish.

Since I would argue that his second point—not showing negative emotions when it would put us at a disadvantage—is the most critical for our purposes, I wanted to get some real-world advice on how one might accomplish that. I told this business owner my opening story of becoming mortifyingly emotional when faced with those unexpected accusations from presumed allies. I asked how I could have managed to edit those emotions so I didn't show them. He answered:

> I think it is analogous to what a politician does. Politicians know they will get antagonistic questions about beliefs and policies that are very personally important to them. And it is always a surprise and it is very personal. So they prepare ahead of time for how they might answer various scenarios. And I think most guys do that: They prepare mental scripts. I'm betting that since you were in that situation that you have scripted it over and over in your head—how you wished you would have handled it differently.

I responded, "Of course. But part of the problem was that I would never have expected to be criticized in that meeting. If I'm expecting a tough meeting, scripts are doable. But what happens when it *is* unexpected? What do *you* do?" He replied.

> Here is a great example. When our daughters were little, they played softball, and the coach always told them, "When the ball is hit to the outfield always take your first step back." Their inclination is to take their first step forward and run toward it, but by that time they cannot really adjust and the ball is over their head. This is just like that.
>
> No matter what comes at me, I always take my first step back emotionally. I've learned that I have to, to give myself some space to think, and get my emotions under control.
>
> So if you had to do it over again, you might have scripted your remarks by listening to their criticism and then even asking for a few minutes to process what they said and think

it through. Or you could just say, "Let's establish some common ground here. Obviously there are strong opinions in the room about what I've written. I want to start with common ground about sharing what my intentions were, and hear what you think they were."

I've found his advice about taking a step back to be helpful. As he added, "Your first goal is to pull the fuse off the stick of dynamite that is in the room so it does not explode. Your second goal is to give yourself a chance to respond in a way that is rational and can add some benefit to the situation rather than in an emotional way that does not. And it will help to *plan* to do that whenever you are blindsided. That becomes your script."

> "Give yourself a chance to respond in a way that is rational and can add some benefit to the situation rather than in an emotional way that does not."

Managing the Perceptions of Others

As I've drilled down into the advice from the men in my interviews, there are probably two main ways that women can manage the perceptions of men so that they don't see women as emotional—even when we might be wrestling with those emotions, inside. The first entails what might be called "forced calmness." The second requires being very aware of possible misperceptions and taking rapid action to head them off.

FORCED CALMNESS

From all accounts, it seems as if the best thing women can do for themselves (in most cases) is to project a façade of calm when we feel ourselves getting upset. This has the dual benefit of pulling the fuse out of the stick of dynamite and of helping us feel the inner peace that we are projecting.

Geoff, the Fortune 500 CMO quoted in earlier chapters, said, "Women at senior levels have to understand that sometimes men overreact big too. And women can't overreact to that overreaction. Remember, he'll be done in ten minutes and won't think about it the rest of the day."

I should note that projecting an attitude of calmness does *not* mean filtering our emotions out so ruthlessly that we eliminate our natural strength in interpersonal dynamics, or become callous. As one man said, "There is a risk of trying to compartmentalize too much, when that doesn't come naturally. Like the women who—pardon my French—become ballbusters because they come in and entirely de-emotionalize every situation. And so they rip people to shreds and do not understand why there is this carnage in their wake. And everybody is just waiting for them to fall down an elevator shaft."

BE AWARE OF POSSIBLE PERCEPTIONS, AND TAKE RAPID ACTION TO HEAD OFF ANY THAT ARE INACCURATE OR NEGATIVE

In my second year at Harvard's Kennedy School, I was one of two graduate students from my program asked to be a full member of the admissions committee. It was a fascinating experience. And one of the most valuable lessons I learned is that in the absence of information, an observer has to make an assumption. If the situation is a negative one (your GPA slipped your senior year), that assumption is probably not to your benefit ("this guy was slacking off"). But if you move to provide an explanation ("My mother passed away my senior year, and I had to help with my younger siblings"), the negative assumption is countered or never gets made in the first place—and is often turned into a positive ("Wow, this is a responsible guy").

It works the same way for women when managing perceptions in the workplace—not just with men, of course, but that's what we are focusing on here. Since women are particularly well-equipped to notice interpersonal perceptions, it follows that we should also be able to be aware of the things that men think of as "getting emotional" and demonstrate that we're not acting that way. When we suspect that a negative perception may be arising ("She's getting too upset—I'll bet she's missing things") we can move to counter it. ("Listen, I know I'm passionate about this, but Bob, you just made points A, B, and C, and here's why I'm concerned about how B might work. . . .")

It is worth keeping a particularly close eye on situations where women might be assumed to be jumping to conclusions. One of my close friends is a female consultant in a largely male-dominated field, and she is usually tapped as the team leader. She has found that when she states an opinion, there's no problem if the men on her team are immediately on board with her viewpoint. But if she senses that they aren't, she has found that she has to make a point of sitting down with them and sharing the steps of her reasoning so that they follow what might otherwise seem a rather hasty, instinctive process.

Similarly, it is worth being aware of situations where a man might assume that women are being dragged into an interpersonal conflict, and demonstrate otherwise by explaining the business impact of the situation—and your recommendation for what to do about it. For example, the woman who raises concern about a fellow leader's brusque approach with her employees and is told "you just have to work it out between the two of you" clearly is not being understood and has to shift strategies.

I relayed that exact example to one retired banker who suggested instead:

> You will absolutely catch any leader's attention if you start with the fact that the situation is affecting performance. Is quality down? Is the morale problem affecting service delivery? Is productivity affected? If it's just bitching and whining, then forget it—you just have to work it out. But if it's affecting performance, then it's a different deal.

Obviously, many men care just as much about interpersonal dynamics and morale as women do, and will have seen the same signals, and therefore won't need this approach. But if you are getting the feeling that your male boss may not be seeing the same things you are and you want to address it, it makes sense to use the approach least likely to be labeled an emotional one.

TURNING A PERCEIVED WEAKNESS INTO A STRENGTH

It is likely that men will continue to view women as more emotional—and in truth, given our hardwiring, we are. But that is not a bad thing. I believe we are each built the way we are for a reason, and that the key to success—for either men or women—is to leverage those strengths, while recognizing and compensating for any areas that could negatively impact how we are perceived. And a woman's relatively greater emotional wiring is one such area.

Once again, let's hear Cole's perspective:

> I think what makes a great executive is somebody who can get emotional about the needs of their subordinates and

their peers but does not get emotional about their own needs. And where women may at times fail is that they become emotional around their own needs and less emotional around the needs of others.

But it doesn't always happen that way, obviously. Many women already tend to have a high relational ability that serves them well; those women who also manage emotion well can be very, very effective.

CHAPTER 6

"If I Let Down My Guard, the World Will Stop Spinning"

The Secret Inner Belief of Every Man

As we've seen, many men have some common expectations about how the business world works. What took me a long time was figuring out *why*. One reason stems from male-female differences in the brain, certain instinctive or social predispositions, and so on. But there is another factor in play as well.

I first became aware of it in researching my first book about relationships, *For Women Only*. I was interviewing a small group of men at a coffee shop. The men were describing how *compulsive* they felt about the need to provide for their families, and how often— even in an economic boom—they would think or worry about their jobs and their ability to bring home a paycheck (the surprising answer: all the time).

I asked, "What makes that mental pressure to provide for your family worse?" I listened, confused, as they shared examples of seemingly minor, unrelated work issues. One man talked about a colleague who took too long to get to the point in her explanations; another mentioned an error in a key spreadsheet that required hours to redo; another described an interoffice squabble between two key employees. When I admitted that I didn't get what these things had to do with the topic under discussion, one man tried to elaborate:

Any interruption at work feels like it might prevent me from being able to provide for my family. I know that sounds crazy. While my direct reports are arguing with each other in a meeting, I'm thinking, *Don't you get it? While you're fussing about something irrelevant, my work is not getting done! And if my work is not done, I'm going to lose this client and my numbers will drop. And if my numbers drop, I'm going to get fired. And if I get fired, I'm going to go bankrupt, and I won't be able to provide for my family and my wife will leave me and the glaciers will melt and the world will stop spinning on its axis, and life on earth will cease to exist as we know it.*

The other men laughed, then looked very thoughtful. "Yep," one said. "That about describes it."

THE EMOTION THAT DRIVES MEN

Although men pride themselves on being rational and unemotional, the truth is that both genders have plenty of irrationality to go around. Both women *and* men have issues that tend to make us feel secretly emotional—they just tend to be different ones. And as irrational as men know it is, most of the men on my survey shared a visceral fear that their working world might shortly come crashing down if they—and those around them—don't focus all their energy on being productive all the time. In fact, 80 percent of the men I surveyed agreed with the statement "If everyone doesn't pull together and keep things moving forward every single day, things will break down."[1]

> *Both women and men have issues that tend to make us feel emotional—they just tend to be different ones.*

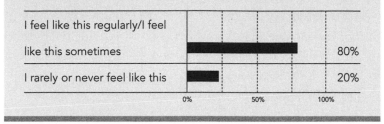

"If everyone doesn't pull together and keep things moving forward every single day, things will break down."

I feel like this regularly/I feel like this sometimes		80%
I rarely or never feel like this		20%

As one man put it, "If I don't bust my butt today, I may be bankrupt tomorrow. We know it's stupid, so you'll never hear us talk about it, but that is kind of how every guy feels."

> "If I don't bust my butt today,
> I may be bankrupt tomorrow."

The Fear Behind the "Rules" of the Workplace

It was clear in my interviews with men that many—perhaps most—of their work expectations and perceptions can be traced back to this rarely expressed but very real fear. On one long airplane ride, an engineering company manager had agreed to take a look at a list of ten findings about men I had tentatively developed early on, and was continuing to test. The first hypothesis listed on the paper I handed him was the one that eventually led to this current chapter. It was labeled "The World Will Stop Spinning":

1. Men have an unspoken fear that their working world might come crashing down tomorrow if they—and those around them—don't focus all their energy on being productive today.

Other hypotheses on the list included statements about how "it's not personal; it's business," how men view emotions, and the importance of "letting it go."

My seatmate counted all the way down the list, then handed the pages back and tapped the "world stops spinning" statement. He said:

> Just so you know, all but two of your subjects are *because* of this first one. The reason men value letting it go is because they feel like if they don't, they'll be bankrupt tomorrow. The reason we have all these Robert's Rules of Order for the business world is that if we don't, disorder and entropy will take over and we'll soon be out on the street. Anytime a man says, "This is just the way business works," you can bet that this fear is behind it.

ANATOMY OF MEN'S FEAR

When I got the survey data back, the thing that surprised me most was not that the fear that a man's world would end *existed* (too many men had confirmed it), but just how universal it was. I had thought this fear would be most prevalent among white-collar workers, particularly the business owners and principals who do in fact carry the ultimate responsibility for the business. I had also, unfortunately, stereotyped blue-collar workers as more likely to have a sense of just putting in their hours. But my survey results found that this fear exists at roughly the same rates whether the men were blue collar or white collar, old or young, company presidents or part-time administrative help, and across the entire occupational spectrum. The slight differences, in fact, were often counterintuitive to my stereotypes. For example, blue-collar work-ers were actually a bit *more* likely to have this concern than white-collar men.

As far as I can tell anecdotally, if a man *doesn't* have this fear, it seems more related to working under a system that completely eliminates the need for it (such as working for a large bureaucratic organization that protects underperformers, and doesn't particu-larly reward those who excel).

What Men's Fear Feels Like

So what does this concern feel like? It appears to be made up of four instinctive feelings.

1. THE NATURAL ORDER OF THINGS IS TO BREAK DOWN

The engineering company manager I referenced earlier used a word that seemed to perfectly describe the physics behind the men's feel-ings: "entropy." One law of thermodynamics essentially states that the universe is running down: no new energy is created, decay hap-pens, things tend to break down and need to be fixed—they don't spontaneously fix themselves. As one definition puts it, entropy is "a measure of the disorder of a system. Systems tend to go from a state of order (low entropy) to a state of maximum disorder (high entropy)."[2]

Men feel this strongly in the working world, and they feel very pressured by it. Left to its own devices, they feel, their area of re-sponsibility will quickly decay or break down. As noted, eight in ten men experienced that feeling.

As one company president, Richard, put it, "A guy has a view that if he doesn't kill himself today he might be bankrupt tomor-row. It's all part of why we're performance oriented. The natural course of events is for things to break or decay, and if I'm not hard at work reaching goals and ensuring we're on task we're likely to be broke tomorrow."

2. CONSTANT VIGILANCE IS NEEDED

That naturally leads to the deep, instinctive belief that constant vigilance is needed, and that they can never truly relax. I was surprised when I heard this comment from an extremely successful and wealthy businessman: "No matter how successful I get, I still feel a bit like I'm pushing a rock uphill—gravity is still there, working against me. I have to be vigilant or I'll slip backwards."

> "No matter how successful I get, I still feel a bit like I'm pushing a rock uphill—gravity is still there, working against me. I have to be vigilant or I'll slip backwards."

When I shared that comment on the survey, three out of four men said they felt exactly the same way.

Similarly, 76 percent of the men surveyed agreed with the comment "I feel like a juggler who is trying to keep a dozen balls in the air; if I lose my focus it will all come crashing down around me."

Now, just because a man believes that constant vigilance or focus is needed, doesn't mean he will ever look like it. As we'll see in another chapter, most men hate looking like they aren't in control. And no one wants to work constantly, every minute of the day. Yet even when a man is socializing at work, or joking with a colleague about last night's game, or relaxing at home on the weekend, he never really feels fully "off the hook." As one man put it, "There is always that low-grade buzz in the back of my mind: *What happens if I lose that customer? What happens if my industry tanks? Will my company make it? Will I be able to provide for my family?*"

One attorney explained it this way: "Most men have this internal pressure. They don't want to be in work mode every second, but when they *aren't* they mentally know there is a trade-off. I'm having a little fun right now, but I do know I'm going to have to pay for it later."

3. SUCCESS DOESN'T PROVIDE MUCH BREATHING ROOM

Recognizing that low-grade buzz or need to keep the pressure on helps to explain why the workplace (the male-dominated workplace in particular) seems so attuned to the question "What have you done for me lately?"

I've often thought of that dynamic as counterproductive. Yet it must seem entirely logical in the face of men's conviction that one is always fighting the tendency of things to decay. Seventy-five percent of the men on the survey agreed, saying that even workplace success doesn't give them much breathing room to relax.

It's a feeling that was perfectly captured by a comment I heard years ago from an old friend of my husband, a very successful independent financial advisor. He described how he would land a big deal or make $25,000 in one transaction, and his wife would say, "Let's go out and celebrate!" To which he would answer, "How can I celebrate? I'm now unemployed. I have to go find the next deal!"

4. "IT ALL DEPENDS ON ME . . ."

Throughout my professional life I have heard men say in a joking tone, "It all depends on me, baby."

But as the men in my interviews described it, it's really not a joke. Fully 85 percent of the men on my survey agreed that they regularly or sometimes felt that everything depended on them—which is a logical feeling for someone who feels like their world could fall apart if they let down their guard. As one of my male advisors put it, "We say 'It all depends on me,' but what we actually mean is, 'The weight of the world is on my shoulders.'" Now, most of us—men and women— have at times felt that if you want something done right, you've got to do it yourself. It's a feeling that usually rears its head when one is unsure of the competency or commitment of others on the team. But the sense of the men I talked to went deeper than that. It was a feeling men seemed to have even when they had a strong team, and were completely confident in those around them.

> *"We say 'It all depends on me,' but what we actually mean is, 'The weight of the world is on my shoulders.'"*

Just as success doesn't give men breathing room, the presence of skilled coworkers doesn't remove the lonely, illogical feeling a man has that the weight of the world is on his shoulders, and that he can't truly depend on anyone other than himself to hold it up.

One COO put it this way: "It's fear. It's not that 'I'm so important' and feeling like I have to be the center of things. It's the opposite of that. It's fear that it'll break if we don't all pull together to keep it moving forward. It's the opposite of feeling confident. Ultimately it's the knowledge that you can only control yourself. And so the ultimate responsibility to keep your part of the world from crashing *has* to rest with you."

WHAT MAKES IT BETTER—AND WORSE

While nothing seems able to *eliminate* men's fear that their world will stop spinning if they let down their guard, they are keenly sensitive to two factors in those around them that can help to relieve that fear and make it more manageable; essentially, two factors that signify that others also feel the weight of the world on their shoulders and are helping to bear it. Conversely, men are keenly sensitive to the reverse of those factors, which makes the weight worse and intensifies their concern that the world will come crashing down.

After I described the premise of this chapter to Allan, the president of an automotive industry supply company, he provided an interesting perspective: "Look, not everyone feels that the world will stop spinning if they let down their guard—but if they *don't* feel that way, I can't trust them to be an effective person or part of my team. If they don't have that same neurosis, I don't think they are taking it seriously enough. We're looking for people who are going to take it as seriously as we do. And when you see someone who doesn't, you think, 'I gotta get this guy out of here. He's killing us.'"

The two primary factors that men seem highly attuned to as signals for whether someone is "taking it seriously enough"?

1. Whether someone achieves and prioritizes results; and

2. Whether someone is "all in" with the team.

When someone exhibits both of these characteristics it makes men think that that person "gets it." Such a person—man or woman—engenders strong feelings of respect and gratitude.

Men believe that every person in the workplace is constantly being scrutinized to see if he or she is sharing the weight of the world and helping to relieve the common pressure. And the men I interviewed largely sensed that other men instinctively understood that. But rightly or wrongly, men often weren't as sure whether a woman realized that or valued the need to relieve that pressure. As a result, they felt all the more respectful of women who visibly signaled that they did. One man on the survey said that his top advice for women was, "Remember that you are being watched and observed by others."

Every person in the workplace is constantly being scrutinized to see if he or she is sharing the weight of the world and helping to relieve the common pressure.

I heard so many men talk about these two signals that I could have written a chapter on each of them—that is how emotionally important they seemed to be. So let's briefly look at them in more detail: both the positive factors that create so much respect among men, and the "red flags" that trigger a man's concern.

Factor #1: Whether Someone Achieves and Prioritizes Results

POSITIVE SIGNAL: YOU ARE FOCUSED ON RESULTS—FOR YOURSELF AND OTHERS

Ultimately, the best antidote for the fear that things will break down is seeing tangible results that things are moving forward. I can't count the number of men who said, "It's all about results," or, "The only thing that really matters to us is, 'Do you deliver?'" Interestingly, this was usually said in the context of explaining that, in today's workplace, skilled and talented women can advance as fast and as far as similarly skilled men if they focus on delivering results. As one man on the survey put it, "Gender is irrelevant—be competent."

One very successful founder of several nationwide businesses provided an interesting—if blunt—perspective from his four decades in the marketplace.

Early on, I think some women in the 1970s and 1980s—and even the government—felt that women deserved different treatment from men. It was business suffrage: I was downtrodden, so now I'm entitled. Business owners used to have to promote a woman primarily *because* she was a woman. I used to have to fill out these government forms stating all the minorities and women I had hired, and present a plan for improving my ratio.

That process didn't last long, because the best grand equalizer happens to be capitalism. Today, if you can deliver, it doesn't matter who you are or what race or gender you are: Capability trumps everything else. And similarly, I can like you a lot as a person, but it doesn't mean I'll hire you or keep you if you haven't earned it. Every business leader today—man or woman—will hire and promote those who perform, period. Because if they don't, they know they won't be around long.

RED FLAG: PRIORITIZING RELATIONSHIP OVER RESULTS

As the business leader above noted, any astute worker—man or woman—likely wants to see that those around them are achieving results. But while men viewed women as just as likely to care about achieving results themselves, they were not as convinced that women were as likely to prioritize results in *others*. A number of men expressed a concern that female managers might preserve a relationship with another worker over results. And that raised the red flag that the woman might not share the same fear that the world could come crashing down.

In an earlier chapter, I quoted Marty and Ronald, the CEO and COO of a $5.5 billion organization. After years spent modernizing the company and advancing women, Marty still saw a dynamic that troubled him:

MARTY: For men, performance speaks for itself. They want to be respected on the basis of what they do, not by being able to incur favor. In other words, you do not want to be advancing because someone likes you more than someone else, but because they perceive that you have greater worth.

RONALD: We want our actions to speak for themselves.

Does that mean, I asked, that you think "actions speaking for themselves" matters more to men than to women?

MARTY: I think so. Because with many women, what I truly see valued is relationship over actions. It is a peculiar thing, because they will be more tolerant of inappropriate actions or substandard delivery to preserve a relationship. The man will usually cut loose a nonperformer much more quickly than a woman. A man may find that easier. It doesn't matter that he may have some existing relationship with that person. With women, I think it does matter.

RONALD: With men, I frankly think we care too *little* about the relationship. We default back to being just completion-driven, outcome-driven, so everything doesn't fall apart. We're neurotic cavemen. And someone's got to bring home the mastodon.

Now, clearly, there may be some factor in play in the women's judgment that the men aren't recognizing as related to "performance." For example, the women managers they reference may have perceived a business value in prioritizing a relationship. As always, the key for women is to be aware of how men may be perceiving certain actions, so we can proactively address any misperception, if necessary.

RED FLAG: SLOWING DOWN RESULTS

Just as men are sometimes unfairly predisposed to see women managers valuing relationships over results, they are predisposed to see certain female approaches to the workplace as more likely to slow down the drive toward results. Men who feel like the world is about to stop spinning quickly get impatient with anything they view as likely to interfere with their ability to keep it moving.

The most common examples I heard were of female colleagues who "slow things down" via some of the patterns discussed elsewhere in this book. For example, allowing emotion to get in the way of business; taking things too personally; sharing too many details instead of getting quickly to the point; or allowing themselves to get enmeshed in inter-office squabbles. In most cases, it was telling that my interviewees viewed these things as not just irritating, but irrelevant to an alarming degree. Several reasonable and even-keeled businessmen became quite passionate about this, revealing how much they view it as an encumbrance to getting the work done. As one normally calm senior executive memorably put it, "It makes you crazy when the two women down the hallway are bitching at each other and I'm like 'What!? We're going to be broke tomorrow! Go get that report out, make that phone call, get me that next client!'"

Factor #2: Whether Someone Is "All In" with the Team

POSITIVE SIGNAL: YOU ARE FULLY COMMITTED

Every one of us knows that results matter. But we would be making a big mistake to think that results are *all* that matter. Despite the number of men who said, "It's all about results," those same men shared examples of another aspect of business that I think is vitally important to them: the intangible sense that the other worker is fully committed to the team and equally sharing the unspoken weight on their shoulders.

> *Every one of us knows that results matter. But we would be making a big mistake to think that results are all that matter.*

Understanding how to demonstrate that sense of being "all in" is one of the most overlooked ways a woman can create a deep sense of loyalty among her male colleagues. Conversely, a woman who unintentionally sends the opposite signal will damage her perception among her male colleagues, without intending to.

Several signals told the men that another employee was taking the job just as seriously as they were:

The worker makes an effort to learn and adapt to the culture and rules of their particular workplace. Essentially, the person signals to the group that they understand and respect the unwritten rules of the organization's culture.

In my interview with Allan, the automotive industry supplier, he uttered the classic "performance is what matters" viewpoint. But before long, he also gave me an example of a valuable and highly results-oriented new female executive who still created a negative impression. When I pressed him about why, he said, "Well, it's not *just* the results that matter. You are also expected to work within the office dynamic. You can't have the attitude of 'I'm getting my job done, so the other stuff doesn't matter.' Especially if you are new and have a learning curve coming in—and so you probably aren't able to deliver immediately—you have to watch out. In every company I've been with, there is a dynamic and a culture that you need to work within. Men are usually fairly cognizant of it. But it's been my impression that women don't care as much about the dynamic as long as they are getting their job done. That is going to be to their detriment, at least in the eyes of the men. If you really want to be accepted by the team and if you really want to move up, don't just deliver the results: Figure out what the rules are and work with them."

In demanding jobs or during demanding times, the employee makes it clear that he or she shares the same pain as everyone else. I will cover the next two points more extensively in chapter 8, but they are worth mentioning here as signals of someone who is willing to "share the weight of the world."

From their days sweating it out together during two-a-day practices in full gear at summer football camp (or whatever the sport), men create a sense of teamwork and commitment by sharing the same discomfort. No high school star would say, "Coach, this is crazy. I'm going to skip these pointless extra practices. What matters is whether I can catch the long bomb when the game is on the line—and I can do it every time." As anyone who has played team sports knows, the common commitment and shared pain are emotionally important to the sense of being on the same team.

In the same way, few men would say what I have heard from many women: "It shouldn't matter if I leave at four o'clock to get the kids, or I can't put in the 'face time,' as long as I'm getting my work done." While I personally would agree with that statement, in a subtle way, most of the men I spoke with wouldn't. Any man will say that it makes sense, logically. But emotionally they feel that such a person isn't really sharing the same commitment to the team.

> Few men would say what I have heard from many women: "It shouldn't matter if I leave at four o'clock as long as I'm getting my work done."

One software development manager described it this way: "Results are important, but there is also something about a shared burden and feeling the pain together. If we're in the middle of a big project, and there is someone in the department who still has to leave at three p.m. every day to pick her kids up—but I know that from nine to midnight she's actually going to be intensively working and doing the stuff she was unable to do from three to six with the rest of the team, then I have no problem. I know she's feeling the same pain; she's just spreading it out over different hours. It isn't necessarily whether or not she has to leave early if we have agreed to that—but whether she's feeling the same pain."

Then he grimaced, and added, "But there's a problem even with that. It's really hard to show that you're feeling the same pain if you're not at the office. Anyone who works long hours gets really good at cutting through the B.S. about whether the pain is really being shared. I had one female colleague who scooted out every day at five o'clock—which for us is really early. But then I'd get these croaking voice mails from her timed at one a.m. to prove how hard she was working from home. OK, fine—but there was never any document in my in-box in the morning. So if she *was* working those hours it didn't translate into results."

The employee shows that he or she is fully invested in shared goals, by a consistent willingness to sacrifice something of value (time with family, sleep, money, and so on) for the sake of achieving those goals. In a similar way, men (and many women, for that matter) are constantly watching to see whether other workers seem fully "invested"—whether they intimately care about the same goals. Quite a few men mentioned the importance of "loyalty" (as one man put it, "the feeling that you can trust someone to be loyal is an invaluable thing"), but it took me a while to realize that what they often meant by loyalty was, in actuality, being invested in and caring about the same goals.

And the primary signal to show how much someone cares seems to be whether they are willing to sacrifice something of value for it. Whenever there is extra work to be done, is the person willing to give up sleep, time with family, or those much-looked-forward-to tickets to the big game? In a partnership, or an entrepreneurial venture, are they willing to spend their own money or put in some sweat equity instead of taking a regular salary? When they get their own work done, instead of heading out the door, are they willing to chip in and ask their boss or coworkers, "What can I do to help you, so we can both get out of here before dinner?"

Now, this "willingness to sacrifice" dynamic may not always be a healthy one. Some people end up feeling like they have no choice but to give up family time for the sake of demonstrating commitment to their job. I love it when I see talented and *committed* women being a part of changing those unbalanced expectations.

But regardless of what decision we make about how to handle it, it is important to understand what signals we are sending our colleagues, bosses, and employees.

RED FLAG: "THEY'RE DOING THE JOB, BUT NOT PART OF THE TEAM"

Allan, the automotive supply company president, offered an example that captures the viewpoint of many men who feel the need to keep the world spinning every moment—and shows the value placed on signaling that one is not just doing the job, but is part of the team. His candid recollection is lengthy, but may be particularly helpful for any woman needing flexibility in her schedule.

Men recognize skill. But anyone who comes into a new situation would also do well to understand the workplace dynamic and seek some feedback on "am I fitting into it" *before* people start getting concerned behind the scenes and think you're not a team player. Because you'll have to perform even more if you have dug yourself that hole. It's like jumping a hurdle: There's always going to be a certain performance threshold or skill set that you are expected to meet. But if you don't comprehend the workplace dynamic and you operate outside of it, you've started by digging yourself a hole—so now you're on an even worse footing and have to jump even higher to meet expectations. And no one needs negative help like that.

I hired a new woman executive a year ago, and she's dynamite—but she got off on the wrong foot. We hired her because we needed someone to help us network into sales calls at a higher level. We're a bunch of engineers and we have a certain way of approaching people—we're not smooth. She's not the same sort of engineer and will never be able to do the same technical stuff, but she is used to working with higher-level people. And that is the skill set I hired her for.

She knew we had a relatively flexible workplace, which she needed, to be able to pick her kids up after school. And she said she would work from home instead. We were OK with that. But then there were all these school days off, when she couldn't come in. And then one of the kids was having doctor's visits, or there were special trips, so she would be gone for hours in the middle of the day, or not in at all. And she never asked enough questions about how this fit into our workplace dynamic, or what people were thinking.

It's hard to see how hard someone is working from her

home office. At first, we thought she wasn't listening to us because she was operating outside even our usual flexible parameters. So the buzz in the office was, "She's taking advantage of how flexible we are." And then there was this office chitchat, so then I was annoyed that she was distracting everyone to the point that their chitchat about her not getting her work done meant that they weren't getting their work done either!

Finally, we had to actually sit down and talk to her, and have the conversation of, "Look, we're here in our expectations—and you're way over here."

That friction lasted until recently, when she started delivering these huge wins. For example, she just got us a meeting with someone we've been wanting to get in front of for two years. So now all the guys in the office recognize her skill and they are ecstatic. Results-oriented people are always watching to see whether anything is falling through the cracks. But now her fantastic deliverables have proven that nothing is falling through the cracks, and have redeemed her lack of time commitment in the office. The men can accept even operating outside the workplace dynamic when they see these huge results.

We now realize that what she has to get done for work has never been sacrificed for her personal schedule. Now that the guys see her big results, they now recognize that she's never said, "I can't call so-and-so because of my kids." But it took us a while to see that, because we felt that she was always gone.

It would have been so much better to not have to sit her down and say, "You need to rein this in" and instead have *her* ask, "How are things going? What do I need to do to gain everyone's confidence?" And that would have given me a chance to say what any manager would love to be able to say in that situation: "I want you to learn our expectations quickly, because we have a vested interest in making you successful."

CHAPTER 7

The Little Things
That Drive Men Crazy

For just this one time in the book, I'm going to break my rule of only including quotes from men who seemed to genuinely care about women's advancement, and relay a comment I overheard in a crowded airline club room. A fifty-something businessman was on a conference call on his cell phone, sitting a few feet from me, and I could hear everything he was saying. I ignored him as best I could until the topic of the call turned to a woman he worked with.

I overheard him say, "Yeah, but she just makes such a big deal of it if you bring something up; it just becomes too big of a fuss to manage. [Listening] I just can't handle it anymore. Better to *not* deal with it and maybe she'll find it difficult enough that she'll look elsewhere on her own."

I quietly pulled out my quote notebook, resisted the temptation to whack him upside the head with it, and began to record what he was saying. Because the irritation unfolding in front of me exemplified something I've heard from many men: All too often, it is the little things that most drive them crazy. The big-picture issues (like whether someone doesn't seem to share the fear that the world will stop spinning) may have a major impact in how a man perceives someone, but they don't necessarily *irritate* him. The little things, however, all too easily rub a man the wrong way, and over time they seem to have a disproportionate impact.

Thankfully, because they are relatively minor issues, they are also relatively easily addressed . . . as long as one is aware of them.

THE LITTLE THINGS

There are undoubtedly dozens of "little things" that irritate men (and women, for that matter). In this chapter, I will cover three that I heard frequently and that seem most representative of this dynamic:

1. Get to the point

2. Don't overreact

3. Let it go

1. Get to the Point

Speaking at a women's event, I was amused when the event organizer recounted a favorite phrase of her boss: "Don't tell me about the pain; just show me the baby."

> *"Don't tell me about the pain; just show me the baby."*

That pretty much sums up how men expect discussions in the working world to operate. As you saw in chapter 3 and 4, while they may listen to details, stories, and long recountings in Personal World, they don't expect to do so in the workplace. In the workplace, efficiency dominates and, men tell me, they have neither the natural wiring to process a lot of details nor the patience for them.

As many men put it, "Give me the conclusion up front, and if I need more detail, I'll ask."

This is not likely to be a surprise; most women have probably heard this in their careers. But I was surprised at the level of frustration or impatience men felt at seemingly "minor inconveniences" like having to wait for the end of a story to hear the conclusion, wade through unwanted details, or endure unrelated conversation at the beginning of a meeting. The men I interviewed and surveyed helped me to understand the reasons why those three nuisances are perceived so poorly. Let's tackle each of them briefly.

"GIVE ME THE CONCLUSION UP FRONT . . ."

The way many of the men I interviewed described it to me, they prefer the conclusion or the bottom line up front because it helps them listen—and if they don't get it, it makes it hard for them to absorb the information.

> *Men prefer the conclusion or the bottom line up front because it helps them listen.*

One executive explained:

There's something about a male brain that wants the end of the story so he knows why he's listening. He's already focused on one thing, and if he's switching to another he needs to know what it is. And if he knows, it actually helps him listen. It's comforting to him. Versus when you wonder "Where is she going with this?" There is an actual discomfort in not knowing.

For example, this morning one woman was describing something that happened with a client, and she was telling me this story, and I didn't know if she was going to end with, "So isn't that funny?" or "So we lost the account." Listening that way is hard and uncomfortable for a guy. If you can come in and make it immediately clear what you're talking about, and how it relates to what he's doing, it will make a big difference. Men are much more patient with moving their focus, when there is clarity.

Another executive tied this to men's relative difficulty with multitasking, saying, "When you start a story, guys are trying to understand the relevance and context. And we really can't do that and listen well at the same time. So if he's wondering, 'Why are you telling me this?' he's not going to be hearing you properly."

On my survey, 60 percent of men agreed—and that percentage was higher the more senior the men were and the larger their company. Of executives in companies with more than $20 million in annual revenues, 70 percent said they feel like it is harder to listen and follow what someone is saying if they don't state the point up front.

". . . AND IF I NEED MORE DETAILS, I'LL ASK"

In *Why Men Don't Listen and Women Can't Read Maps*, Barbara and Allan Pease nail the reason for men's frequent request for fewer details. "Women's brains are process-oriented *and they enjoy the process of communicating*. [Emphasis mine.] Men find this lack of structure and purpose very disconcerting."[1]

Every branch of science studying how men and women communicate has found that women tend to process externally (they think something through by talking it through), while men tend to process internally (while they are thinking it through, they often *can't* talk about it). In large measure, this is due to the differences in brain structure covered in chapters 3 and 5.

To a man, however, the woman who is processing verbally may simply look scatterbrained. And it is all too easy for him to get exasperated. (*"I can't follow this." "Why is she wasting my time?"*) As one man put it, "I'm impatient with people who make me have to work out what the heck they are talking about. You're making me work too hard to understand you."

> *To a man, the woman who is processing verbally may simply look scatterbrained.*

Women presumably share the details because (as verbal processors) we instinctively assume that our listener similarly needs to hear our thought process to understand that we thought through all the permutations. Men, however, are used to processing internally and not hearing all those permutations—and they usually prefer not to.

One man advised, "Start with the end of the story, and work backwards," sharing only a few details about how you got there. By doing that, he said, you are essentially putting both parties at the same starting point. And the man can ask for more details as needed going forward.

Look at this representative comment from the vice president of human resources at a large technology company. "I think a man wants to know, 'What is the bottom line?' A woman wants to tell a story and for a man, that is just a waste of time. If there is important context to be shared, then OK. But nine times out of ten, just start with the bottom line and if I want more, I will tell you."

He went on, "I do not need to know the whole story and the rest of the problem. I just need to know that for a $10 million budget, we look like we will be $500,000 off. OK, start with that. Now I understand the problem, and I am definitely listening. Next, I need to understand why we're $500,000 off and how we got there.

But do not start with how we got there. Start with the bottom line and then work backward. Get me on the same page with you. And then I may ask for more."

Now, there is one important caveat to this "If I need more details I will ask" rule: It appears limited primarily to a supervisor-subordinate relationship. As we'll see in later chapters, junior men and even peers may not feel comfortable admitting they don't understand something or need additional details. But even the more junior men said that they need others to start with the bottom line and limit details to some degree. Especially in response to a question.

One manager gave me an example of what that looks like. "I told a new female hire, 'It would help if you could first just answer the question that I have asked you. If you need to give me the additional information, fine, but first answer the question.' I guess no one had ever been willing to bring that up with her before. But she instantly got it, and I am really enjoying working with her now. There's not that frustration in the background."

To some men, verbal processing can even make the speaker look insecure. Randal, the CFO of a small New York media company, told me:

I have several women who work in my department who seem to want to tell me their process so I can appreciate all the hard work that they did. But men assume that if you have got there, then you have done all of that. I also frankly think there is an insecurity that I am going to reject what they are saying if they don't give all the details, that I'm not going to give it enough weight.

By contrast, there is another woman I work with closely who is really great about summarizing. She will say to me, "These are the options and this is what I think." That is very effective. It is sort of a hybrid approach; she can get out the details that she thinks are critical, but gives me the bottom line.

It is ironic that the detailed processing that some men experience as frustrating and irrelevant can actually be a strength in women—one that men can easily miss. Here is a revealing comment from Matthew, the North American sales manager for a medical equipment supplier:

> Men sometimes talk about things forever too, but generally, if it were just men, it would be a ten-minute meeting: "OK, what do you guys want to do? Good. Let's go do it." But women need to download what is in their brain to process it, so you throw in a few women and you have added forty-five minutes to that meeting. So there seems to be a lot of wasted time as far as the man can see.
>
> Now, that said, men's eyes need to be opened to things that may be foreign to them, but are often very valuable. One of women's strengths is that there may be good things that come out of that extra forty-five minutes that would not have happened otherwise. Guys could go out of the ten-minute meeting and just completely botch the job because they did not spend enough time in analyzing the problem. There is benefit to be had from that additional deliberation. There is strength in how women handle things, but for men to understand it and perceive it that way is the issue.

As one of the men I spoke with put it, "It is clearly selfish for me to ask a woman to cut out all those details, since they are significant to her. But I have to know that they are significant to me, and in most cases, they are more significant to how she got there and I don't need to hear them. I know this is selfish behavior on my part, but almost every guy can identify with it."

CUTTING OUT UNRELATED CONVERSATIONS

One of the main logistical ramifications of men seeing a strict separation between Personal World and Work World, and of women seeing things more holistically (chapter 3), is that women find value in building relationships with coworkers through touching base or catching up on personal matters before getting down to business. Many men, on the other hand, tend to see such "small talk" as completely irrelevant to the business, and an exasperating way to squander limited time. They largely have the same impression of discussions that are work-related but have nothing to do with the purpose of that particular meeting.

When I asked the men on my survey if there were things they saw talented women do to undermine themselves with men, one survey-taker answered, "This sounds terrible, but [it is] the chatting. All the mindless talking that seems to take up the first half of any conversation."

As Jeffery Tobias Halter, author of *Selling to Men, Selling to Women*, put it in a recent talk, "As a rule of thumb, 80 percent of the time, men are transactional and women are relational. You can always tell transactional people from relational people by walking into a meeting and asking, 'How was your weekend?' The relational person will tell you they went to the lake with their kids, and open up an opportunity for you to ask, 'How many kids do you have?' And talk back and forth for a few minutes. The transactional person will answer, 'Fine.' If they are the senior person in the meeting, that is your cue to avoid the relational talk at all costs. Otherwise, they'll think you are wasting their time."[2]

This is another area where women might legitimately perceive a business value in spending time on issues beyond the immediate work matter at hand. For example, in conference calls or in meetings I personally am very transactional. I have very little margin in my schedule, so I can easily get impatient with time spent on conversation that I view as extraneous. Yet all the women who work for me are very relationship oriented, and when we start our biweekly morning-long staff meetings it is common to spend a few minutes catching up on kids or weekend plans, or a husband's job situation. This was torture for me, and I kept trying to eliminate it, until my staff director took me aside and told me bluntly, "Your team needs this. We are scattered doing all these different things. To continue to enjoy our jobs and enjoy working together, we need this time together to hear what is going on in each other's lives. And we need to hear what is going on in yours. Take the extra five minutes and tell us about what happened at your event last weekend. That is part of what keeps us cohesive and motivated."

Once I was willing to relax a bit and not try to hurry to get down to business, I saw that my staff director was correct. I imagine that many women have had that conversation with a male boss (and some female bosses, for that matter), who has probably seen the same results. Yet until you attempt to address it directly, and in terms of value, it is important to be aware how negatively the "extra conversation" is likely to be perceived by many of your male colleagues.

Two-thirds of men on the survey said that if a female colleague came into their office to talk one-on-one about issues beyond the workplace, they either were "likely to have" or "may have" the feeling, *I should discuss it with her, to show that I care . . . but privately, I'd really rather not, because I fear I'll get sucked into a personal conversation, and I just don't have time for that here.*

Whether the topic under discussion is personal or is related to other work issues, men appear likely to view the person who doesn't immediately get down to the business at hand as not only non-businesslike, but high maintenance.

The media company CFO, Randal, provided an example that he viewed as "fairly common."

We had just acquired a company and I was running an integration project with two team leaders, one woman and one man. With the woman, I had to spend an amount of time just sitting and listening to her, and that was really frustrating. She would come to me, explaining her issues with her team that I had assigned to her. She was very in touch with her emotional side, and I have to tell you that there were times when what was coming to mind was, "I do not need two wives to listen to—I already have one!" I honestly didn't think the issues were that big of a deal, but I had to deal with it.

But with the male team leader, I had actually given him a much more difficult team, with a bunch of different work styles he was going to have to blend. He had a bunch of what we would call the old-timers in this field, late forties and fifties, who were resisting doing things the new way. And I gave them this thirty-something guy as a leader.

And he has this whole bunch of dynamics that was far beyond what he could envision, but he would come to me and simply tell me what the problem was and how he had solved it or was planning on solving it. He would briefly fill me in, or bounce something off me to make sure I was OK with what he was planning to do. And that was just so much better, honestly. He was a much more low-maintenance employee than she was. I found her a high-maintenance employee. That is not to discount how talented she was and how hard she tried, how much time she invested in doing her role. But if I had to choose who I would rather work with, I would work with the guy.

2. Don't Overreact

As we saw in chapters 3, 4, and 5 (and the story at the beginning of this chapter), men place a high value on being able to address concerns or offer a criticism directly, without worrying about how someone is going to react. The men I interviewed told me that once they started having to worry about that, it was hard not to let their wariness color all of their interactions with that person.

> *Men place a high value on being able to address concerns or offer a criticism directly, without worrying about how someone is going to react.*

One of the men on the survey provided this example: "My co-worker actually got emotional in a meeting when asked to explain her testing technique. Instead of answering the question as a matter of informing the guy, she assumed he was questioning her skills. I ended up having to rephrase the question for her to understand it from a nonconfrontational viewpoint. Now to this day a lot of the programmers are wary of getting her involved in discussion and assume she can't handle pressure well."

When I asked the survey-takers what women might do to undermine their perception with men, many male survey-takers used their space to address the "don't overreact" issue. Their answers included everything from "Get overly upset when someone disagrees with them" to "Take suggestions of how to improve things too personally" to "Become overly heated during a simple exchange of ideas."

The concern about "overreacting" is inextricably tied up with men's comments in earlier chapters about not taking things personally and not getting emotional. As discussed in those chapters, managing how we are perceived requires a purposeful "edit" of our reactions, before we let anything show.

That said, many men told me that their lifelong practice of editing their reactions doesn't mean that a man won't sometimes lose it—including for effect. Geoff, the Fortune 500 CMO said, "Women at senior levels have to understand that sometimes, men overreact big too. And women can't overreact to their overreaction. Remember, he'll be done in ten minutes and won't think about it the rest of the day. Some men will even overreact for effect. Not long ago [our CEO] got mad in a senior meeting. He never swears, but he used the F-bomb with a direct report, to make a point. The guy the anger was directed at didn't overreact, didn't take it to HR, and I saw them having lunch three days later. So if men overreact they don't mean it forever."

And that leads to the third issue commonly mentioned by the men I interviewed.

3. Let It Go

This is one of the "little things" that men found the most inexplicable: the tendency of a worker (most frequently a woman) to essentially hold a grudge against another worker. Because men tend to think of Work World as a place where you essentially become your position and take your personal self out of it, men rarely show personal animus as the result of a workplace conflict. And they are not only irritated but alarmed when women do, viewing an unwill-

ingness (or inability) to "let it go" as a character flaw and potential
threat to the business.

> Men view an unwillingness (or inability) to
> "let it go" as a character flaw and potential
> threat to the business.

When asked what a talented woman might do to undermine
her perception with men, one survey-taker answered, "Two women
may get into an emotional confrontation, and may not forgive each
other for it. The aftereffect is that a man that works between their
two departments will have to suffer the hostility and bitterness between the two women, making them seem less desirable employees
to upper management."

A business owner I was speaking with brought this subject up,
describing such a situation as a "personal conflict." His colleague
jumped in: "Actually, it may look personal. But the man's mind
moves it immediately out of the personal category to the business
category. The man isn't looking at two women having a catfight.
He's looking at a threat to the business. That's the impact it has."

The business owner added, "It is the same threat if a man is doing it. Our chief technology officer didn't let things go, and it was
viewed as a serious character flaw, and we had to fire him."

I asked the men on the survey a series of questions about their
perceptions in this area, and their answers were stark. On average three out of four men looked quite negatively at someone who
did not let a conflict go, perceiving that as a big problem for the
company and an individual's career. Rather than summarize these
perceptions, I'm going to include the full list here. In the question,
I was not specifically asking about women, but about anyone who
expressed annoyance with another coworker over time.

Consider times in your working life when you have seen two co-workers have a work-related conflict and then begin to express annoyance with each other over time. Did you have any of the following perceptions about the situation and those coworkers? (Choose one answer on each row below.)

	I DID THINK THAT	I DID NOT THINK THAT
a. Getting personal in the workplace is not appropriate	77	23
b. This is wasting time and hurting the organization's efficiency	82	18
c. It makes me think they are choosing to not set this aside	73	27
d. It makes me think that they are incapable of setting this aside	61	39
e. Handling things this way could limit their professional opportunities	79	21
f. Whatever else I think about it, I do not want to get dragged in	74	26
g. It won't negatively impact the business, so it's fine if they process things this way	19	81

On the survey, 49 percent of men said that "if people become annoyed with each other, it is important for them to be able to express it openly, in their own way." Yet I believe this is an example of men who were trying to be sensitive and politically correct, but didn't actually believe what they were saying. *Fully 80 percent of those same men* said that continuing to express annoyance after a conflict (which presumably was an example of someone "expressing it openly, in their own way") wasted time and hurt the organization's efficiency. Even more telling, 79 percent of those men essentially felt that although the person "should" be able to express themselves openly, *actually doing so* would hurt the person's career.

Although the men were straightforward about the harm of not letting something go after a conflict, the men were significantly more cautious when I asked whether that was more likely with men or women:

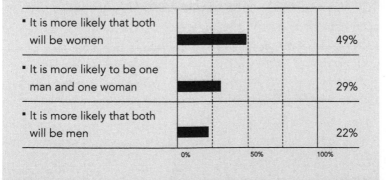

Now, this is a sensitive question, but your anonymous input will be helpful. In the type of scenario you recollected for the [previous question], in your experience what is more likely to be the gender of those expressing annoyance? (Choose one answer.)

• It is more likely that both will be women	49%
• It is more likely to be one man and one woman	29%
• It is more likely that both will be men	22%

In my personal interviews, nearly all the men I spoke with said that, realistically, such a two-sided scenario of continued annoyance was primarily observed among two female colleagues. While only half of the men on the survey put it that way, nearly eight in ten men did indicate that when those situations occurred, a woman would be involved. It was much less likely to be seen among two men.

Ironically, although the male survey-takers were cautious about naming women as those most often observed in that behavior, the control group of female survey-takers wasn't. Among the female survey-takers, fully 73 percent said both parties would likely be women, 20 percent said it would be one man and one woman, and just 7 percent said it was likely for both parties to be men.

WHAT LEADS TO "NOT LETTING IT GO"?

What leads to the tendency to not let things go? And why is this something that men *don't* seem to struggle with? From what I can tell, it appears to be an unconscious response to our multitasking female brain. Our research for *For Men Only* found that 81 percent of women have difficulty closing "mental windows" on issues that are bothering them. The concern tends to pop back up until whatever caused the concern is resolved. By contrast, men find it easy to compartmentalize and, if they judge this particular concern as unlikely to be a problem for the business, they can completely ignore the concern and let it go.

To men in business, therefore, a woman's "open mental windows" can easily look like holding a grudge. As one man put it, "Women have very long memories. And those emotions often continue to gyrate long after the issue should have been put to bed."

My husband, Jeff, who coauthored and researched *For Men Only* with me, provided a helpful perspective:

As guys we tend not to talk about interpersonal conflicts to others. We clam up. If a guy is actually talking about it, that means it is such a big deal that he hasn't been able to stuff it, he hasn't been able to compartmentalize it. So if I see a woman talking about these conflicts, I assume this is such a huge thing for her that she can't *not* talk about it. But it's really just a difference in perception. I look at the conflict and think, "Why is this such a huge deal for her?," when she may actually be experiencing the exact same feeling as I am, but just handling it differently.

The problem is that to a guy, her reaction could look like a lack of self-control, or as if she *could* be letting this go but is choosing not to. Or that she is making something a big deal that shouldn't be a big deal. And unfortunately, any of those could be seen as a weakness.

Men's need to let it go appears to be heightened by social pressure. An executive of a multinational company described how men handle such concerns:

Among men, there is something unmanly about remembering something. It shows a weakness in yourself. It shows that your armor was chinked in that conflict and you remember it. Why would you want to bring something up that happened two weeks ago or two months ago or two years ago? You forget it because you move on. And you move on because to do otherwise shows weakness. It is like: You fall, skin your knee, shake it off, and move on. In business, it happened, it is done, there's no need to deliberate about it, forget it. So you go have a few drinks and everything is done.

"Among men, there is something unmanly about remembering something. You move on because to do otherwise shows weakness."

HOW MEN VIEW NOT "LETTING IT GO"

When men see *anyone* holding on to an issue, it both irritates them and can have subtle, more negative ramifications. Dominic, the owner of a fifty-person manufacturing company, gave me an example of this sense of irritation, recounting the spats and misunderstandings between two of his executives, a man and a woman.

DOMINIC: After a while I would tell them that they needed to work on their communication skills. For crying out loud, you're twenty feet apart; stop using e-mail where you misinterpret and misread things. Just get out of your chair and go down and talk to this person—see the look on his face, hear the inflection in his voice. You know, I think I've spent more time wearing my striped shirt and referee hat once I got these women in there, in director roles.

ME: But this can't really be just something women specifically need to know, if men do it too.

DOMINIC: (Pause) I will say this: When I have two men in key roles, I don't have those conversations. Ever. I don't mean to suggest that when it was one man and one woman that it was all the woman's fault. I'm just saying there was more noise that I had to deal with when a woman was involved. I was looking forward to hiring women, and I will do it again. A woman can be extremely productive in our particular field. But to be frank with you, there just are things that you deal with, with women, that you don't usually deal with, with guys.

Matthew, the medical equipment sales manager I quoted earlier, provided a sobering example of the fallout that can result from high-maintenance friction in the workplace, saying, "I have known a lot of men, high-level men, who have chosen to leave management because they do not like to manage the emotional personalities. There is one guy that I work with now who used to be a hospital administrator. And most of his direct reports were women—he had ten women under his charge. He never told me this at the time, but as he describes it to me now, he says, 'I would come home and my nerves would be rubbed totally raw by the end of the day and I just had to get out.' He was managing personalities, managing slights of one form or another, and he would spend half of his day arbitrating one dispute or another and he finally said, 'I just do not want to do that.' Obviously, I am not suggesting that every office has these scenarios. But that is one of the actual examples I've seen."

Beyond being "rubbed raw," here are some of the deeper ramifications of a man viewing a woman as not likely to let something go, according to Cole, the executive search leader I quoted in the previous chapters:

COLE: I think men know that they can engage in this significant work-related conflict and generally not carry emotional baggage away from a conflict event. But men fear that if they engage in the similar level of intense conflict with a woman, that there will be emotional baggage that is carried away that will come back negatively in the future whether as resentment or as retaliation or revenge. They begin to be concerned that there will be an occasion all of a sudden, three weeks later in a meeting, where she will seize the opportunity to take a dig, thinking that this is a chance to even the score for something the guy thought was just a business conflict.

ME: How is that perceived by the other people in the room?

COLE: The other people in the room typically do not have the context. So, truthfully, the revenge may work. It usually makes a fool of the man—or it could be another woman, too. But what happens then is that the guy is unwilling to engage in the same level of business conflict because the future repercussions are not entirely predictable. And over time, the consequences of that will actually go deep for the woman who took the dig, and for the company. Because if he's not willing to engage her, then he has to try to find ways to bypass her. And eventually the woman is marginalized or the business doesn't function properly.

WHAT IS THE SOLUTION?

In the men's minds, the solution is to address an issue of concern directly, and then simply not bring it up again. Three out of four men on the survey chose that approach. Another 22 percent said one should "stuff" the feeling of annoyance, or should never have allowed oneself those feelings to begin with. Only 3 percent of men said it was acceptable to continue to express feelings of annoyance and let the situation naturally run its course.

But such a simple solution isn't always as easy to put into effect. How does a woman address something from the past that truly *needs* to be addressed for a business purpose, without being perceived poorly? I asked that of the multinational executive I quoted earlier:

ME: Suppose that a woman is ticked off that a colleague did something he shouldn't have. And the next year the guy is up for promotion and she feels the issue will affect the business. How can she raise it?

HIM: I would want to see that there is a sterile analysis of it. It is not an emotional analysis of it. So her first problem is that people saw her getting ticked about the situation to begin with. If she hadn't done that, her analysis a year later would seem a lot more credible. You need to show that when you look at it, you are looking at it through the lens of "We have these pros and these cons. This guy has delivered these results but there is this problem from last year." You can enumerate the problems but you look at it rationally in a detached fashion, not emotionally. You are not getting bent about it.

Another man responded with a different example:

We do have a problem with someone who seems to be keeping the pot stirred. But we're not robots. If I have had a business problem with someone, I'll move past it, but it doesn't mean that the problem is erased from my memory bank. We're not necessarily starting from a blank slate on the next deal. I'm just not going to let it impinge on what I'm doing today. It's a choice I have to make.

Letting it go doesn't mean that I've forgotten it and expect a problematic colleague to be different next time. If I've found him to be untrustworthy once I assume he'll still be untrustworthy next time. So I won't go back to him next time with a similar thing. But on everything else, we may not like each other or see eye to eye, but we can put the personal stuff aside and focus on what needs to be done.

> *"Letting it go doesn't mean that I've forgotten it and expect a problematic colleague to be different next time."*

Thankfully, the men I interviewed clearly felt that when professional women handle it the same way, they are well placed to capitalize on the situation instead of being dinged for it. Here is the encouraging perspective from one business owner:

> For companies to be successful, if you make mistakes, you learn from them and you move forward. I think men do keep scorecards, and they essentially expect that everyone else will too. But they expect it to be in a detailed and organized way, not an emotional way. They expect it to be solely on issues affecting the business.
>
> Men keep up with those things, but they use their scorecard to make specific work-related decisions going forward. With women, I don't perceive them doing that as often. They don't seem as likely to set aside the personal aspect to make business decisions going forward.
>
> Now, if a woman makes it clear that that *is* what she is doing, the perception will completely change. Women can sometimes be more observant. If she shows that she has observed something *and* she is taking her personal feelings out of it and putting it purely in a business scorecard context, that would be immensely valuable. Instead of being looked at as a gossip or as lacking maturity, she will be seen as someone who has excellent corporate intelligence and who uses it well.

CHAPTER 8

"Suck It Up"

Getting It Done No Matter What

When boys play even an informal game of football or basketball they usually play hard. They may be on the grass of the city park or a half-court by the old fire station, but they play like it's televised on ESPN. They block each other hard, trip each other to the ground, and inevitably, it seems, someone gets hurt. A face is badly scratched, a nose is bloodied, or someone gets the wind knocked out of them. When that happens, do the others stop play? Do they crowd around, asking, "You OK?"

If the boy is unconscious or coughing up blood, maybe. Otherwise, the expectation of everyone—including the wounded soldier—is the same: Suck it up and continue the game. No excuses, no complaining, and no asking for special consideration.

The same expectation holds in business. When I asked the men I interviewed what advice they would give to women in business, or how they felt about certain situations in the workplace, sports-related analogies came up over and over again. I realized that understanding the "suck it up" mind-set that comes with it is absolutely critical for women who want to know what their male colleagues (and even many female colleagues) are privately thinking. It has implications for everything from how men view flextime to what they expect from you as you rise through the ranks of the company to how they expect the boss-subordinate relationship to work.

Men seldom express these private expectations out loud. Of all the insights I gained from my interviews, several of the points in this chapter were those on which men were most uncomfortable being direct.

Let's take a look at what feeds the "suck it up" mind-set and the workplace expectations that come with it.

ACCOMMODATION IS FINE, BUT NOT EQUAL

To understand how the "suck it up" mind-set affects how women may be perceived, it is critical to understand just how much men see the world in terms of competition. For most men, everyday life is seen in terms of you versus me, us versus them, and even me against myself if there's no other competition around at the moment. All the expectations in this chapter would be merely academic if it weren't for the fact that workers do in fact compete for compensation, promotion, and prestige. Even men in collaborative, team-oriented jobs see themselves in competition to get ahead—not just with that other company across town, but with the other members of the team.

This is why, as you will see, men seem so highly attuned to how hard everyone is playing the game, and how well—and whether everyone is playing the game by the same rules. (This is not, as in previous chapters, about the big-picture "rules" or "natural laws" of the workplace—but about whether a man sees all colleagues having a level playing field for the competition between them.) In the end, this mind-set lends itself to the workplace expectations that I'll outline in the rest of this chapter—expectations that, in some cases, may be hard to hear. As always, though, knowing what they are (even if we disagree) is essential for making the truly informed choices that are right for us.

To most men (and quite a few women), the "suck it up" mentality means:

- You don't let personal or professional obstacles stop you from getting the job done

- You don't complain

- You resist asking for help or explanation

- You don't ask for different standards unless you also adjust your expectations

Let's look at each of these expectations in detail.

EXPECTATION 1: YOU DON'T LET PERSONAL OR PROFESSIONAL OBSTACLES STOP YOU FROM GETTING THE JOB DONE

From the earliest age, boys on the field of play recognize that the expectations of those around them (coaches and teammates)—and their own internal drive—create the most fundamental rule of any competitive endeavor: If you have accepted a particular spot on the team, you don't let obstacles stop you from getting that job done. If you're the starting halfback, and have to play on a twisted ankle or with a gashed chin, that's what you do.

In a man's mind, a business endeavor works the same way. Just as he expects his "first string" teammates to get themselves off the ground and back into the game, he expects his "first string" colleagues to push themselves to get the job done—despite the flu, difficult clients, personal problems, technology glitches, or the need to attend to a sick child.

When I asked the CFO of a Fortune 500 manufacturer what he would advise women in business to understand about men, he answered, "I played soccer all my life, and if your teammate has a hard collision you may encourage him with a slap on the back, but you say, 'Let's get it done.' And certainly when *you* take a hit, you know you'd *better* get up and keep playing. If you're really hurt, you take yourself out of the game. So if someone doesn't take themselves out, you don't expect to see them limping along at half speed. You get your act together or get off the field. Men naturally expect that mind-set from other men—and, in today's workplace, from women as well."

Although this comment may seem harsh, this man was, in fact, a relatively sensitive individual. As I saw in many of my interviews, the "suck it up" mentality exists even when the man is caring and sympathetic.

The reason men hold this mind-set, as one engineer put it, is because "you *expect* to have to prove yourself, every day. It's not just about competence but your ability to get the job done, that day. When we're in the business equivalent of third and ten, and the game is on the line, I'm going to put in the person who has proved he or she can get it done, period. I'm simply not going to put in someone who has shown that they can't always be there at 100 percent capacity. And if you're at all aware of how business works, there is no way that should be controversial, or a surprise."

> *"When we're in the business equivalent of third and ten, and the game is on the line, I'm going to put in the person who has proved he or she can get it done, period."*

Over and over, the men emphasized that it's not the gender of the person but their performance that makes the difference. As one man put it, "I don't care if the person on the line is a man, woman, or little green-eyed monster. They get my respect when they prove themselves." There are several factors that contribute to earning such respect.

Pushing Through Obstacles

A man respects a person whom he sees as pushing through obstacles. And, in fact, a person's willingness and ability to do so is a large part of what makes him consider someone a reliable or key player instead of a marginal one. At the same time, the colleague who does so does not necessarily receive applause or appreciation. To other men, the colleague is merely adhering to the rules of the work world and doing what everyone should be expected to do. Conversely, if it appears that a colleague is not meeting that expectation—by letting those obstacles "defeat" them (letting those obstacles prevent the job from getting done well)—the man loses respect for that person, questions whether they are a dependable member of the team, and often mentally puts them "on the bench" to some degree. Privately, they may not consider that person a "first string player" while that pattern persists.

On the national survey I conducted, when I asked men what women might do that unintentionally undermines how they are perceived by the men they worked with, one survey-taker answered, "When a woman has major responsibilities and does not show up because of minor physical or emotional problems. In other words, she doesn't work through her obstacles to do her job."

I read that quote to a male colleague, who shook his head. "The problem is, who gets to say that a physical or emotional problem is 'minor'? Unfortunately for women, men often don't understand many of the issues women deal with, and so often view those issues as minor when they're not."

The reality, though, is that even when a man views an outside issue as important, it is still supposed to take a backseat to the person's workplace responsibilities. Here is what one test survey-taker advised women on avoiding perception problems: "Women should be cautious how they bring discussions of children's issues into the workplace. We all love our children! We all must also make provisions for them when they're sick or need help at school. And while many of us only 'work to live,' while we're at work, it is expected that work comes first. [Giving] 100 percent while at work is the rule."

Right-Sizing Expectations

If a worker is hindered by obstacles that can't be worked through, he or she will retain (or even increase) a man's respect by adjusting their expectations away from first-string play for a time. If a person acknowledges that they are encountering obstacles that will hinder the team's chances of "winning" (for example, landing the deal or getting the report in on time), they may be able to carve out a less-demanding role for a period of time. That person is much more likely to be viewed with respect than the person who continually insists that they can get it done, and then doesn't.

As one man explained, "Honest self-assessment is a value for guys. And getting it done is a value for guys—and a lot of women, too, obviously. So being able to self-assess that 'I'm not going to be able to do this well right now' says 'I'm putting the team and the business first.' But if you say you can do it and then you don't, what you're saying is, 'I was more important than the team.' It's selfish and it hurts everyone else."

In a private meeting with a group of managers at a huge household name company, the female hiring director described a "talk" that she has had to have with many more up-and-coming women than men. She said that when women with children rise through the ranks, they often come to a crisis point. She privately takes them aside and tells them, "You're going to have to choose whether you are going to prioritize your family or your career right now. Because you've gotten high enough up that by trying to prioritize both, you're doing neither well. Your work is suffering. If you want to keep doing this job well and keep rising in your career right now, your family has to take a backseat. Or, if you want to prioritize your family, you need to adjust your job track. You have to make whatever choice is right for you—but very soon now, you're going to have to make a choice."

> *"You have to make whatever choice is right for you—but very soon now, you're going to have to make a choice."*

Hearing that story, one ambitious female friend of mine who does not have children said, indignantly, "How has that company not been sued? How can she get away with that?" A more senior woman who was listening in said, "It's because it's true! She's giving a woman the chance to think it through and be purposeful about a decision, before the decision is made for her by being fired or humiliated within the organization. Or before her family falls apart. It's *better* for women if we're honest and realistic with ourselves. And each other."

It is worth noting at this point that although that corporation's hiring director correctly described this issue as affecting women more than men, quite a few men told me they felt a similar need to be "realistic with themselves" about their work-life balance situation. (Multiple studies have investigated the many reasons *why* women are more likely than men to face this need, but that discussion goes beyond what we can tackle in this book.)

Signaling Day-to-Day Commitment

Since men expect colleagues or subordinates to "get their act together" when they encounter obstacles, they certainly expect the person to demonstrate complete commitment during normal times—and to never signal a *lack* of commitment.

Unfortunately, while the men I interviewed said they knew many committed, dedicated male and female workers, they also confessed that when they *had* known workers who signaled a lack of commitment, that person was, in their experience, much more likely to be a woman.

Men would often hasten to say, "But I don't think this is a gender issue—I'm sure men do this too." And every single time, when I asked, "Can you give me an example of when you've seen a man do this?," their answer was always, "Well . . . no."

One main difference, apparently, is that men are more likely to have learned how to hide any apathy or difficulty they might have, instead of broadcasting it. Here is a conversation I had with Brad, a junior partner at a large national law firm:

ME: Have you ever looked at the way a woman said or did something and thought to yourself, "Why is she shooting herself in the foot?"

BRAD: I see this a fair amount, where a woman comes out of law school and has no intention of staying to become a partner. Maybe without intending to, she broadcasts an attitude of "I'm only going to be here three years, six years; at some point I'm going to ramp down my schedule when I have kids." OK, more power to her; that's her choice. But then you see this winding down of mental commitment to the job.

I'm thankful that we live in an age where a woman can be just as valued for choosing to be a mom, instead of looked down on. My wife is making that choice while our kids are young. But maybe because there isn't a stigma anymore, there's also often no filter. Sometimes, younger women don't think they need to play the game of making people think they are mentally invested.

ME: What is it that a female colleague might do, to make you think she's not invested?

BRAD: She's smart, but she's not spending the time you would expect her to spend to get the job done properly. For example, she'll leave a project for a more senior person to correct and finish. Or she won't go the extra mile to figure out something technical. It makes it look like she doesn't have pride in getting the work done, with the long term in mind.

ME: Do you see that in guys?

BRAD: No, I see the opposite. Now, remember that I see many committed women, too. But still, percentagewise, guys are more likely to take it the extra mile and show that commitment. Look, I don't love learning certain technicalities of Delaware tax law. But it's a pill I know I need to swallow because I'm going to be doing this as a foundation, as my career, to provide for my family, and so I need to build my skill set. If I saw a man not taking the extra time, I would think he's checking out and he's about to move to another job. And it unfolds within a month from when I first see it.

EXPECTATION 2: YOU DON'T COMPLAIN

Just as men believe you suck it up and get the job done despite any obstacles, they also believe that you don't draw attention to or complain about those obstacles. Part of sucking it up involves dealing with all hindrances with aplomb, pushing through them by working harder—and not drawing attention to how much you have to deal with. Doing otherwise is akin to crying on the football field, "Coach, that big, mean linebacker hit me too hard!" Even when there is something legitimate to complain about, it just isn't done.

In one focus group, a female management consultant shared a story of a former colleague who had been in a difficult situation: Her husband was having cancer treatments during the day, so this woman was having to work crazy hours late at night, and regularly mentioned it. The female consultant I was talking to described how she and many of her male associates were initially sympathetic to her difficult situation, but eventually grew frustrated with how much the woman raised the issue.

"She did what was needed, but complained," said another businessman. "Either don't do it, or *do* do it and don't complain! Complaining does not qualify as sucking it up. If it happens too often, that person will be mentally sidelined."

While most of us recognize that complaining is not viewed well, what we may not realize is that, to a man, complaining is far more than just saying, "This is unfair." There are many words and phrases that are viewed the same way. One example is blaming institutional bias—including gender bias.

When a woman mentions, even in passing, that things are difficult for a woman, men felt it can come across as being "whiny." An investment company executive I spoke with said:

If the men at my company get annoyed that the higher-ups seem biased in favor of promoting folks from Ivy League business schools, the other guys say, "Well, OK, then I have to suck it up and work harder and prove that I can compete." If you complain instead, then you are seen as self-condemning, deficient, not capable of winning on your own merits. That is a behavior that the average guy would despise. Suck it up, fight the battle, win on your merits rather than positioning yourself as a victim. Guys think, *What guy with testosterone in his body would go out there claiming to be a victim?* And they essentially expect that any woman who is serious will handle things the same way.

> "If you complain you are seen as not capable of winning on your own merits."

What I found fascinating is that he (and other men I spoke with) tended to view complaining as "claiming to be a victim," which undermines how confident that person is perceived to be in their skills and abilities.

Talking About How Hard You Are Working

In a man's eyes, this is akin to complaining. One survey-taker advised, "Don't act like you're having to work harder, even if you are."

Now, in my previous hometown of New York City, people put in insane hours and gained a sick sort of satisfaction and kudos from working more hours than anyone else. But in order to not brag directly ("I was working on the Becker merger until two a.m."), employees would come up with creative ways to get the message across. The e-mail or voice mail sent to the boss at 1:14 a.m. was a well-worked strategy. Given the pressure to work around the clock, a savvy worker would often resort to the *appearance* of face time in order to sneak out "early" at nine p.m., such as leaving the office lights on and the suit coat visibly draped across the back of his or her chair. Or—my personal favorite—calling back in to the office at midnight and having yourself paged, so that "Bill Smith, you have a call on Line Three," would resound through the office for everyone else to hear.

I'm certainly not advocating such pathological behavior. But it does point out just how out of whack the "suck it up" expectations at work can be.

Seeming Uptight or Overly Focused on Little Problems

One thing that raises the specter of a "whiny" individual is getting agitated or stressed about little problems or minor issues, instead of dealing with them in a calm way. Several of the men I surveyed said this was a relatively common way that women unwittingly undermined themselves with men.

As one survey-taker put it, "My advice to women is: Never complain too much, and don't sweat the small stuff. Once a woman is known as a complainer, management will walk the other way when they see her."

Talking About Personal Problems— or Problems of Any Sort, Really

One of the reasons men expect people to leave personal issues at home is that men think that if they are talking about them at work (in other words, complaining), that they are *affecting* work. One female senior vice president at a major corporation told me that she had a female peer who was going through a divorce—who was advised, "Don't let anyone at work know, or the guys may think you are going to fall apart."

The common denominator in all these examples of "not sucking it up" is sharing one's concerns or situation out loud. One of my experienced female advisors made an astute observation: "You know, men have ways of 'not sucking it up' too—the problem is, it is more obvious with women because women tend to be more verbal." A businessman who was listening nodded in agreement. "Men are more passive-aggressive about it, where women seem to act out more and talk about it more. The ironic thing is: The fact that women talk about it is perceived poorly—but at the end of the day they get it done."

EXPECTATION 3: YOU DON'T ASK FOR HELP OR EXPLANATION

In the basketball movie *Hoosiers*, Gene Hackman, the new coach of a tiny 1952 rural Indiana high school basketball team, institutes a completely new style of play with no explanations as to why he's doing it. Where previous coaches had encouraged players to shoot for the basket whenever they had an opening ("If you don't shoot, you can't score!"), the new coach insists they not try for a basket until they pass the ball at least four times. The team starts off in clumsy fashion and loses its opening games. Frustrated, one of the players defies the coach and begins making baskets without passing. He is yanked from the game by the irate coach, leaving just four players against the other team's five.

At the end of the game, the coach comes down to the locker room and tells the team, "For those of you on the floor at the end, I'm proud of you. You played your guts out. I'm only going to say this one time . . . Think about whether you want to be on this team or not, under the following condition: What I say when it comes to this basketball team *is the law absolutely and with no discussion!*"

The players eventually develop the much broader skills the coach was aiming for, and go on in David and Goliath fashion to win the state championship against much larger schools. But I was fixated on the frustrating start to their season. In exasperation I asked my husband, Jeff, "Why didn't he just tell them *why* he was insisting on four passes before shooting? If he had just explained the reason for the rule the players would have understood, been on board, and wouldn't have gotten frustrated!"

Jeff—who played every conceivable sport in high school—grinned. "That may be how girls think, but not guys. In sports, guys generally don't ask why. And I'm guessing that girls who play competitive sports don't ask why either. The coach *is* the law; he doesn't have to explain himself. That doesn't mean that all questions are off-limits; there is a way to ask questions without seeming to question the coach. But especially when you're under time pressure, you're expected to just do what he says. Guys tend to think that if you don't understand why you're doing something, you should be able to figure it out on your own."

"Guys think that if you don't understand why you're doing something, you should be able to figure it out on your own."

A great many men with whom I've discussed this pointed out the ways this expectation tends to transfer to the workplace:

The Boss Is the Law

Men have been trained, through sports, the classroom, the Boy Scouts, the military, and the business world, to work within a top-down hierarchy. Top-down authority is a system most men in the workforce feel comfortable with; everyone knows his or her relative place. Thus, employees may either love or resent their supervisor, but while that person is the boss, his or her decision is the law—what he or she says, goes. And anyone who doesn't "get" that is viewed as naive about the most basic rules of the road.

As one manager put it, "A lot of guys grow up learning that what the coach says is to be followed absolutely; you don't question it. And we tend to view the edicts of the boss the same way. The boss says jump, your job is to ask how high. And if the boss gives a task on deadline that you don't quite understand, you jump to get started anyway and think to yourself, *I have no idea what I'm doing, but I'll figure it out.*"

You Figure It Out Without Help

And that leads to the second point. Many of my interviewees said that men place a high value on figuring things out on their own. "They will go out of their way to avoid asking for help," explained one businessman, "because asking means they *couldn't* figure it out on their own. So if they see a colleague asking for help or asking, 'What is the point behind this?' they automatically assume that person *can't* do it, *can't* figure it out."

As I discussed this issue with the men I interviewed, I realized this one factor probably affects working women far more than we might realize. Women often have a natural desire to "help" others, and have much less reluctance to ask for help ourselves— whether that means stopping the car to ask for directions or popping into the boss's office to ask for more explanation on how to create the new budget report. For women, asking such questions doesn't carry a stigma. But that often is not the case with men. As a result, both offering help and asking for it can easily be misinterpreted by the men we work with. It doesn't mean we shouldn't ask, but it is important to realize such a request may at times be misperceived.

All that said, many men also acknowledged that there is a significant downside to their mind-set. One senior manager put it to me this way: "Men will definitely lean toward 'You suck it up and do what you need to do,' and may even do it incorrectly instead of sharing problems they are having with getting it done or figuring out whether there's a better way to do it. Men are like, 'Just put me in a cave and let me figure out how to do it.' Men will do that often. I'm not sure that women will."

If There's a Deadline, Figure It Out Fast; Don't Waste Time Trying to Figure Out a Better Way of Doing It

Not surprisingly, if the situation is time-sensitive, the men said, they are *more* exasperated if someone wants to take time to ask, "Wait a minute—is there a better way of doing this?" Their instinct is to dive in and get started, and they may be annoyed or frustrated by our "need" to ask those extra questions.

Personally, I have a huge pet peeve against racing ahead with what seems like a half-baked process when a little extra thought could dramatically improve it and save a lot of time down the road. But although the benefit of that "extra" front-end time may seem obvious to us, that is often not how men view it.

When I asked a managing partner of a Big Four accounting firm, whom I'll call Harold, how a man would view it if someone wanted to take extra time on the process, here's how he answered:

It depends on the perceived crisis by the manager. If someone says, "It has to get done right away," men want to see action steps immediately, and if they see hesitation they think that person can't do it. We're in an emergency room, we need triage right away. Not "Let's get seven doctors in here and have a conference."

But in reality, even with the large, urgent problems, 80 percent of the solution is often defining what the problem is. Over the years I've seen that a woman can often be more effective at helping define the problem, because they are instinctively more willing to take the extra time to do so. Unfortunately, a man may view that as they can't do it on their own.

The female executives I spoke with agreed with Harold's assessment. One woman said, "I have definitely experienced this with some men. If they didn't see a flurry of activity, they wrongly concluded I hadn't prioritized or wasn't taking action."

> One woman said, "If the men I worked with didn't see a flurry of activity, they wrongly concluded I hadn't prioritized or wasn't taking action."

In a mixed-gender focus group that I conducted on these topics, a woman asked the men in the room, "Does 'suck it up' look different for women and men? Or does it mean the same thing to each?" One high-level operations executive answered, "I think it *does* look different. In my experience, even 'get it done'–type women want to talk about it or analyze it first. Men just want to get on with it. We want to be fixers and we think that time constraints mean we *can't* talk about it!"

You Don't Examine or Try to Change the Deadline or Requirements, Even When They Seem Unrealistic

Harold, the Big Four partner, outlined another perceived difference between men and women: When faced with seemingly unrealistic requests, women are far more likely to ask, "Is this deadline hard and fast?" or "Is this requirement really needed?"

"In my experience," he said, "women will compare notes, realize there are some big issues getting in the way, and maybe spend a little bit of time asking, 'Is there a better solution to this?' instead of sucking it up for twenty hours. They have more of a tendency to say, 'Let's go to the client and see if there's a more realistic deadline.' Where a man would say, 'I was told that the deadline was tomorrow, so let's just do it.'"

The rub with these "you don't ask for help" or "you can't spend too much time up front" approaches, of course, is that we may completely disagree with them.

One experienced businesswoman at a major consulting firm, hearing some of these points of friction, pointed out in an e-mail that women shouldn't be quick to change their approach just because others might get impatient with it:

Women need to know that many men will instinctively want to move on instead of asking more questions up front. However, there may be a big price to pay. I interviewed our client executives regarding their satisfaction with our service, team, etc. When clients were very dissatisfied it was because their needs were not understood up front. In many global client loyalty studies, understanding needs and expectations up front drives overall satisfaction by a ratio of two to one. (Chalk one up for the female approach.) We just

need to find a constructive way to approach our male colleagues and clearly communicate that this is all part of the
up-front planning that yields so many dividends.

Many of the men acknowledged that men might benefit from
a different approach. Harold suggested that women counter the
negative impression of a more measured approach before it has a
chance to form, by being proactive about it:

> Don't state your concern or your question first. Instead, you
> should first say, "I know *a, b,* and *c* are the steps we would
> normally take to handle this." So you're demonstrating that
> "I know exactly what to do and could do it right now if I had
> to." *Then* you state your concern. If you first outline the ac
> tion plan that you *could* do, the guy will think, "She knows
> what to do, so there's also probably a reason why we should
> ask these questions first."
>
> When a woman says, "Wait a second, is this the best way to
> do this?" what is missing is a woman's internal logic—that "If
> I do *a, b,* and *c,* it's going to lead to this and I'm not sure that's
> the right outcome." But if she doesn't actually *say* that, the
> other person may think *she doesn't know what has to be done*.
> Meanwhile, she's thought it all through and is back to the
> beginning again. Doing it in a different order totally changes
> the perception about how knowledgeable she is about it.

EXPECTATION 4: YOU DON'T ASK FOR DIFFERENT STANDARDS—UNLESS YOU ARE WILLING TO ADJUST YOUR EXPECTATIONS

This is a very sensitive topic. And for some women, it may be difficult to hear. But it is probably also essential for anyone who feels torn between balancing work and home-life responsibilities. In the minds of men (and many women, for that matter), the need for everyone to play the game by the same rules is one of the most basic "natural laws" of the competitive working world. Even the most compassionate, accommodating men I spoke with shared the conviction that one simply does not ask for different standards—such as fewer working hours or a more flexible schedule than others—*unless* one also adjusts one's expectations to match those different standards.

> *Even the most accommodating men shared the conviction that one simply does not ask for different standards* unless *one also adjusts one's expectations to match.*

The problem, the men said, is that while men seemed to universally understand this "rule" and perceive when a boundary had been crossed, some women did not. In nearly every interview about this, men raised examples of women (usually, those with family responsibilities) appearing to expect equal treatment while asking for *unequal* standards. For example, being less available than other consultants to work nights and weekends, yet expecting the same opportunity to be included on the most exciting or lucrative deals, or being upset if they weren't.

Most of the examples I heard were about working moms in demanding jobs who were torn between the requirements of their job and the requirements of their children. The men were far less likely to have the same perception about women who didn't have children and thus didn't have to manage the same sort of balancing act. Indeed, many childless women had the same perceptions as the men.

Almost every man I interviewed felt he could not openly address this dynamic without being misunderstood. They wanted to be supportive—and said their actions *were* supportive in most cases—yet it unquestionably affected their perception of certain female colleagues. Let me give one representative example.

"When It Comes Time to Make Partner, Let's Not Pretend That Things Were Equal"

One of my first in-depth business interviews was with an old friend from my New York days, now a partner in a major consulting firm, whom I will call Wes. He is a good guy, and a sensitive manager. I figured he would be able to give me a fair-minded but honest reaction to the question of whether women might be doing things that hamper how they are perceived by men, without realizing it.

The resulting discussion was quite long and some points that he raised may be a bit hard for women to hear, but they are very representative of what I heard from dozens of other men.

ME: Is there anything that you or the other men here would consider a relatively common frustration that comes up when working with some women, that doesn't happen as much with men? Is there anything like that that men view as a concern?

WES: (Pause) Can you turn off the tape recorder?

ME: Sure . . . I'll just take notes on my laptop instead.

WES: OK. Yes, there is a very common pet peeve that I've seen. We work hard here, right? We have big deals that come in at the last minute, we sometimes need to pull all-nighters when we're trying to land or finish a project, and we need 100 percent effort from everyone. Now, you know that I'm a family guy. [He gestures to a picture of his wife and kids.] But when the work comes in, you gotta do what you gotta do. The problem is that expectations don't seem to be even.

ME: What do you mean by that?

HIM: We have a lot of associates, men and women. I've been working hard to get female associates hired here, and get them in on
the good deals. But privately, it's just a reality that *if* they have
kids, they are more likely to have to be home at a certain hour.
It's usually not their husband who leaves work to get Johnny
when he's sick at school. It's them. Now, you know me—I personally think family has to take priority. If one of my female
associates has a kid who's sick, I want her to be able to go and
do what she's gotta do. I don't want to make her feel guilty. If
one of my daughters was sick, I would want [my wife's] boss to
be generous about letting her run out to the pediatrician. But
the reality is, of course, that it puts the rest of us in a bad spot.
Someone is going to have to work double time to get that person's work done. No one ever, ever talks about this out loud,
but everyone—men and women—know that it's rarely a man
who has to ask someone else to cover his work because of family
obligations. It's usually a woman. And we're OK with that, but
there are consequences.

This just happened here late yesterday. A big deal finally
crystallized yesterday afternoon, but one of my female associates still had to leave as usual at six o'clock to pick up her son.
And my colleagues Steve and Jack were here at eleven o'clock
at night away from their own families, getting a deal memo put
together without her help. And that's OK, because we want
to be supportive and we would want the same thing for our
wives.

ME: OK.

HIM: (Leaning forward.) *But when it comes time to make partner, let's
not pretend that things are really equal.* That is what really, really

irks men—and some women—around here. We've got some incredibly smart, competent female associates. And some of them are single, or don't have kids, and they will bust their tail at midnight along with anyone else to get it done. But some others—usually the ones with families—simply can't. Or don't. And then they get upset when I don't assign them the best deals! And they make it clear that it's been twelve years and they expect to be making partner, right along with Steve and Jack, who have been here twelve years but working far longer hours. And sometimes they do, honestly, because we're trying to increase our ratio of female partners, or even because our partners know that we could be hit with a discrimination suit. But can you imagine what that says to the folks like Steve and Jack? They've sacrificed their time with their own families, after all.

There is no doubt that the women I'm talking about are just as smart, just as competent, and would be just as good on those deals as anyone else. They are equal in talent. And women want equal treatment. But what Steve and Jack would probably be dying to say is, "Let's not pretend that things really *were* equal."

ME: You think this is a common view?

HIM: (Shrugging) I know it is. Men can't really talk about it, because they'd look like a heel, but I know it is. Privately, it's a very big frustration.

"I DON'T VIEW IT AS THE SAME"

His concern was echoed on the survey I conducted. Even when I proposed a fairly benign (and common) situation where two team members added "great value," but worked from home on Fridays and—due to family obligations—weren't as able to stay late at the office during the week or on weekends, 57 percent of full-time men said their workload simply wasn't the same, when it came to compensation and being promoted.

I actually found it heartening that more than four in ten men *did* view the two family-oriented workers "as exactly the same," and view that as good news for women who endure a difficult work-life balancing act every day. That percentage probably signals the positive experience of men who have seen the benefit of work-life-balance programs over the years. But that said, I am also very aware that the clear majority of survey-takers did *not* view it as the same—and that the real-world examples of frustration from the men I interviewed seemed more common than was apparent on the survey.

"IT DEPENDS ON HOW THEY HANDLE IT"

Men who have the "suck it up" mind-set tend to form a perception of others largely based on how they handle a less-than-ideal situation. On the survey, I continued the previous flextime scenario by asking the men to now suppose that the two workers were in fact compensated differently from everyone else—and protested. Very few of the men (15 percent) viewed the workers positively—and almost half (47 percent) viewed the workers negatively.

That said, I was pleasantly surprised (again) that half of the men *didn't* have a problem with the two flextime workers' protestations. But the fact that half of the men did raises a red flag: For those women who have a flexible work situation, we should realize that many men (and women, for that matter) will be highly attuned to how we handle it. And not everyone may be on the same page.

> Many men will be highly attuned to how we handle flexible work situations.

No, All Our Progress Has Not Been Wasted!

As a working mom myself, who is torn every day between the demands of my job and the needs of my two small children, I know some of the comments I have relayed may be disconcerting or exasperating to hear. It would be easy to wonder whether years of progress in building more family-friendly and flexible work plans have been for nothing if taking advantage of those programs risks damaging the perception of those who use them. It would also be easy to question whether all our efforts at educating corporate leadership (often, men) have been wasted.

It is important to reaffirm that the progress is real. My research was not intended as a comprehensive review of how men feel about all flextime programs, but was an attempt to gauge how men felt about one type of scenario (when even valuable flextime workers simply couldn't put in as many hours or be available at the same times). Regardless, many studies have demonstrated that family-friendly programs have indeed made it easier (if still not easy) for working mothers to juggle the demands of work and family. And the ability to take advantage of them is something many women are thankful for.

Women need to continue to make the work choices that are right for their individual situation—but also continue to ensure that those choices are deliberate and informed, taking into account how they may be perceived by others we work for and with.

Further, the perceptions I'm passing along are not as negative as they may appear at first glance. Based on my research, the increased attention to and awareness of family-friendly programs has clearly improved men's private perceptions of them, even if it didn't change the overall feeling that such programs represented different standards. It is also important to note that the men I interviewed and surveyed were often quite torn about this subject. They recognized the dilemma that talented women were being placed in, since, statistically, female colleagues were more likely to be the ones with primary child-care responsibilities, and thus more likely to be put in a position to have to ask for those perceived different standards.

Different Standards = Special Treatment

While women might not think of flextime, for example, as equal to "different standards" or "special treatment," men often do. Ironically, many women who take advantage of family-friendly programs (like those providing flexible working hours) see them as "leveling the playing field," since they give women an equal chance to compete with men who don't have the same family constraints. But men's perception is often the opposite.

> *While women might not think of flextime, for example, as equal to "different standards" or "special treatment," men often do.*

As one survey-taker opined on the survey scenario about the two team members who worked from home on Fridays, "Realistically, if the work being done remotely requires communication, it usually seems to take more time from other team members to compensate—or we could all work remotely regularly."

Many male observers feel that giving special treatment to one person creates its own alternative dilemma: By default, it puts another person at a relative disadvantage. And out of the same desire for fairness that motivates women, the men I interviewed said anyone should be aware that special treatment is being asked for.

In my interviews with men, there was a clear undercurrent of frustration regarding women who, they felt, didn't see that they were asking to play by different rules. That didn't mean that the men were unwilling to accommodate those special needs—they just wanted the woman to recognize that they were. (Which, of course, many women don't agree with!)

One man I know compared the situation to a woman playing competitive golf with the guys; she hits off the women's tee closer to the green and sees it as leveling the playing field so she can compete equally—without recognizing that the men see it as competing unequally. My interviewee mentioned a mutual female friend who is a former Olympian and very athletic. When she plays golf with men, she plays off the men's tee rather than the women's tee, and in doing so earns their astonished respect. But as he pointed out:

In most cases, though, women hit off the women's tee when they play, and we're fine with that. It is an accommodation, but it's fine. It's sort of like that in business—most men aren't at all opposed to making an accommodation for children or recognizing that a colleague may have a difficult family situation, and cutting her a break. We're not heartless! The problem is that we as guys don't usually ask for a similar accommodation from other guys. Or if we do, we *know* it is an accommodation.

In golf, a guy who doesn't have as much arm strength as other guys would never ask to hit from the women's tee. And in business, many men would never ask for what some women ask for. We are willing to give her that—it's just that in the minds of some men, at least, she's not competing equally. I know this is going to sound harsh, but it's like, if you worked fewer hours and produced less but got the same bonus, I can be pleased for you—but just don't fool yourself into thinking that you got it fair and square.

Factors That Improve the Perception

Thankfully, even though "asking for different standards" can be viewed negatively, there were several factors that dramatically changed how different standards were perceived: acknowledgment instead of denial, a willingness to adjust expectations wherever output changed, and a realistic accounting for impact. Those factors were so powerful that in many cases, the men said, the different standards became a nonissue.

ACKNOWLEDGMENT INSTEAD OF DENIAL

First, as noted, men respect when someone accurately assesses the situation and is willing either to acknowledge that they are asking for special treatment and compensate for it in some other way (like serving on the dreaded interdepartment committee in return for working fewer hours on Friday) or to acknowledge that they may need to adjust their expectations for projects, pay, and promotions during the period when they can't work as many hours as others.

> *Men respect when someone accurately assesses that they are asking for special treatment, and compensate for it.*

WILLINGNESS TO ADJUST EXPECTATIONS ALONG WITH OUTPUT

Second, the men emphasized that there was no reason to adjust expectations if someone's production or hours of availability remained unchanged. But *if* an accommodation goes hand in hand with unequal availability or output, men expect an agreement that differences in compensation, promotion, or opportunity would be understandable if they occur.

However, one often-overlooked factor is the opportunities that *lead* to higher pay and promotion potential. My conversation with Harold, the Big Four managing partner, provided an illuminating example:

In a professional services firm like this one, you essentially have three things going on: one, service delivery; two, people development; and three, business development and sales. In other words, you have to handle clients, develop people who are coming up (it's an up-and-out profession), and then you have business development—you have to find new clients.

Business development will give you the best pay and advancement, but it's also the most time-intensive and unpredictable. And among management there has been an understanding that there's clearly an uneven playing field between women, who historically had to balance family responsibilities, and everyone else. Men would say, "This is a difficult client situation; we should probably put Joe on it instead of Mary. She has flextime and if the people underneath have problems and she's not here, I'm going to have to step in." There were sometimes similar issues on personnel development.

The result is that in this office, the last time we looked at it, the ratio of men to women was about fifty-fifty on service delivery, sixty-forty on people development, and by the time you got to business development, it was seventy-five to twenty-five. The women with families could come in and do the work but simply didn't have time to grow the practice.

Adding those percentages up, men would believe that more men than women were qualified, capable, responsible, and deserving at the highest level. And where it starts to rub a little bit is where a guy who works hard and makes partner in twelve years sees a woman make partner in thirteen years, who essentially took five years off the partnership or business-development track. There's definitely some resentment.

But on the other hand, when you turn around and look at it from the broader perspective, you say that realistically, if you're going to get women in the workforce, and many of them will have these breaks, it might be fifteen or sixteen years until they make partner—and that just doesn't work. So in most cases, people aren't sitting there with a calendar and saying, "Jane, you lost a busy season here, so you need to pay with an extra year or three." Instead they decide to look at "Is she ready to move up and can she contribute as a partner."

As one of my businesswomen friends notes, "The good news in this perspective, for women, is that over time, 'equality' will mean the demonstration of equal *capability*, not equal contributions or equal results or equal time."

And more and more of these "adjusted" situations are creating opportunities for women who actively *want* to use and further develop their skills, but don't want the time pressure and stress of trying to climb the corporate ladder right then, because of family responsibilities. In many partnership organizations such as law, consulting, and investment banking, new career tracks have been developed over the last ten or fifteen years, providing alternative partner-type opportunities (such as nonequity "employee partners") for those who deserved advancement because of their seniority and skill but weren't able or willing to put in the hours it took to become an equity partner.

One executive recruiter told me that his company and his client companies are thrilled with the depth of talent available among skilled and educated women who have taken five or ten years off to raise kids, and are jumping back into the workforce part-time. As he put it, "We have two such women working for us part-time, and they are the best employees in the office. Our staff spends a lot of time on the phone with top corporate clients, and because of their maturity these women are totally comfortable joking with the CEO on the line—much more than our young MBA types are. It's just terrific. We recognize that we are getting an extraordinary asset for a part-time salary, and because that is also what these women want, it totally works."

REALISTIC ACCOUNTING FOR IMPACT

The third factor that affects men's perception of "different standards" in the workplace, of course, goes back to the "It's all about results" mantra.

To be perceived well, the men said, women who are accommodated in the workplace need to accurately estimate the impact of their flexible situation, and ensure that they are able to get the agreed-upon amount of work done on time and with no larger-than-expected disruption to the team. And if that happens, the perception of a double standard disappears.

Interestingly, many men told me that the reason their perception of flextime plans had improved was that they had seen workers who were willing to adjust their expectations—but then returned so much productivity under the flextime arrangement that there was no longer a *need* to adjust their expectations!

As my New York friend Wes put it, "Although I've never had someone work for me who is technically part-time, I do have one woman who is full-time but works from home two days a week. And it works really well—and she is paid the same as others her level—

for two reasons: She takes it seriously, and she doesn't appear to take advantage."

I interviewed one high-level businesswoman from a Fortune 50 company who had requested—while her kids were young—to work only four days a week, with only three of those days in the office. Nearly everyone else on her team was male, and she said there was a lot of quiet resentment at first. But it largely vanished when they saw that her numbers remained exactly the same, despite the cut in her work hours. (In other words, her productivity had increased.) And that protected the team's overall position in the company. It also helped, she said, that she openly acknowledged that her two days of absence from the office made the situation more complicated for those who remained, and went out of her way to minimize those complications. Because of her approach, her bonus ended up being just as high as that of the other top producers in the office.

Those are the good examples. But I also heard quite a few negative ones. I was surprised at the number of examples where a woman was realistic about the fact that she was asking for a special accommodation (to work from home on Fridays, for example) and was willing to adjust her expectations for pay or promotion—but was not at all realistic about what would be needed to ensure that her arrangement did not hinder her work or that of the office. In such cases, the end result was a net negative for everyone. One man mentioned an analyst who regularly overestimated how much work she could get done at home on Fridays between her baby's nap times. She was completely willing to take a cut in pay, but she was *still* viewed negatively because she was regularly unable to meet her deadlines.

Accommodations That Were Not Family Related Risked Being Viewed More Negatively

Although family responsibilities clearly accounted for most cases where women asked for different standards, it was clear that *anything* that prevented someone from working the same hours, the same way, could be viewed by the men in the office as unequal. And if it *wasn't* related to family responsibilities (or serious illness) there was a risk it could be viewed far more negatively.

For example, Barry, the CMO of a well-known business in a mountainous area, explained that one of his key hires was a woman who loved to ski in the winter and go rock-climbing in the summer. When she was hired, she negotiated getting quite a few Fridays off for her outdoor pursuits, making up the hours by working late other days. But here is his perception of how that arrangement had worked out, a year later:

> As the COO and I slave over complex documents with her subordinate because she's skiing, you can't help but have a little bit of bitterness. She negotiated that, but it isn't really OK. If she was attending to a child, it would be different.

To show just how differently such an accommodation was viewed when it was a result of a family oriented issue (and was acknowledged), Barry then shared this story:

> A few years back, a key female employee came to me and said her eight-year-old daughter was struggling academically at her private school and was on the verge of being asked to leave. Her husband was a busy traveling salesman and simply wasn't home enough to spend extra time with her. So this key employee came to me and said she really needed to switch to a

three-and-a-half-day workweek to spend the rest of the work-week at the school, working with her daughter. I moved her down just slightly with regards to her trajectory here, but I thought that it was a sign of great character that she was willing to say, "I know this will affect my career for a few years, but this is more important." I really respected how she handled it.

Many of the men I interviewed said they personally supported and appreciated the choice an employee was making in putting her family first—as long as the person was realistic about the effects on their performance and that of the rest of the office.

PUTTING IT IN PERSPECTIVE

I must admit that as I tackled the issue of men's "suck it up" mind-set in the workplace, I initially found myself quite stressed and conflicted. So many women feel that they are already doing all that is humanly possible to meet the expectations of others. And many of these women are among those most pressed to balance the conflicting priorities of work and home. Any further pressure would seem to take us in utterly the wrong direction.

I was able to regain some perspective by recognizing several key facts.

There's No "Perfect Solution" to Balancing Work and Home

The tension over balancing work and family has no perfect solution. Competing priorities such as time at work and time with our kids are, by definition, both important and often mutually exclusive. There's no one "right answer" that will work for everyone. The only thing we do know is that wishful thinking about how *much* we can balance is usually a recipe for anxiety and distress on both fronts. As most working moms (me included) have found out the hard way, you really can't get that report out on time when you have a five-year-old tugging at your sleeve and saying, "Mommy, I'm hungry." Or "Mommy, the video is over, can you play with me now?"

> *Wishful thinking about how much we can balance is usually a recipe for anxiety and distress on both fronts.*

As modern women, we are blessed to live in an era when we can "have it all"—but as many of us have discovered, that doesn't necessarily mean having it all, all at the same time. Here is how Meredith Vieira, in a 2006 interview with *Time* magazine, responded when the reporter asked her, "What do you say to women who want to have it all?"

> I hate that expression. When I left *60 Minutes* [to focus on my family], I had women who came up to me very angry and said, "You know, you were proof you could have it all. How dare you leave?" I thought that was ridiculous—I would lie to myself to create a lie for everybody else? You have to prioritize. If you can fit in a job and kids and be comfortable with it, great. At that point, I realized I couldn't do it and give my kids and husband what they needed.[1]

Later, of course, when her children were older, she became the host of *The View* and then the *Today* show. As her example indicates, I think women may experience less stress when we purposely recognize and plan for the fact that time with one priority may mean *not* having as much time for the other priority. That way we can actively choose the path that is right for us, instead of feeling constantly disappointed by trying to meet our own and others' unrealistic expectations.

The Desire Toward Family and the Desire Toward Career Impact Are Both Legitimate

It also helped me to see this balancing act as something women have personally struggled with in every decade since women first strode into the professional workplace in great numbers. Not every woman experiences this tension, but for those who do it helps to recognize that the desire to "spend more time with the kids" is noble and is just as legitimate as the desire to do great things in our career. (Obviously, many would say the need to invest in family is even more important—hence the astute parable that at the end of life, you are unlikely to regret that you didn't spend more time at the office.)

Here is how Harold, the Big Four managing partner, brought the issue into perspective:

> [Auditing and consulting] is a profession that attracts a good number of women, and we did these flex work plans thirty years ago. Early on the firm was 20 to 30 percent female, but for the last twenty years it's grown to at least 50 percent female. And when you realize that more than half your working population is female, you realize that you need to do whatever you can do to attract and retain them.
>
> But all those programs can only *help* women with the tension of balancing work and family—they don't miraculously *solve* it. Men feel that tension too, but realistically, in my experience, the women are simply more likely to be the ones *wanting* to place more priority on their children. My niece

is a doctor. She says, "I love my profession but I can't stand being away from the kids."

I have worked with many, many women here who said "I'm going to keep working with no change," but when their child was born they told me that they didn't *want* to be away that much, and so needed to leave the firm or have a flex work arrangement. And if that is how they felt, I have always taken the position of "You're absolutely right."

I had that conversation in 1975 and two weeks ago. Some things have lasted for thirty-five years and the internal tension is no different for women today than it was then.

> "I had that conversation about work-life tension in 1975 and two weeks ago. Some things have lasted for thirty-five years and the internal tension is no different today."

The Most Important Expectations to Meet Are Your Own

I realized anew what I have mentioned many times in this book: Just because certain expectations exist in the workplace doesn't mean we have to meet them, or allow them to pressure us into a course that is demonstrably not right for us. Many women are comfortable with prioritizing the career fast track, and accepting the trade-off to their personal lives, and many others are not.

Multiple studies over the last five or ten years have found that even highly educated, fast-rising women with top prospects are becoming less willing to sacrifice time with their families for the sake of career expectations—at least while they have children at home. It looks likely that at least half of the notorious "wage gap" between men's and women's wages (where full-time women make about eighty cents for every dollar made by full-time men for the same job)[2] can be explained by the fact that many women are either proactively or by default choosing the "trade-off" in wage expectations discussed in this chapter.[3]

For example, one of my close female friends is an extremely competent project manager who is invaluable to her firm. Now that she has small children, however, she has told her firm that she can take on only a limited amount of travel. By contrast, her male peer at the firm took his job knowing it would require quite a large amount of travel, including long international trips away from his own family. Not surprisingly, my friend realistically knows that her peer will be paid more for that extra work sacrifice. And she is fine with that. Nonetheless, the discrepancy between their wages is counted as part of the "wage gap" of unequal pay for equal work—when in fact it reflects different pay for different work.

Now, that said, the reverse is also true. I have another close friend who is invaluable to her corporation, and is able to work many long hours because her kids are grown—and yet continues to see less-senior, less-talented men promoted and paid over her simply because her male bosses seem to prefer to promote other men. There are many cases where the bias-based wage gap continues to stubbornly persist.

Yet even as companies work to eradicate that bias, we should acknowledge the very real progress women have made in being able to have the option to choose alternative work standards and compensation packages when that is better for us and our families.

The Good News: Things Are Changing

According to the men I've talked with, the entrenched "default" workplace expectations of men appear to be slowly changing—in large part because so many people are taking part in alternative work arrangements. The men frequently said the old-guard expectations are not best for them, either. Many men expressed regret about being beholden to "face time" expectations—which they described as not only unhealthy but as sometimes unnecessary and unproductive, as well.

> *The men frequently said the old-guard expectations are not best for them, either.*

For example, here is how one highly successful male entrepreneur who runs a private venture capital fund described his own choice:

My daughters are all teens and preteens now, and I realized that these are the last years they will be living at home. Other people can do things at the office if necessary, but nobody else can be a dad to my girls. So I have throttled back the pursuit of my business ambition over the next five years, so I can get things right at home. I haven't said "I'm going to try to have everything that I want in my business *and* everything that I want at home." Sure, I'd love to make the same income I did last year, but you can't have it all. So I have made a conscious decision to make a trade-off.

There is no doubt that workaholics and totally driven people usually do better in business—those are the companies I often end up investing in. But those people have a trade-off at home, sometimes a serious one. I don't want to run my life like that.

Given all these factors, I believe we should continue to live out a healthy and purposeful work-life balance, press toward the evolution of different default expectations, and demonstrate how productive they can be. It would be ironic if we traded away our hard-won ability to make choices just to fit old-guard beliefs that desperately need to be changed to begin with.

While the tension between family and career will likely always be with us, and there will always be some who feel pressured to (as the venture capitalist put it) completely "trade-off at home," recent studies have documented increasing numbers of both women and men who are championing an alternative workplace model—and an alternative workplace perception. Not through the sort of wishful thinking that is ultimately damaging to self, family, *and* career, but through the clear-eyed decision to prioritize that which we believe is most important for us and then doing what we *choose* to do, well.

CHAPTER 9

The Confidence Game

Men's Inner Insecurity—and How It Can Affect You

Men and women equally want to get ahead. But in the corporate world, a man's ego is a much bigger issue. . . . You can give women feedback and they'll take it well. Women can help people work as a team and not see everyone as a threat. But women also tend to forget that not everyone is like them. The one universal thing is a man's ego—and the heart of that is fear.

—AIDAN, a male partner in a global consulting firm
who manages a large number of women

At the opening of the book, I described a conversation I had on a flight with an executive-level leadership consultant, who just a few hours before had watched a female executive unintentionally make a poor impression with her male colleagues.

The story he told me described a seemingly trivial situation. But it serves as an indicator to something larger—even critical—that some women may be missing.

This consultant had been at an all-day meeting in the executive conference room of a well-known sports-related corporation, where about thirty of the company's most senior executives took turns presenting their business strategies for the next year. Most of the executives were men, with a small sprinkling of women.

The strategy session took place on the same day that major sports-related news was breaking, which required intermittent attention from people in the room. From time to time someone would crack open the door and gesture to an executive in the room that they were needed outside for a moment.

Apparently, that happened several times as a female senior vice president—I'll call her Carol—was making her presentation. Several times she glanced sideways, gave a small sigh of exasperation at being interrupted, and then continued her presentation.

At the end of the day, after the others had left, the consultant was working with the CEO and the COO. An executive vice president slot was about to open up, and ideally they wanted to fill it with one of the people who had been in the room that day.

They looked at the profile of each senior vice president in detail, and none were really feasible—until they came to Carol. This consultant was thrilled to see that she had exactly the experience and skill set that they were looking for. Moreover, the corporation had been actively trying to move more women into leadership positions. He told the CEO, "Carol is perfect. She's got the right education, the right capabilities, and you'd get all these connections with partner companies—"

But the CEO shook his head. "We can't promote her," he said. "I wish we could."

"Why not?"

The CEO thought for a second and said, "Well . . . did you see what happened when she was interrupted? That little sigh of annoyance?"

"Yes."

The CEO said with regret, "She has a tendency to make every man she works with feel like an idiot. We can't promote her. She would be a negative presence on the executive team."

A few hours later, sitting next to me on the airplane, the consultant told me he had been confused as to why Carol would shoot herself in the foot in her interactions with her male colleagues. But, in talking to me, he realized that she probably did not recognize what she was doing.

So what *was* she doing? What was it that made "every man she worked with feel like an idiot"? Why would something so subtle as a sigh of exasperation be described as representative of a "negative presence"—a description that the male consultant I was talking with immediately understood and agreed with?

The answer to those questions (which I address later in the chapter) can only be understood in light of a complex truth about men, one that requires venturing deep into the emotional land-scape of the male psyche.

TOUCHING A HIDDEN NERVE

One of the most fundamental misunderstandings that women have about men relates to what we call the "male ego." Women observe how men interact with the world and tend to conclude that some men have an inflated view of themselves. Yet underneath the ex-ternal confidence that men project is a more complex and nuanced truth than we might realize.

In my survey, most men echoed what I regularly heard in my in-terviews: that they sometimes felt like an impostor. Seven out of ten men on the survey said that no matter how much confidence they projected, they sometimes or regularly felt lost. The men agreed that they are thinking, "I hope I can figure this thing out before someone realizes that I'm not sure what I'm doing!"[1] With the men I spoke to, that sense of uncertainty veered uncomfortably close to a feeling of inadequacy, and that is an unusually painful feeling for a man, one that he prefers to avoid at all costs.

I believe understanding this inner uncertainty can unlock many of the frustrating dynamics that women experience in the workplace—for example, the double standard that strong men are seen as "assertive," while strong women are seen as "difficult" (or worse).

Men instinctively understand that they all suffer from self-doubt at times, no matter how much confidence they project. As a result they instinctively try to avoid hitting that nerve in other men. And when they *do* hit it, they are often doing so on purpose; they know exactly what they have done, and why. But unless they are deliberately *trying* to undermine each other, there is an unspoken social agreement between men regarding what one says or doesn't say, to avoid hitting that nerve.

> Understanding this inner uncertainty unlocks many frustrating dynamics, such as the double standard that strong men are "assertive" while strong women are "difficult."

Many women don't recognize this hidden self-doubt and the underlying social contract. As a result, they are far more likely to say things in a way that another man never would, create hard feelings or a poor perception, and even become someone that men go out of their way to avoid—without realizing what is really going on.

If women do sense those hard feelings they tend to dismiss them, attributing them to the fact that the man in question is being oversensitive, or is feeling threatened by the presence of a strong and capable woman. It may be helpful for women to realize that *most* men are "oversensitive" in this way—but not just with women. They are oversensitive with each other, as well. Which is why they built up these expectations of how colleagues should interact and relate with each other to begin with.

One of the most senior men I interviewed, Warren, is the president of a well-known Fortune 50 corporation. Over the years as he rose through the ranks of his company, he worked with countless women in different departments. Here's what he told me when I asked him if he had one piece of advice that he would have wanted to share with them along the way:

> It is the same thing I used to tell everyone back in my years in sales, or in our international division: Know your audience. Know how your audience is going to perceive how you are saying this. Women innately know how another woman is going to perceive something. They don't innately know how a man is going to perceive something. It is no use saying "They shouldn't perceive it that way," when they do. But once you learn your audience then you can gear yourself to be responsive to that audience.

"Women innately know how another woman is going to perceive something. They don't innately know how a man is going to perceive something."

Now, avoiding this hidden nerve in men does not mean a woman has to walk on eggshells, any more than you would approach a colleague or client from a foreign culture on eggshells. Nor does the existence of this sensitivity in men mean that they expect others to cater to them. But it does make sense to understand the "male culture" enough to recognize that such sensitivities exist. It's up to you to decide what, if anything, you want to do or say differently in those cases where you think it might increase your effectiveness in that culture.

THE UNDERLYING FEELINGS

Men's underlying sensitivity is one of the most complex and deep-rooted areas I investigated, with a host of implications for women in the workplace. I want to touch on just the broadest ramifications, since every man is different and women's individual experiences will vary.

There are four underlying concerns behind this sensitivity and vulnerability in men:

1. Most men like to tackle challenges, but at the same time, they harbor a painful degree of self-doubt, and a fear of being discovered as inadequate in the process.

2. Ironically, one of men's most intense emotional needs is to feel adequate—to know that they are respected and trusted by others.

3. As a result, men tend to be ultrasensitive to signals that someone views them as inadequate or not up to par and therefore does not respect them. They will sometimes see such signals even when they are not intended.

4. Most men tend to be highly attuned to and have a deep mutual respect for those who respect them, even when the other person is raising concerns or questions that need to be addressed.

Concern #1: Most Men Like to Be Challenged, but Fear Being Seen as Inadequate in the Process

In the survey I conducted, 76 percent of men agreed that they sometimes or regularly feel, "I'm not always as confident as I look."[2] This vulnerability stems from two deeply embedded and contradictory feelings.

First, men often thrive on tackling new challenges, regardless of how many bumps and bruises might come their way. The same instinct that compels my kindergarten-age son to hurtle himself down ten stairs and try to land on his feet compels adult men to tackle a more grown-up version of that challenge.

In adulthood, however, the stakes are no longer physical, but emotional. What is at stake is not "Will I break an ankle?" but "Will someone discover that I am not adequate to the task?" And that leads to an inherent male tension, because the feeling of or fear of inadequacy is not just uncomfortable—for a man it is a particularly painful sensation.

Aidan, the change management partner I quoted at the beginning of the chapter, summarized the tension this way: "The one universal thing is a man's ego—and the heart of that is fear."

Let's explore the tension between the desire to dash forward headlong, and the fear of being found out as inadequate in the process.

"GET ON WITH IT"

Thanks to testosterone and an aggression-oriented brain structure, men have a biological bent toward wanting to push things forward in the face of daunting obstacles; they often tend to turn everything into a competition. As one man put it, "Guys are focused on progress and we would much rather see something move forward and mess up than just sit idle or use the time making contingency plans. Sitting in meetings, going over stuff . . . for me that is torture. It's like 'Let's make a decision and just get on with it and we'll figure out what the consequences are when we get there.'"

This "push forward" mentality is intensified by men's competitive nature. A recently retired executive in the international development arena put it this way:

> Men judge success by doing something, period. If you're able to do it you're successful, and your *degree* of success is also easily measured. For example, "How much money did I make on my deal versus how much did he make on his deal?"

"ASKING FOR HELP IS A SIGN OF WEAKNESS AND FAILURE"
Here is how one credit-card-company manager, Sean, explained the conundrum between figuring it out as you go, and the fear of humiliation:

> No guy wants to admit that he does not have an answer. That is why guys do not ask for help at work, and tend to try and solve everything on their own. Asking for help is a sign of weakness and failure. Particularly in a work environment, because it is very competitive and it is where guys' identity is defined in many ways by their performance. They don't ever want to admit that they are not up to the task—and they think they can *make themselves* up to the task—so they sometimes tend to take on tasks that they are not capable of doing easily. They think, "I'll just try to do the best I can, and when I get to the point where I can't do any more, I'll figure something out then." Most men have a certain degree of confidence in our resourcefulness that way. But we

also know we could be totally humiliated if we can't figure it out.

That was a very big part of my experience, particularly early in my career. If someone assigned you something you just went back to your desk and tried to figure it out. You would never come forward and admit that you weren't sure—and I hate to say it, but some of us find uncertainty particularly hard to admit if our boss is a woman.

"IT COMES DOWN TO FEAR"

Not surprisingly, a man who lives with the tension of wanting to leap forward but wanting to avoid failure in the eyes of others finds that fear of possible humiliation always on his shoulder. One C-level executive explained, "A man's greatest fear is being seen as incompetent."

Sean had spent years rising through the ranks at a huge credit-card-services company, and had mentored dozens of other successful, ambitious businessmen. Yet when we sat in his office in New York behind a closed door, he gave me example after example of how isolated these men often felt. "As they get up the ladder they have fears and private failures and this fear of being exposed, but no one to share with. The insecurity is that you'll be found out as incompetent. That at some point someone is going to turn over a leaf and realize, 'This guy has no idea what he is doing.'"

According to one management consultant I interviewed, fear drives a great deal of men's thoughts and actions:

I have this one incredibly successful client at a telecom company. When he's had a few beers, he admits he's a total impostor. It all comes down to fear. Fear of being found out. Fear of being fired, and that you aren't a good provider. Fear that your family wouldn't have enough to get by. Fear of failure from that point of view. . . . Even the most successful men have an underlying fear of being laid off.

Here is a perspective from a fast-rising broadcasting executive:

When I was younger I used to feel invincible: I can do anything! Now, I sit in this office and I go, *I cannot believe that I am here*. I feel like somebody is going to walk in and say, "What are you doing here? Get out of here, you don't belong here!" That sense of invincibility has disappeared over time, because the higher up you get, the more you see all of the different pitfalls and all the things that you do not know—and that you have to rely on other people for. In fact now, I rely almost entirely on everybody else, which then makes you think that you are even more of a fraud, because you are not an expert in any of the substantive areas anymore! I recently heard a retired CEO confess to a similar feeling during his years at the top, and that was actually a relief to hear.

> "The insecurity is that you'll be found out as incompetent. That at some point someone is going to realize, 'This guy has no idea what he is doing.'"

All that said, when a man has spent years in the same position, building a sense of expertise and doing the same thing every day, the resulting sense of confidence can override or mute that feeling of insecurity and fear. Here is a more "settled" perspective from a long-time regional manager at a major big-box retail chain: "You eventually get to a point in the process where you arrive and you look back and go, *Wow, I know what I'm talking about*. Confidence! Earlier on, I did lie, did fake it, and had no idea what I was talking about. But if you do the same thing long enough, the insecurity eventually does get better. But it never goes away entirely."

As one marketing director, Thomas, confided, "When a man comes in with presuppositions and fears that 'I'm not doing well,' certain reactions from those above me just confirm my fears."

I have known Thomas casually for about ten years, and sought him out for an interview because he was so well respected professionally, and because I had heard through the grapevine that he was having a hard time working for a well-respected woman whom I will call Sheri. I wanted to find out what was behind his unhappiness. He explained, "As a man I want to be seen as good at my job. I'm sure women do too. But when Sheri has a concern about something her natural reaction is fight, not flight. When she gets defensive, or angry, it just confirms my private fears that I'm *not* good at my job. Even that little expression of disbelief makes you feel so stupid. You can handle it sometimes, but when it happens constantly it wears you down."

Thomas went on to confide that he was interviewing for other jobs, and I told him I was sure his company would be really disappointed to lose him. He answered, "I'll be disappointed too. I don't want to have to leave. I enjoy what I am doing, but I just can't work like this." And indeed, several months later, he e-mailed me to tell me he had moved on.

Clarence, the owner of an analysis and research company, offered another example of what triggers the feeling of insecurity or inadequacy:

In general, anyone who is taking a risk will be thrown into a position of insecurity. I went into this big sales situation about two weeks ago, knowing that what the client wants is something we've never done before. Bigger, more complex, more international, and just flat out more demanding. I walked right in and said, "Let's sit down and talk about what we can do for you." Am I insecure about that? The answer is: kind of. It's not acute, because at the moment I'm more excited about landing the client and trying something new. I have a reputation to protect, but I'm willing to take the risk to grow the company.

But the moment I land the client and start working on tasking out my people . . . that's when the insecurity hits. I can be completely secure in my abilities on one level, and on another there's a little voice that is telling me I'm a total fraud.

On the national survey we conducted, regardless of how I asked the question, roughly three-quarters of the men who responded admitted to self-doubt or fear. In one question regarding what if any types of insecurity the men experienced, 74 percent said that one or more applied to them, particularly concerns about how they were viewed by others or their employability in their workplace.[3] It is worth noting that this survey was conducted in 2008, when the market was at a high point and jobs were plentiful, *before* the economy and employment fell off a cliff.

Concern #2: One of Men's Most Intense Emotional Needs Is to Feel Adequate and to Know That They Are Respected and Trusted by Others

We all want to be respected in the workplace. For most men, this is not just a "want to have," but one of the things that most intensely drives them.

In my book *For Women Only*, three out of four men on the survey I conducted about their personal relationships said that if they had to make a choice they would *give up* feeling loved if that was what it took to feel respected and adequate. "I'll feel unloved if I have to," one man said. "Just don't make me feel inadequate."

The same internal makeup is still present when the man goes to work. Regardless of the situation, according to my interviews, men want and are more motivated by respect, trust, and appreciation than by, for example, whether someone likes them as a person. Which explains to a large degree why I sometimes see men brushing off things that women might take personally, but getting defensive about other issues that might not bother me.

Despite men's claim that one shouldn't take things personally in business, this is one of the things that they seem much more likely to take personally than women—even if they never show it.

As one businessman put it, "Most men could care less whether someone likes or dislikes them unless it serves a business purpose. But they care deeply whether someone respects them. I know that I keep many of my customers simply because they like me and enjoy working with me. But it really doesn't matter if my coworker in the next cube seems to dislike me for some reason. I'd prefer cordial relationships. But it matters more that he knows I'm the guy who will get the job done."

And the sense of whether someone does or doesn't think that makes a big impression. As one man explained, "My assessment of an individual is not impacted by whether or not this person likes me or will like me, but it is heavily impacted by whether I think this person does or doesn't respect me."

"My assessment of an individual is not impacted by whether or not this person likes me, but it is heavily impacted by whether I think this person does or doesn't respect me."

It is worth noting that several men brought up a downside to this dynamic. One prominent COO quoted in an earlier chapter, Ronald, noted that "being liked is often a business good that we miss; it is why, I think, women sometimes work harder to seek the win-wins than the men do. A man is sometimes too focused on his own performance and competing for the win, and whether the other party thinks he is good at his job."

THE TIE BETWEEN INSECURITY AND RESPECT

One of the main reasons men crave respect is because it mitigates their underlying sense of insecurity.

One day, out with several other couples for dinner, two friends who are well-regarded businessmen ended up talking about the relationship between respect and insecurity. One man whom I will call Gary offered a vivid metaphor:

> Insecurity is sort of like having a bad back, where the disability is always chronic. You've learned to live with it. You don't like it, but you do things to compensate for it. Versus disrespect, which is where someone comes along and slugs me right on the sensitive part of my back and the pain is sharp. I can manage the constant ache of the insecurity, but I'm going to do whatever I can to avoid that intense pain.
>
> And the business world is largely set up to meet that need. Respect is essentially built into the corporate structure. It is expected that you show respect for each other, automatically. It's just the way it works.

SIGNALS ARE NEVER SMALL OR ISOLATED: THEY ARE A LARGE CLUE

Even what women might view as a minor comment could loom large in a man's mind—if he assumes it is a signal of how someone views him. Similarly, women might view a particular comment or concern as isolated, thinking, "Well, I respect my boss in all these areas, but just not in this one." But for many men, it doesn't work that way. In their minds, the other person either respects them and their overall judgment (even if he or she disagrees with certain points), or the other person only respects them when they are doing something perfectly—which means he or she doesn't really respect them at all.

One industry expert drew from an analogy from business guru Tom Peters, saying, "Airline passengers are very attuned to signs of whether the airplane is being cared for. In their mind, coffee stains on the seats mean the engines aren't being maintained. And a clean, fresh look in the cabin means they don't have anything to worry about. That is similar to what it is like with a guy. For good or for bad, we're attuned to these small signals from those around us as a clue of something bigger."

Ben, who runs a large division of a global company, put it this way:

> Our area has a high percentage of women. They are just as willing to ask the tough questions, and many of them know just how to do it. They do it in a way that respects the other person's judgment—which shows they respect the person's judgment overall, not just on that issue.
>
> But there are other women that I wish I could take aside and give advice to, to help them understand that questioning anything to do with leadership is a sensitive subject. You can easily hit a hot button of seeming to be questioning their decisions and how they are running things. Because if you are questioning my ability to make the right decision on the "minor" issues, you certainly don't believe I am capable of making the right decision on the major ones. I don't mind the questions at all. I do mind if you question my abilities. So how you approach it is crucial.

Now, no one in the workplace—man or woman—expects meaningless affirmation in the face of mistakes. Nor do rational people expect others to blindly trust them for the sake of preserving their ego. The key is to be aware of a man's tendency to see small signals as a clue of the larger issue: whether someone has an overall respect for them or not.

Concern #3: Men May See Signals That Someone Views Them as Inadequate, That Are Not Intended

This gets to the heart of the issue that women need to be aware of. Men are aware that they share a finely tuned "disrespect radar," and they have learned how to avoid triggering it. When they do trigger it, they know exactly what they are doing and why (to undermine or send a harsh message to the other person). But if a woman is not conscious of men's sensitivity, she can send damaging signals without realizing it.

> *If a woman is not conscious of men's sensitivity, she can send damaging signals without realizing it.*

As one business owner wryly confirmed, "Yes, men can see disrespect where none is intended. This is a skill that we have. An ability we have evolved."

Geoff, the Fortune 500 CMO, put it this way: "Men are inherently defensive about everything and women are not. Men are the wary hunters. We are defensive by nature and have to learn that we don't have to be."

That defensive nature, combined with what many men described as having their identity wrapped up with their work—and the fact that respect is expected to be a "default" rule of the workplace—means that men in the workplace are likely to have a particularly negative (although often hidden) knee-jerk reaction to perceived disrespect, or to being viewed as inadequate. In my research, the most common reaction seems to be unexpressed irritation or anger—anger that is kept under wraps because overtly showing such emotions would violate one of the other common expectations of the workplace, which is that you remain levelheaded and don't take things personally.

Sometimes, in fact, the man isn't even sure why he is irritated over a remark or comment. One man told me, "Until you and I talked about this feeling of inadequacy, I didn't know where to put this feeling I tend to have around this one female associate. I would never have been able to articulate why I did not like her approach. But this issue is exactly it; when she says in that sort of comforting, overly patient tone, 'Doug, don't worry, we'll get there,' it seems like she is talking down to me. But I would not have been able to put a finger on it, and I certainly would never have been able to explain it to her."

Many men told me that even when they do identify what they are feeling as inadequacy or disrespect, they push it down because they "shouldn't feel that way." Yet they remain wary of someone who has been the source of that painful feeling. And that wariness is likely to make them even *more* likely to see signals of disrespect in the future.

Since "the absence of disrespect" is the emotional issue that matters most to many men in the workplace, we need to understand what men are likely to perceive as disrespect in the first place. Many disrespectful signals are obvious. Here are some of the most common *unintentional* ones.

Seven Unintentional Signals of Disrespect

First and foremost, context is key to how a comment or remark will be perceived by another party. Dozens of men told me, "It is not *what* you say, but *how* you say it."

Here is how Aidan put it: "Everyone needs to be able to ask questions or challenge potential problems. It is not *that* you question me, but *how* you question me that makes me think you are questioning my ability to lead this practice area. For example, if it is done to try to understand, then that is a whole lot easier than stating your point of view assertively."

Here are seven "how you do it" situations that men (and some women, for that matter), based on my research, are likely to perceive poorly.

1. A DIRECT, BRUSQUE APPROACH

Surprisingly (and contrary to much of the advice women receive during business coaching), it is easy for men to experience a direct approach—especially a question—as a confrontation or attack.

I got a great example of this when I had the first working session with my survey designer, Chuck Cowan, on the survey questions for my earliest relationship book. I had drafted a question for the men that read, "Do you know how to put together [a particular type of event]?"

CHUCK: That question won't work because you're starting off in attack mode.

ME: Huh?

CHUCK: You're starting off suggesting the man is inept.

ME (thinking to myself): *Suggesting the man is inept? What is he talking about?*

CHUCK: Soften it a bit—put it in a context that isn't so blatant.

Simply by adding a context sentence to the beginning—"Suppose you had to plan an event . . . Do you know how . . . ?"— the very same question was no longer perceived as an attack on a man's adequacy.

Since I had always thought of men as more likely to be direct, I was surprised at the number of men who said something similar to Geoff: "Women are brusque communicators and men are more likely to build up to it. For example, a woman recently sent me an e-mail saying, 'This ad sucks.' If they work with men, women have to communicate the way a man does. They don't have to emulate men, they just have to not threaten. You can count on men over-reacting to that. Women don't, but men will."

When I (politely) challenged the notion that women are more brusque, every man I interviewed said essentially the same thing: Men are direct, yes, but most men purposefully do not *confront*, unless they are *trying* to throw the other person off balance. One executive I spoke with made this distinction:

> First, a man will be far more direct one on one than he would be in front of others. In a group such directness would be public humiliation. But even when it is one on one, a male manager will be direct in a way a guy can hear. He'll say, "Bob, you've hit us some great home runs this past year, and I'm still in awe of how you landed the Hansel deal—but this was one boneheaded move on the Greene merger. How are you going to fix it?"
>
> In a group, though, he will find a way to be direct but not make it a confrontation. He'll say something like, "I'm still in awe of how you landed the Hansel deal, but you missed this one on the Greene merger. So let's figure out how to scramble to fix it." He'll convey his message that way un-less he's the sort of guy who rules by fear and is trying for a scorched-earth approach. Or unless he has no social skills.

All this said, my research and personal experience makes me skeptical that women are in fact more direct than men, although it is clear that many men do handle directness differently from women.

But there may be another factor at play here, as well: Some men may be far more sensitive to a direct approach from a woman, and perceive it differently than if that same exact approach came from a man. I'll discuss that possibility in more detail later.

2. BELIEVING A DECISION WASN'T BASED ON A LEGITIMATE REASON

I daresay that each of us—whether in our work or personal life—has at some point said in frustration, "What was he (or she) thinking?" The translation of that, of course, is *He wasn't thinking*. And when that assumption creeps into our conscious or subconscious thoughts in the workplace, it can quickly lead to words or actions that any-one, man or woman, would legitimately perceive as disrespectful— because our underlying assumption is a disrespectful one.

Here's an example that serves as both a good case study of the as-sumption, and an alternative route that might have been chosen.

FROM A SENIOR PARTNER AT A $1 BILLION PROFESSIONAL SERVICES FIRM

In our practice area, we have a few partners like me who are in their forties or fifties, and a lot of eager up-and-coming associates. One junior associate, Wendy, has a lot of potential, but she caused a huge headache for me—and herself—last summer when I chose not to bring her on a sales situation. In our business, the partner going to a client development meeting picks one associate to go along. Those opportunities are rare and every associate wants to be the one invited, because helping land deals is how you get ahead.

Last summer we had taken on a contractor in his fifties, Drew, for a few months' work. Near the end of his three-month contract, I landed a big sales meeting, and took him with me. Wendy was offended that she didn't get to go—but she told others, not me.

I heard afterward that she had been talking to a few colleagues about not getting to go and that she resented that she'd been there and busting her tail for two years and hadn't been to many sales meetings, and he's not even an employee, but he's older and a man, and he gets to go.

Obviously, I thought she was questioning my judgment. She thought I was biased and had favorites, that I didn't have a legitimate reason for what I did. The fact that she didn't even come to me and *ask* implies that she doesn't think she'd get a fair hearing. Very disrespectful. Not to mention that she told others. If I needed to question a man's decision I would do it one to one and make sure he knew I had his best interest at heart. I would only question him to others if I wanted to undermine him.

It would have completely changed my perception of Wendy if she had come to me and said, "I'm sure you've made the right decision here, but I just want to understand why you've made it."

I would then have told her, in confidence, that I was trying to decide whether to take on Drew full-time. In his three months, I had seen him in every other situation, and this would be my only chance to see how he did in a sales situation. And based on his performance that day, I decided not to hire him.

Even if Wendy wasn't comfortable coming in straight on and saying, "Help me understand this," she still could have addressed it while avoiding the specific example. She could have said, "I'd like to go with you to a sales situation; this is important to me, so I'm going to keep asking about this." I would think, *She probably saw me taking Drew. And I respect the fact that she's not taking me to task for that. That she respects my decision and trusts me with it, even if she didn't know what my reasoning was.*

Even when you are risk averse and don't want to confront the other person directly, you need to state what you want: "I'd love to go to more selling situations. I know you're a great salesperson and so the next sales situation you get, I'd like to go with you." That flattery works incredibly well with guys. And if the guy is at all smart, he'll understand what she's not saying.

Quite a few men expressed frustration at any assumption by women who worked for them that their hiring, pay, promotion, or project-allocation decisions were affected by antifemale bias instead of legitimate business reasons. That was also a common theme among the men on the survey. Of course, gender discrimination is indeed a very real issue in some workplace environments. But a surprising number of men who were clearly women's advocates recounted examples of women who saw even them as biased. And that signal of distrust caused them to view those women more negatively.

Malcolm, the president of a well-known midsize company, for example, mentioned one woman in his organization who he felt had "a chip on her shoulder" about men, and he didn't understand why:

> I'm sure there are workplaces where discrimination does become an issue, where a competent woman doesn't get the promotion just because she's a woman. But in this place, I've been in lots of different roles over twenty years and I've honestly never seen it. But our female HR director is convinced that it happens all the time.
>
> The women here who have a chip on their shoulder tend to think, *It's his chip that is the problem. He doesn't like dealing with a strong female.* I can tell her that we've spent all this time and money to add more women in leadership, and my pointing this out just bounces off her.
>
> Recently, we were looking at candidates for a job—a key person who would network with some of our grassroots customer groups. Our four final candidates were two white women, a white man, and a black man. And the senior VP and the leadership group who were making the decision are in their thirties and forties and are totally on board with women

in leadership. Totally gender blind. They are looking for competency, period. And of the four candidates, they ended up offering the job to the black man, because he already had tons of these relationships and would hit the ground running.

So our HR director says, "It's all a gender issue." Whenever we have made a hiring decision like that away from a female candidate toward the male candidate, our HR director claims it's not simply about competency. She says, "You guys play golf together." And the irony is, we've got fourteen people on the executive team, and I think only four of them play golf. But that was one of the rumors that got started: "You have to play golf here to get ahead."

As you might imagine, Malcolm and the executive team preferred not to work with an HR director whom they perceived as constantly distrustful of their decisions. A year after my interview, she left the organization, never recognizing that her open distrust of leadership had caused any problems for her.

3. ASKING "WHY" QUESTIONS

As many of the above examples underscore, men are sensitive to words or actions that can be seen as "questioning my judgment"—especially in a group setting. One of the most common ways women unintentionally send that signal is by asking "why" questions ("Why did you choose that pricing?" "Why did you develop the strategy that way?") In my experience, such women are usually just asking for information. Yet all too often—*especially* if it is asked in front of others—men hear even the most benignly phrased "why" question as a challenge.

On the survey I conducted, nearly all the men said that if they were making a proposal in a group situation and a colleague began asking "why" questions, they would likely assume that the colleague was trying to understand. However, nearly two in three said they might *also* feel that "my colleague is questioning my judgment." (Forty-two percent said it would depend on who was asking.)

In one focus group, a man I'll call Neil provided an example that hit home with the businesswomen who were also in the group that day. Neil is an operations executive who specializes in growing businesses. He is an even-keeled person who tends to get along with everyone, making his story even more of a surprise.

Neil: When I was commuting to Seattle to run a consumer products business, there was a woman I worked with who . . . well . . . I just didn't like her. It really became an issue with me, and I couldn't put my finger on why. I'd even be on the phone with my wife and say, "Hi, honey," and she'd ask, "Are you OK?" I'd say, "I'm fine." And she'd pause, then say, "Were you in a meeting with Nicole?"

I really had a hard time with it. And finally my wife tried to help me reconstruct things: "OK, why don't you like Nicole?"

I realized eventually what it was. I don't think Nicole disrespected me, but I *read* disrespect because in our meetings she would always ask "why" questions. Instead of asking "what" questions or "how" questions, it was very much, "But why do you think that?" I felt that she was questioning *me*, and it was very offensive to me.

And finally when I told this to my wife, she said, "She's not challenging you; she's trying to understand. It helps her understand." I'm like, "Really?" It took a while before that sank in. But eventually, Nicole and I ended up becoming very fast friends.

And probably a year later, over dinner, I said, "Do you know, Nicole, you really ticked me off when we first started working together."

And she said, "I know, and I couldn't figure out what was going on. But why?"

"Because I always felt that you were challenging my position."

"But you know I wouldn't do that!"

(Laughing) "No, I didn't know you wouldn't do that—that was the whole point!"

Interestingly, my feeling disrespected by her never occurred in a one-on-one situation. It was only when I felt that she was challenging me in front of others, in a larger meeting. One on one, if she asked, "But why are you thinking that?" it wouldn't bother me. But in a meeting it created a very different dynamic.

In the focus group where Neil told his story, the businesswomen in the room raised the natural follow-up concern: "If asking 'why' can be heard incorrectly, how are we supposed to ask the question?" They also wondered, "Is it that women are more likely to ask 'why' or that men are more bothered by it when a woman asks it?"

One man in the focus group claimed that the actual word "why" is used by women, rather than men. Another man said, "Guys will ask the same question, but we will do it in a different way so that we avoid the word 'why.' " We'll say, "I'm not following the reason for setting it up that way." A third man added, "Or, 'Can you tell me what you're thinking here?' "

The second man said it clearly mattered more when the question was raised in front of others, and suggested, " 'Help me understand where you're going on this one.' It's the equivalent of saying, 'I know you are going somewhere with this and do have a reason. Help me understand what it is.' "

But the first man experienced it in one-on-one meetings, as well:

Yesterday after I got a verbal agreement from a customer, my VP came into my office and asked, "Why did you agree to this price?" To me, she's not just asking a question; she's saying I didn't do my job; she's questioning my judgment as a salesperson. It would have been totally different if she would have said, "I've got to understand your thinking on this."

"Or, 'Help me understand your reasoning on this deal,'" another chimed in. "Not—"
All the men, laughing:
"WHY?"

4. PUSHING TOO MUCH

As you have seen in earlier chapters, quite a number of the men I interviewed raised "pushing" as an issue. For many men, when someone disagrees with their decision and won't let it go or "pushes too forcefully" to change it, they hear a challenge to their authority or judgment. Disagreement itself doesn't convey disrespect—the key, they said, is the other person's manner and length of time in expressing it. In their experience, women were more likely to "push" than a man was. (Ironically, many women I interviewed agreed.)

> *Disagreement itself doesn't convey disrespect—the key, they said, is the other person's manner and length of time in expressing it.*

Kevin, the human resources director I have quoted in other chapters, gave me this example.

Several women who worked for me over the years would argue opinions until I was literally blue in the face and could not take it anymore. And I am not the type that is just going to say, "We are going to do it my way." If I feel strongly about something I am going to let you see my rationale and all the different reasons why I think this is the right answer.

Usually, people come around to, "OK, I disagree, but I get your perspective and I understand why you want to do it this way." But several of these women wouldn't do that. They finally had to tell me, "You just need to tell me to do it your way because you are the boss." Which is totally not my style.

My first thought in these situations is, "Why can't this person wrap her mind around this topic and see it in another way? Why is she dead set on being right?" And then what goes through my brain is, "She has got her own opinion and is not willing to give in. She does not respect my opinion."

5. EXASPERATION

Exasperation with a boss's decision would make anyone in the workplace feel disrespected. It's also unprofessional. So I was surprised at the number of times men brought it up. I eventually realized that what they were talking about were nonverbal, body-language cues—presumably unintentional, and mostly given by women.

One C-level executive at a well-known multinational printing company claimed, "Men are not affected by body language by other men. But they are very attuned to the body language of women."

A university administrator gave me his perspective. "Exasperation is something you feel for your toddler when he throws his third tantrum in the store. And no man wants to feel that he's being treated like a three-year-old. Even the most subtle roll of the eyes will do it, whether it is his wife or his female colleague. You will almost never see a man in a work setting make an exasperated sound or roll his eyes, or listen with crossed arms and an irritated look on his face. You do see a few women. It never works out well for them."

This is also the answer to why, in our opening story, the female executive's small sound of exasperation at being interrupted was viewed so poorly. It was apparently just part of a pattern of behavior that made (in the words of the CEO) "every man she worked with feel like an idiot." And it cost her the promotion to EVP.

6. MICROMANAGEMENT

Overmanaging can make anyone feel disrespected. But it is worth mentioning here because quite a few men raised it as an issue with women—mostly providing examples that I would not have seen as micromanagement.

One man told me, "Micromanagement can sometimes be subtle. If she wants to be included in everything, or is offended at being left out, that's a lack of trust. And I think it is partially why women more often write a long e-mail versus a guy who writes one line. It's not that we as guys are incapable of thinking through the same paragraphs and providing the clarification; it's that we trust the person receiving the e-mail. Most of the time, guys are going to feel like they can understand why they are getting this e-mail without the extra three paragraphs."

One senior IT consultant I met in an airport gave me an example of something that he noticed when he went from being the CIO of his company to being a consultant.

When I started thinking about retiring and transitioned to consulting work, a new female manager had just come in, who didn't know me well. And she gave me lots of directives. It made it more difficult to feel like a contributor. Everyone wants to feel like they've had an impact on the decision and when that is denied, they think, "Well, I guess I should be working in a factory." In a younger guy, it could impact his self-worth.

For me, today, all I want to do is have someone set the direction and let me do what I know I need to do to get there. She should knock down the hurdles, but don't tell me how to do it. Don't give me every step on the path.

I had one woman manager who I would have killed for. She cleared the path, set the direction, and let me set the goals. That's all I ever ask for.

7. DIRECT DISAGREEMENT

Direct disagreement—and sometimes even making suggestions in a group setting—can be easily misperceived. The key is the manner of expressing it.

I asked Toby, a partner in a midsize advertising company, whether he had seen female colleagues do things that were misperceived by men. "Any type of corrective actions or corrective suggestions," he said. "Like, 'You need to go more in this direction,' or 'You need to think about this a different way,' or 'You need to focus on the important, not the urgent.'" Toby said it makes a guy think, "Are you threatening my job?"

I was surprised that simply making corrective suggestions would be perceived as threatening his job. He explained, "It is entirely about how the corrective suggestions are given. 'You need to' is rarely a good start. Admittedly, that is more difficult for a man to take from a woman, because he immediately tends to relate that to his personal home situation, and it drives a guy nuts when his wife says that. It is totally unfair to his female colleague that his mind goes there. But I suppose it is better if she realizes that it might.

"She could just as easily have said, 'I know these things are urgent, but we can't afford to miss these more important ones. Let's tackle these first.'"

Of course, open disagreement is even more charged. I asked Hugh, the sales director for a $1 billion manufacturing company, what he would suggest a woman do who had an actual criticism or disagreement with her male boss. Here's how he answered:

> Bottom line, the man needs to feel that she is saying, "I respect your ideas, I just don't necessarily agree with them in this case." Now, some guys will still take the straightforward approach: "That idea stinks, but what about this?" Men can be sensitive to that approach from other men, but won't say it. But they can be especially sensitive to that approach from women. So if the woman walks in and doesn't like it, it would benefit her to develop the skill set to say that in a way men can hear.

> *"Bottom line, the man needs to feel that she is saying, 'I respect your ideas, I just don't necessarily agree with them in this case.'"*

One business owner interrupted our interview to take a call from his lead software developer, and when he put down the phone he said, "That was a perfect example of how men tend to approach other men. I had told my developer I wanted to do something one way, and he just said, 'Can I offer a suggestion for how we might do it differently?'"

Hugh continued the earlier conversation with this suggestion:

> Know where you want to go and ask the right question at the right time to lead him down the path to get there. To help *him* realize that this is where he needs to go. Whether the decision-maker is a man or a woman, the best ideas are the ones the boss can develop and get invested in. If you can deliver up your solution in a way that is more palatable, he can seize on it.

I recently proposed a new sales organizational structure, and one of my women sales leaders didn't like it—she thought I didn't have enough sales leaders to manage the sales reps. But she didn't tell me that right away, and she didn't say, "You're wrong." Instead, she said, "You know I was looking at your suggestions and seeing you wanted a ratio of one sales leader to eight sellers. What's your reasoning on that?" So it's obvious she's not quite on the same page, without saying so. Then after I told her my reasons, she asked me, "Have you done a work/time study to find out how much time a sales leader spends in the field? That might help us find out whether the sales leader actually has time to manage eight people. I can do that if you'd like."

I said, "Great suggestion, go and do it." And so then she came up with the facts to show that we needed a different ratio. That is what I mean by helping the man adapt to it for himself. Be more of a partner, instead of challenging him head on. Do it in a nonthreatening way. Because as soon as he feels that challenge, he shuts down—the window shade is down. And then it becomes a battle of the wills, and he's got the title, so shut up and do it. But asking the question and then listening works really well. It's what I train all my salespeople to do to close a sale, after all. If a woman develops that skill set she will do very well. Especially since women tend to be able to listen better anyway.

THE COMPLICATION FOR WOMEN

As we've seen, as unfair as the situation is, a certain percentage of men are simply more sensitive to signs of disrespect from a woman than from a man. While this did not appear to apply to the majority of men I talked with (I would guess that I heard it from perhaps one in five men interviewed on this subject), the fact that it exists at all is worth discussing briefly.

> As unfair as the situation is, a certain percentage of men are simply more sensitive to signs of disrespect from a woman than from a man.

Hugh explained it this way:

A lot of men are intimidated by women because they don't understand women or know how to communicate with them. So they just shut them down. I don't think it's conscious or with forethought or malice. It's just inherent in our nature.

But it does add to this huge double standard I still see in corporate America, where a guy can say something to other guys that wouldn't be perceived as disrespectful, but if a woman says it, it would be. Also, in a leadership-subordinate relationship a woman can't be as tough with a man as a man can be with another man. Women still have a tough time managing men.

Toby explained that his advertising partnership was run by a woman named Miranda, someone with a type-A personality who mostly had men working for her. He said:

My wife has a very strong, type-A personality too, but I find myself responding differently to Miranda. The reactions can be different in a work environment, and I think the reason is that men are so focused on work as the essence of who they are. Because of that, there is an even greater tendency for men to potentially overreact to a woman exerting her rightful authority in a workplace. The smallest things can be perceived as much larger than what they really are. And, as a result, it takes even more work for a woman to be able to manage a man well and have a positive and respectful relationship in a work environment.

With his wife, a man can sometimes brush things aside and say, "Honey, you are blowing that way out of proportion." But it is just the opposite in a work environment, where men are the ones who tend to blow things out of proportion when a female superior tries to guide them or correct them or give them suggestions.

All that said, in my interviews it was difficult to tell how much of this oversensitivity to women (especially women superiors) is due to the fact that they are *women*, or due to the way women approach the interaction. Based on the feedback I heard, it seemed to me that most of the time the real culprit was the difference in approach. But that difference was definitely exacerbated in quite a few cases by the gender difference.

While this occasional oversensitivity that some men have to women is intensely frustrating, for what it is worth, there is a side to it that can occasionally work in a woman's favor. I frequently heard a caveat such as what this executive mentioned.

Remember, even today, guys are still highly intimidated by smart, together women. They will treat her differently. Even to the point that they will be more forgiving of the woman than of another man. I see it all the time. If two reps are performing poorly, one woman, one man, they'll try harder to fix and help the woman. More training, and so on. Where with the guy, they'll pull out the gun and shoot him.

Concern #4: Men Tend to Respect Those Who Respect Them

As you can tell from many of the stories above, men have an obvious appreciation and respect for those who make a point of showing their respect—especially when concerns or criticisms are raised. Just as men can be overly sensitive to feeling inadequate, they can be deeply attuned to signs of respect. They don't necessarily *expect* it, but they recognize and appreciate it when they see it.

A man seems particularly attuned to signs that a colleague's respect is not conditional (in other words, it does not change in the face of the occasional mistake), that the colleague signals respect for him in front of others, and that he or she is purposeful about raising an objection or holding to a firm position in a way that is not offensive.

RESPECT THAT IS UNCONDITIONAL

One key for many men is feeling that the other person's respect is not conditional, but rather is a lasting appreciation for their overall competency that won't change in the face of an occasional mistake.

In the first case study in this chapter, a female associate undermined her perception with her managing partner when she assumed he was biased for taking an older male contractor on a sales call instead of her. Later in the same interview, the partner went on to share an example of a very different reaction from a woman when *he* was the one to make a mistake.

We were at a big meeting with multiple offices of our firm and talking about our business lines for the following year. We had five business lines all presenting and competing for resources, and I was feeling pretty competitive since I know I'm a good presenter and I had a fantastic team of people behind me—most of whom were women. But I had poor judgment that day. I had a list of our distinctives, and then I jokingly added, "And my team is much better-looking than any other team."

After the meeting, someone on my team had the guts to walk into my office and say, "You have always told us you want feedback. I appreciate how you have fought for women at this firm, but what you just did today perpetuated the sense that women are there to be looked at."

She was totally right, and I had to go apologize to each of the women on my team. And I thought: If she had the guts to tell me something I didn't want to hear, that makes me think that she's brave and that anything she says is likely to be good and honest. She didn't try to undermine me in front of others, she didn't lodge a complaint with the other partners, and she didn't imply that I was inherently biased. She respected my advocacy of women enough to point out a way that I had undermined it, and then trusted me to make it right. Which, hopefully, I tried to do.

That fast-tracked the relationship with me—that one incident of being brave and giving me some genuine feedback, but in a respectful way.

"That fast-tracked her relationship with me— that one incident of being brave and giving me some genuine feedback, but in a respectful way."

As an investor relations executive put it, "What the man wants is to *be* respected, not treated with respect as if an actor has learned his lines. He does best when you expect the best of him."

Now clearly, not everyone has that sort of fundamental respect for their coworkers or bosses. So I asked the executive how a woman might navigate such a situation. He chuckled and pointed out,

"There are limits to transparency. The worst thing she can do for her career if she doesn't respect a male colleague or superior is to make that clear. And I'm guessing that even in that situation she can find things to respect. Maybe he's the classic visionary head honcho who is all over the place, and has no operational ability and is constantly messing things up for the operations people. But she can admire the fact that he's a man of vision and has this entrepreneurial drive. You can still respect the person. And if you just can't find anything to respect, well—respect his position. He's still the boss."

SEEING AFFIRMATION IN FRONT OF OTHERS

One thing I frequently heard mentioned is a man's appreciation for someone who shows genuine appreciation in front of others.

A senior businessman I interviewed in the public-relations field, Ferdinand, explained that he works closely with a female colleague whom he deeply respects and appreciates. When I asked him why that is, he answered:

> Claudia is totally willing to acknowledge that my strengths complement certain weaknesses that she has. She is slightly senior to me in her role here, but I've had a longer tenure in the industry. So there could be some tension between us, but there isn't—largely because she is so careful to make me feel that my greater experience is appreciated. In public meetings with clients or whatever, she will acknowledge that "Ferdinand is the one who is detail-oriented. So he will take care of this operational piece."
>
> That is also important in our staff meetings, because my personality is low-key and Claudia tends to jump over me sometimes. And because of that the junior staff could always perceive her as the only leader. So she is making a conscious

effort to change that perception, and acknowledge more of my leadership qualities in meetings with them.

A male communications specialist who had recently switched firms provided another example. "In my last job, my boss was a woman, and she was totally safe. I could talk to her, share ways I'd messed up, get her input for going forward. It was a very productive situation." When I asked him what his previous boss did that made him feel "safe," he said, "I felt like she was for me. She would brag on my behalf to her peers in the firm. Or tell potential clients about things I had done." In his current firm, he said, he worked almost entirely with women—but he didn't get any of those affirmation signals to let him know whether or not they thought he was doing a good job. As a result, he told me, "I can't share with anyone what I am thinking. I am afraid for them to know."

VOICING OBJECTIONS OR HOLDING FIRM IN A WAY THAT IS RESPECTFUL, RATHER THAN CHALLENGING

Most of the men I interviewed had enormous respect for women who were able to stand strong on a particular issue, raise objections, or completely disagree with them—and do it in a way that was not offensive. Men are grateful to have a professional business inter- action that does not contain a subtle undercurrent of questioning their adequacy, but instead allows them to singlemindedly tackle a situation purely on its merits.

Several times, men I interviewed shared examples of female colleagues who seemed to have a "chip on the shoulder"—which would normally make me wonder if they were prejudiced against women. But shortly thereafter each man also gave me examples that proved otherwise, including this helpful story of a woman who, this man felt, handled a big meeting with a large group of men very well, by being strong but focusing entirely on the business at hand.

We'd just gone through the budgeting process and our CIO could not attend this critical one-day session, so he sent his right-hand person, Teresa. So she is thirty-something, and she is in this annual executive budget meeting with ten senior executives who are all men and we are going through a very tough discussion of how we will allocate out $240 million. And the big issue is IT, which she is representing. I was totally impressed at the way she stood toe to toe with these guys, to the point that I thought to myself, "She is someone to watch." I saw really good leadership. She didn't kowtow, she didn't back out, and she didn't get harsh, either. She was just calm and bold and gutsy and would say, "Well, I have to disagree with you on that one, because of X, Y, and Z."

Everyone said later, "I really respect the way she handled that." So, that was the common thread: "Man, she was *good*."

I said, "That's what a guy would say about another guy!"
"Exactly!"

THE BENEFIT OF A DIFFERENT APPROACH

Most corporate training and business coaching does a good job of bolstering women's confidence and effectiveness in the workplace. But it can subtly backfire if it doesn't take into account how an approach will be perceived by male colleagues who are dealing with their own doubts and insecurities.

I happened to stumble across an example of this several years ago, after I'd already done hundreds of interviews with men. I was looking at a website with popular business coaching tools, including online videos for women in business. Clicking on one at random, I watched a well-known female coach say: "Women, you've got to be aggressive, you've got to be assertive! No one in business is going to give you anything. If you want that corner office, you have to take it!"

Staring at the screen, I could practically hear the echo of hundreds of male voices in my head saying, "Yes, but . . . !"

In a coffee shop a week later, I showed that video to a male executive whom I have known for years, someone who is an advocate of women in the workplace. His reaction?

> *"Women in business shouldn't assume anyone is going to hand them anything. They should be aware, they should be assertive. The question is how."*

I think women in business need to do all those things the corporate trainers suggest. They shouldn't assume anyone is going to hand them anything. They should be aware, they should be assertive. The question is *how*. Business still is, unfortunately, very male-centric. But if women understand how men are wired, they can be the type of star that others will want to bring through the ranks with them.

Several men I interviewed raised another intriguing point: that just as men have natural inclinations and perceptions, so do women. And some of those inclinations (such as the often-mentioned "natural listening ability" or "desire to be liked") could be a benefit in trying to navigate the minefield of male sensitivity in the workplace—and in gaining men's trust.

One COO of a very well-known organization gave me an example of that, one that has been powerfully affirming to a number of businesswomen I have relayed it to:

The desire and need to be liked seems to be greater in women. Not all women, of course. But many women in business have been made to feel that that is a bad thing, that such a desire is totally inappropriate in business. But I think it is totally rational.

Women instinctively realize that if they aren't liked, the cards are really stacked against them in a male-centered environment. So they figure out how to weave their way through the system and confront problems and yet still be liked and appreciated. In an environment where a woman is dealing with male egos, a woman who does that will find it a much greater value than being a tough contrarian. As long as she is not prioritizing being liked over the good of the business, if it is her genuine personality, she doesn't have to try to squash it. Because that is a strength she can use to offset what is, at times, a man's weakness.

Geoff, the CMO, shared a similar reaction. "If your boss is a man, if your colleagues are men, learn how men communicate. Once you get on that team, where a man extends real opportunity, figure out how to be influential without being threatening. It's a delicate art, not a science. It's the words you pick, your body language, the words you write. Clearly those first hurdles are hard. You have to understand how men communicate. But women are particularly well-suited to do that. And once you figure it out, you're in."

CHAPTER 10

The Visual Trap

Why That Low-Cut Blouse Can Undercut Your Career

As I'm writing these words, I'm sitting at a café in a bustling business area, watching an interesting dynamic unfold at a table nearby. Around me in the lunch rush, several groups of men and women are continuing business discussions over their soups and salads. At the table across from me, a stylish thirty-something woman is eating with three men, arguing a passionate point that has something to do with risk management. But I'm betting that the men are missing a substantial amount of what she's saying.

Why? Because her stylish professional outfit includes a low neckline and cleavage. And among the thousands of men and women I have interviewed and surveyed over the years, I have found no subject more universally misunderstood than what a man thinks when he sees a woman overtly showing a good figure.

Women tend to think, *I want to feel good about myself . . . look stylish . . . make a good impression.* When we hear someone caution us that we should watch what we wear around men, we have the indignant thought, *It's none of his business what I'm wearing. He shouldn't be looking.*

But the man thinks, *She wants me to look at her body. No, look at her face. Is she flirting with me? Shoot, what did she just say about the loan failure rate? I missed it.*

"MEN ARE VISUAL"

The subject of a man's visual nature can be awkward and sensitive to discuss. It may engender strong reactions. Some women just shrug and say "What's the big deal?" while others find it offensive. Many women are quite cautious in how they present themselves, while others may not be completely sure what being cautious entails. As mentioned, still others may think, *It's none of his business what I'm wearing—he shouldn't be looking.*

Regardless of where each woman lands on that spectrum, the data in this chapter is designed solely to bring women up to speed on a reality that men think we already know but that, in fact, is often misunderstood. This is one of the starkest examples of an arena where we may or may not be in agreement with commonly held male perceptions, yet realize it is definitely in our best interest not to be in the dark about them.

We are frequently told "men are visual"—but I've realized that many women don't know what that actually means. According to brain scientists and researchers such as Michael Gurian, some percent of women—perhaps as high as 25 percent—are visual in a similar way to men.[1] If you're in that category you are more likely to instinctively understand men's reactions. But the other 75 percent of women who aren't that "visual" have very little concept, literally, of how men see them.

In 2001, when I was first interviewing a few trusted male friends for my novel, this is the subject that woke me up to how much I didn't know about men. And, ironically, the scene that opened my eyes—that I was describing for the men—was a business situation. I had placed my male character, Doug, in a conference room listening to whiteboard presentations from a series of executives, one of whom was a woman. I described her as all business, but also as very attractive and wearing a suit or blouse that showed off her figure in some way—a low-cut shirt or a tight skirt. Then I asked each man I interviewed, "If you were in Doug's place, what would be going through your mind as the female executive made her presentation?" I was stunned to hear the men's responses:

- *"Great body . . . Stop it! What am I thinking?"*

- *"I feel an instant tightening in my gut."*

- *"I'll bet she's using those curves to sell this deal."*

- *"Look at her face, look at her face, look at her face . . ."*

- *"I wonder what's under that nice suit? Stop it. Concentrate on the presentation."*

I was a bit unnerved to hear these comments—and others— especially from happily married men who were respectful of women.

Since that time, I've heard similar reactions from thousands of men—and realized that when it comes to the ways that talented women may unknowingly undermine men's perception of them, this one is near the top of the list. Why? Because of the disproportionate impact it has on a man's thoughts, and how drastically it affects the way the woman is perceived. And yet, in most instances, the woman has no idea what is really going on inside the minds of the men around her.

THE HARDWIRED REALITY

As I'll discuss a bit later, each of us—men or women—probably have individual quirks of our biological wiring that we'd rather not have: temptations, frustrations, impulses, desires. There are facets of our nature that we would love to be able to just turn off at times. I would love, when I'm on a diet, to be able to switch off the quirk in my wiring that becomes utterly attuned to the chocolate cake on the dessert cart whenever I'm at a restaurant. Or at someone's house for dinner. Or in the grocery store . . . As someone who has to watch my weight (as opposed to those maddening "naturally thin" people), it is frustrating to not be able to turn off my sweet tooth when I want to. Instead, I have to work to ignore it.

The visual wiring men have presents a similar temptation that men say they often don't want and wish they could turn off—especially in a business setting. Their visual nature is highly attuned to and predisposed to take in appealing images, including images of an appealing woman. And if that woman is dressing in a way that emphasizes her assets, that fact is not only noticed but often begins a train of thought that most men in business would rather not have.

But their visual nature isn't something that can be turned off. Just as I am incredibly aware of the chocolate cake across the room and must work to ignore it, it takes an effort of will for a man to counter a visual distraction and stop his train of thought. And while most of the men I spoke with make that effort (as opposed to the few who clearly preferred the visual thrills), they would far rather not have to deal with the situation to begin with.

> *Their visual nature isn't something that can be turned off . . . they would far rather not have to deal with the situation to begin with.*

In talking to men, I found most were incredibly puzzled as to why the *woman* wouldn't want to avoid the situation. Why, the men wonder, is a professional woman dressing in a way that is likely to cause men to be distracted and miss some of what she's saying? And the answer, of course, is that most women have no intention of causing that sort of a distraction, and don't realize that they are doing so.

The Male-Female Disconnect

To test the difference in men's and women's perceptions in this area, I asked men what they would think if they saw a woman dressing in a way that emphasized or showed off her figure in some way, such as a low-cut top or a tight skirt. Then I asked white-collar women who said they sometimes dressed in that way what was actually going through their minds. Here are the starkly differing results. Seventy-six percent of the men felt the woman wanted the men around her to look at her body. Yet only 23 percent of the women actually felt that way. In other words, three out of four women said that was *not* what they were thinking at all!

In one interview I knew that the man worked alongside many women. When I asked him if he ever saw women do things to hold themselves back in the eyes of men, he paused, then gingerly said, "There is a mistake I've seen women make . . . How people perceive you is important in business, whether you're a man or a woman. And certainly, first impressions are even more important. The immediate appearance of a person walking into a meeting or a business situation: How that person presents themselves is critical."

"OK," I responded.

"And women more than men have some subtle ways of maybe not looking as professional."

"In what way?"

Looking uncomfortable, he gestured to his shirt.

"Like a woman's shirt that is unbuttoned too low. Or is tight. You know what I'm saying? I think a woman in a business situation that is dressed simply and not trying to call attention to herself is received better. A guy can relax in that situation a little more than if . . . well, if the lady is trying to call attention to herself. And subconsciously, I'm sorry, but the message comes across. She's looking for that attention. And it can be really distracting."

Almost everyone in business wants to make a good impression, and most of us work hard at doing so. The problem isn't that we don't know that it is important. The problem is that we simply may not realize that the visual impression we are making is not the one we intend. Based on the seven nationally representative surveys I've commissioned over the years for my books, I can almost guarantee that the businesswoman who puts on a figure-framing crossover blouse under her suit isn't "looking for attention" or trying to "send a message." But that is how almost every man perceives it.

To understand why, let's look at the visual wiring that is a part of so many men, and the ways in which that differs from the average woman's physiological makeup.

THE VISUAL BRAIN

To put it at its most basic, the average man's brain structure and chemical mix make it impossible for him to not be visually oriented. That visual orientation is especially attuned to stimuli that he perceives as sexual, and his initial reaction to it is much more likely to be visceral, instinctive, and automatic than it would be in a woman.

Men Are More Visually Oriented

Neuroscientists have consistently found that more areas of the male brain are devoted to visual-spatial processing than in the female brain.[2] By contrast, more areas of the female brain are devoted to verbal and emotional processing. Where a woman's brain predisposes her to experience the world more relationally, a man's brain predisposes him to experience the world much more visually. Researchers at the University of California, Vanderbilt University, and the Veterans Affairs Medical Center in Minneapolis found that even in a neutral rest state, men's brains are much more attuned to external, visual stimuli, and women's brains are much more attuned to internal sensory stimuli.[3]

Men Are More Highly Attuned to Stimuli That They Perceive as Sexual

Testosterone increases the assertiveness of a person's sex drive, which is why men (with more testosterone) tend to have a greater desire to initiate or pursue sex. But as Michael Gurian describes in *What Could He Be Thinking?* their visual nature, combined with more testosterone, combined with more vasopressin and dopamine (brain chemicals that affect memory, sexual bonding, and emotions), also makes men far more visually aware of sexual stimuli, and far more likely to perceive certain stimuli as sexual in the first place.[4]

> *Men are far more likely to perceive the sight of an attractive person of the opposite sex as sexual.*

In particular, men are far more likely to perceive the sight of an attractive person of the opposite sex as sexual. A group of scientists from Massachusetts General Hospital, Harvard Medical School, and Massachusetts Institute of Technology found through functional MRI scans (fMRIs) that men's brains are affected at a very primal level when they look at pictures of women they perceive as attractive.[5] As ABC's John Stossel put it when he reported on this study in 2002, "The same part of the brain [the nucleus accumbens] lights up when a young man sees a picture of a beautiful woman as when a hungry person sees food, or a gambler eyes cash, or a drug addict sees a fix."[6] The gut reaction: *I want that.*

Men's Initial Reactions to Those Stimuli Are Stronger, More Visceral, and More Automatic

Thus, far more than with women, a man who encounters visual sexual stimuli (that is, stimuli he perceives as sexual) has an automatic tendency to become aroused. While men have a choice in what they do from that point (how they choose to handle their instinctive reaction), their initial response is often purely biological, rather than voluntary. As David M. Buss, a professor of psychology at the University of Texas at Austin, says, "Telling men not to become aroused by signs of beauty, youth, and health is like telling them not to experience sugar as sweet."[7]

According to a study by Emory University researchers published in the professional journal *Nature: Neuroscience,* when men and women see sexual stimuli, a man's amygdala (which regulates emotion and aggression) and hypothalamus (which primes a hormonal response) are more strongly activated. In other words, men simply have stronger biological responses to such stimuli than women.[8]

Men also store and recall visual, sexual stimuli very differently than women do. First, as noted by Dr. Richard M. Restak, a professor of neurology at George Washington Hospital University School of Medicine, visual experiences are more likely than any other sensory input to be retained in memory.[9] And men experience the world much more visually in the first place. Finally, remembering that the male amygdala is much larger and more active than in the female, consider how Dr. Walt Larimore's book *His Brain, Her Brain* explains what happens in a person's memory with regard to sexually attractive images:

> The amygdala amplifies memories which are pleasant. . . . It communicates to the hippocampus which memories need to be locked in place. . . . In men, these areas of the limbic system are far better connected to the spinal cord [the instinctive, visceral center] than they are to the cortex [the thinking center].[10]

In other words, when men or women see or remember a sexually attractive member of the opposite sex, women are more likely to think to themselves, *He's an attractive man* (a more "thought-oriented" response), where men are more likely to feel a gut-level sense of desire that they then have to bring under their intellectual control. (*Stop it. Look at her face.*)

But since the more gut-level responses are far more likely to be tied to memory, by the time the man's intellect kicks in, the visual image is likely to have been stamped into the man's memory.

And those memories in men can resurface. I'll explain how this works in practice in the following pages, but Joseph LeDoux, a neuroscientist at the Center for Neural Science at New York University, was the first to identify a sort of shortcut from the hypothalamus to the amygdala for certain memories that entirely bypasses the thinking centers of the brain. In effect the amygdala acts as a kind of repository for gut-level impressions and memories tied to gut-level responses. And those memories can again bypass the thinking centers to involuntarily pop back up in a person's mind.[11] Where a woman (more oriented toward processing emotion) is more likely to have emotional pop-up memories, men are more likely to have visual pop-up memories.

WHAT THAT MEANS IN PRACTICE

So what does this mean in terms of how men visually experience day-to-day life in the workplace?

Reality #1: He Can't Not Notice

In my research, women's fundamental misconception about men's visual nature is the notion that men can somehow turn off their initial sexual awareness and attraction if a woman's body is being emphasized by her attire. Based on the responses I've gotten in my interviews and surveys, it appears that if a man is heterosexual, he can't not notice.

> *Based on my interviews and surveys, it appears that if a man is heterosexual, he can't not notice.*

He can, however, choose whether or not to *look*. And he can make decisions about how he will handle the situation once he notices, but there is an involuntary component to his initial awareness and attraction. In other words, men can't just "turn off" their visual nature.

Many women think, *It's none of their business what I'm wearing or what I look like.* They don't realize that once they select clothes that are revealing (even if they don't think of it that way), they have made it a man's business. Yes, I grant you, this is a hard thing for most women to accept.

The clearest evidence I can provide of this comes from one of the surveys I conducted on the "relationship" side of things for my book *For Women Only*. This is helpful because it provides a non-business-setting control group of men who weren't affected by the inherent wariness of answering business-related questions. Take a look at the situation I painted for male survey-takers:

Imagine you are sitting alone in a train station and a woman with a great body walks in and stands in a nearby line. What is your reaction to the woman? (Choose one answer.)

a. I openly stare at her.	▰	4%
b. I'm drawn to look at her, and I sneak a peek or glance at her from the corner of my eye.	▰▰▰▰▰	76%
c. It is impossible not to be aware that she is there, but I try to stop myself from looking.	▰▰	18%
d. Nothing happens; it doesn't affect me.	▪	2%

0%   50%   100%

As you can see, nearly all the men put their response to an eye-catching woman in the "can't *not* be attracted" categories.

It is hard for us as women to understand exactly what such a visual orientation is like. Here is an example that might help you to identify with it.

Start by looking at the letters in this box—but whatever you do, don't read the words:

Don't read this.

Were you able to look at the letters, but not read the words?

It's impossible, right? Your brain read the words before you could stop it, even if you were trying *not* to. Well, based on my research with men, that is what it is like for a man when (for example) an attractive woman with a figure-hugging outfit knocks on his office door, asking whether the Coleman report is ready for review. His brain reads "*Great body*" before his intellect can override his biology.

I'll examine the ramifications of this shortly. But in the meantime, let's look at this critical caveat.

IF THE WOMAN'S FIGURE ISN'T EMPHASIZED, A MAN'S INVOLUNTARY SEXUAL RESPONSE ISN'T TRIGGERED

In other words, a woman can be very attractive—and very attractively dressed—and yet trigger none of that involuntary sexual response in a man. The key question is whether her clothing choices—such as the proverbial low-cut top I keep mentioning—draw overt attention to her body or not.

Now, that doesn't mean that a man can't *choose* to stir up his visual nature, regardless of how careful the woman is, but that is an entirely different discussion that goes beyond her control, and beyond the scope of this book.

Reality #2: Some Images in a Man's Brain Can "Pop Up" Later

One of the most perplexing elements of a man's visual nature that most of us as women don't understand, simply because we have no equivalent to it, is that the appealing images a man sees—especially images he perceives as sexual—can become stored in his brain, like picture files stored on a computer. And these images can pop up in his mind without warning. (They can also be called up at will.)

Most women know what it is like to have thoughts and feelings "pop up" in their minds: those concerns, worries, and "what if" scenarios that arise in our minds seemingly out of nowhere.

That is very similar to how men describe their visual memories, only what pops up is equivalent to a picture, image, or live-action video. A man may be sitting at his desk, reviewing the latest marketing plan, when suddenly the screen of his mind replays a sensual scene from a movie he saw last week. Or he can be in a long meeting about how to cut fuel costs, but when his attractive female colleague stands up to work some numbers at the whiteboard, it suddenly triggers an image of what she looked like *last* week in that tight skirt.

Now, a man can push these unwanted visual memories down by forcing himself to think about or visualize something less distracting, just as we do with our emotional pop-ups. But to do so, he has to overcome another biological drive.

Reality #3: Men Often Have Sexual Thoughts

For many men, the moment they become aware of a sexually attractive woman they are confronted with a gut-level temptation to entertain sexual thoughts or images about her.

This is the point where the automatic, involuntary aspect ends, and the decision element begins. And most men have had years of practice at managing that process along a spectrum of possible choices. The way the men I talked to describe it, they can't entirely avoid the temptation arising, but the more they choose to wrench their thoughts away and think about something else, the less frequently such thoughts intrude over the long run.

But the reverse is also true: The more frequently the man follows the temptation to think along sexual lines, the more likely it is that such sexual responses will arise over the long run.

What is important to remember here is that a man can't just turn off his visual-sexual nature. Here is how one man put it:

Women need to understand something: *We don't fundamentally change how we see certain things just because we are at work instead of somewhere else.* I'd rather not have noticed that my colleague is wearing a black bra this morning underneath her blouse, but there's nothing I can do about that now. All I can do is to try to keep out of her way.

THE RAMIFICATIONS FOR WOMEN

When a woman dresses in a way that a *man* considers revealing, here are some of the common ramifications:

Ramification 1: "It's Distracting— and I'm Missing Some of What She's Saying"

The ramification that is of most concern to professional women is the "distraction" factor. The man is trying so hard to "not notice" (*Look at her face*) that he's distracted from the task at hand, and is missing some of what the woman is saying.

> *The man is trying so hard to "not notice" that he's distracted and is missing some of what the woman is saying.*

As one survey-taker explained it, a woman can undermine herself if she "dresses in a way that distracts her male workers. Not that she intends for this to happen; it's just a natural reaction that lowers her perceived effectiveness."

One sales director for a $1 billion company provided an example of how this plays out. "I have a twenty-something saleswoman on my sales team; she's extremely competent but she's also extremely attractive, and has a tendency to wear high fashion, *Sex in the City*–type outfits. On one sales call, I accompanied her for our first presentation to the customer, who was a forty-something guy, and I thought she did a phenomenal job. A few days later, I was in a different meeting with that customer and asked him a few questions, and realized: This guy didn't remember a thing from the first meeting about our product or our corporate capabilities. So a week later, I had a male sales rep make the exact same presentation as the woman had—and the customer had a laundry list of questions throughout the meeting. It was the same damn presentation and he didn't remember a thing."

Two-thirds of the men on the survey—and nearly every man I've interviewed—agreed there would be a distraction factor. Take a look at the survey results to the scenario I created, on the following page.

Two out of three men said that they would be missing either "quite a bit" or "some" of what the woman was saying. Only one third said they would be able to concentrate fully on her presentation. And nearly every man to whom I have shown this has expressed amused skepticism about the latter number.

One man chuckled, pointed to the 36 percent "I'm not affected" number, and said, "That is the 'liar, liar, pants on fire' cohort."

Imagine you are in a business meeting, and a woman with a great body stands up to give a presentation. She is all business, but she is wearing a suit and blouse that show off her figure in some way (for example, a low-cut blouse or tight skirt). Which answer below most closely describes the likely impact of that on your ability to concentrate on her presentation? (Choose one answer.)

a. I'm instinctively drawn to look at her body, and sneak in peeks when she won't notice—so I'm missing quite a bit of what she says

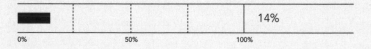

14%

0%   50%   100%

b. I try to concentrate, but I'm distracted from trying to look at her face and not her body—so I miss some of what she says

50%

0%   50%   100%

c. I'm not affected; I can concentrate fully on her presentation

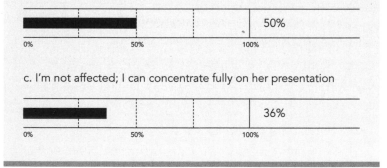

36%

0%   50%   100%

Now, to be fair, on a survey question with no visuals, different men have different perceptions of what the woman in question looked like and what she was wearing. And the men I interviewed universally agreed that there were different degrees of distraction depending on what the woman wore and how she wore it. (To read more about this, go to my website, TheMaleFactorBook.com, where I will add more specifics over time.)

But regardless, at the heart of this issue lies one immovable fact: A man's efforts to pull his mind off the visual stimuli in front of him makes it difficult for him to be as focused as he wants to be on the business matter at hand. This is probably why the issue of how women dressed was one of the top five subjects my interviewees mentioned most often.

Here are quotes from two representative survey-takers who said they had seen talented women sometimes undermine themselves with men, and who tagged this issue as the reason why:

- "Professional business dress for men and women is different. Current fashion trends are pushing female fashion to a more provocative style—tighter clothes, shorter skirts, etc. While attempting to be 'fashionable,' even a skilled woman may unintentionally dress in a manner that demeans her talent and position in the eyes of her male colleagues. Men are by nature visually stimulated and improper dress by female coworkers can cause a distraction if done on a regular basis. I have also seen it cause the woman to be taken less seriously in all aspects of her business relationships."

- "When giving a presentation she might wear something provocative or distracting to the men in the room—who would not be paying attention to what she is talking about at all."

Most women (seven out of ten on the survey) wouldn't be distracted in such a situation. Here is an analogy that might help us to understand what this is like from a man's point of view.

"HER CLEAVAGE IS TALKING"

Watching the 2008 Super Bowl, my husband, friends, and I were almost as intent on reviewing the commercials as we were on the game. One particular ad, for Tide to Go stain remover, stood out by showing a comical job interview situation. The interviewee had a noticeable stain on his shirt, and as he talked to the manager across the desk, the stain grew a big pair of lips and began "talking" in nonsense words—essentially making it impossible for the manager (or the TV viewer) to concentrate on what the interviewee was saying. It was a memorable ad and a clever way to make the case for the Tide product.

As that commercial was wrapping up, one of the men in the room (who knew I was researching the effect of the "visual" aspect on men) turned to me and pointed at the television. "That is *exactly* what it is like when a woman's outfit shows cleavage," he said. "It's like her cleavage is talking. And you aren't able to concentrate on a word she's saying."

In an out-of-town interview a few weeks later, a different man again brought up the same commercial. He added,

> By the way, it's not just cleavage. If she's attractive, it is any emphasis to her figure. Or even if it's a tattoo! It is hard to concentrate when the tattoo is peeking out. I had one lady working for me who was incredibly bright and personable. During a wilder part of her life, she had gotten a tattoo. I didn't even know it was there until she came in one day wearing something more summery. And then you start wondering, *How low does that go?*

This man agreed that men's visual nature can be easily distracted by other things that aren't sexual at all. For example, as he put it, "there's a thing among some of my younger staff members about not just tattoos but facial piercings. Like nose studs. But it is really hard to take someone seriously when their nose is blinking at you."

THE VISUAL EXPERIMENT

Once I realized the importance of men's visual nature, and the role it can play in unintentionally undermining men's ability to concentrate on a woman's business purpose, I wanted to see if I could estimate what the actual distraction factor was.

While there was no way to feasibly re-create and test my survey question in a live environment, I could at least examine the impact of a video clip and assume that the actual impact would likely be greater in a real-world situation. Working with my survey designer, my research assistants, and a team of studio and online specialists, I created two ninety-second videos of an attractive businesswoman wearing a suit, presenting "the four top customer suggestions" for a fictitious retail clothing company. The presenter introduces herself as Laurie Boss, Director of Customer Service. The only difference between the two videos is that in one she wears her cross-over top low to show her cleavage; in the other she wears it high, eliminating cleavage.

We then created a short survey about the content of the four top customer suggestions she was presenting. Without knowing what was being tested, 409 men took this survey online, randomly seeing one of the two videos. The results? There was a clear difference in what they absorbed and retained. For example, the percentage of men who remembered the presenter's name dropped by 25 percent if they saw the more revealing version of the video. More important, the men who watched the woman with the cleavage remembered 25 percent less of the content that she shared: Where 64 percent of men who saw the more conservative video remembered her four points, only 48 percent of those who saw the more revealing version did.

The men who watched the woman with the cleavage remembered 25 percent less of the content that she shared.

Given the artificial distance imposed by watching a short video online, and the memory-jogging assistance of answering multiple questions about it immediately afterward, the distraction factor would almost certainly be higher in a real-life environment.

In fact, at the end of the survey for the more revealing video, several men commented that without the survey questions, they wouldn't have been able to recall much at all about what "Laurie Boss" presented. As one described it, "If I hadn't taken the survey afterward, I wouldn't have remembered anything she said. But tomorrow and a week from now, I would still remember her cleavage."

Overall, when I asked the men who had seen the more revealing video two totally open-ended questions about their impression of "Laurie Boss" and what she could have done to improve her customer service presentation, nearly six in ten volunteered that the most important adjustment would not be adding visual aids, speaking more slowly, or adding more quotes from customers: They said she should change her top. Several of their comments essentially summarize the dilemma for men:

- "I had to avoid looking at the woman's cleavage to better focus on what she was saying."

- "Her top was too revealing, therefore very distracting, so it took a lot of concentration to determine what she was talking about."

- "The speaker's outfit was distracting. A more conservative outfit would assist male viewers to focus more on the information being relayed."

- "Too much cleavage in the announcer. Draws attention away from presentation. I took notes and therefore could listen better without looking."

ATTRACTIVE VS. DISTRACTING VS. SEXUAL

The uncomfortable reality is that men often think women are *trying* to distract them sexually. But many men hastened to add that women can be very attractive and yet never trigger the distraction factor. Douglass, the corporate sponsorship executive I introduced previously, says:

> Realize that breasts can be distracting before they are sexual, and seeing part of a woman's breast is distracting. Conversely, a woman can be extremely attractive, but if she's not showing skin or wearing really form-fitting clothes, the issue doesn't come up. She's just . . . attractive. Women have the ability to be completely beautiful and completely appropriate . . . But there is a line at some point that you cross where it becomes distracting, and another line where it could become sexual. At least that is how it comes across, to me. What you do not want to do is look at her and start down the other path.

"A woman can be extremely attractive, but if she's not showing skin or wearing really form-fitting clothes, the issue doesn't come up."

Ramification 2: He May Think the Woman Wants to Be Viewed Sexually

As I touched on at the beginning of the chapter, the awkward and sobering reality is that men and women have entirely different views on *why* a woman would dress in a way that shows off her figure. My survey and interviews demonstrate that most women are not trying to attract sexual attention. But depending on how revealing the clothing is, and how attractive the woman is, the men often find that difficult to believe. Because men are so visually attuned and sexually aware, they have a tendency to assume that women are too. They assume that a woman in a low-cut top knows (in the words of many men) "exactly what she is doing."

While some of the white-collar women I surveyed did confess to wanting to attract sexual attention, or to manipulate the men around them to their advantage, the vast majority of women who occasionally dress that way aren't thinking about that at all. And in my interviews, most women are horrified that men would think that they were.

Here are the stark differences between how men and women perceive revealing clothing. As we saw at the opening of this chapter, three of four men think the woman "wants the men around her to look at her body." Seventy percent felt the woman was showing off her body in order to create an advantage—when only 16 percent of women said that was their intent.

As you can see, most men think the woman is conscious of showing off her body, does it on purpose to create a business advantage, and wants the men around her to look at her body. Perhaps even more damaging, 67 percent of men said that a woman who dresses to show her figure "does understand how she's being perceived— and she doesn't care."

By contrast, the large majority of white-collar women who did dress that way said their primary motivation was none of those reasons: 89 percent said they simply wanted to look good and wear what is in style.

When I relayed this information to some of the men I interviewed, some replied that they had figured that had to be the case. Others, however, had a hard time believing me. For still others, it explained something that had previously confused them about women's intentions. As one young man told me, "We have five men and one woman on our project team, and the woman is really attractive. She wears these suits with short skirts. She's a happy newlywed, and I've often wondered why she would want to tempt all these other guys to fantasize about her. It helps to know she's just clueless!"

Ramification 3: He May View That Woman with Less Respect

Given the common male assumption that women wear figure-showing outfits to purposefully create sexual thoughts, manipulate their male colleagues, or create a business advantage, it is not surprising that some men view such women with less respect.

I heard this most commonly from men who were meeting the woman on a limited basis (for example, an infrequent sales meeting, or a one-time project), or among those who felt that a female colleague regularly dressed that way and wasn't a top performer. The more regularly a man worked with a female colleague, the more he respected her for her business performance, regardless of what she wore. The man might still be equally distracted by her dress, but he was less likely to think less of the woman because of it.

But in situations where the man either didn't know the woman well, or didn't yet view her as a top performer, men told me that they tended to view her with less respect simply because of her dress. One male survey-taker said a key action that undermined men's perception of women was, when a women would "[dress] inappropriately for the business, but believ[e] she will still be taken seriously during important meetings." And this held true on the video-driven visual survey as well, where one man who saw the more revealing version said, "[Her] cleavage distracted away from the message and made her look silly."

The more regularly a man works with a particular woman, the more he respects her for her business performance, regardless of what she wears. He can still be as distracted by it, but is less likely to think less of her because of it.

Another man who saw that video said this: "Presenter seemed knowledgeable and spoke well. First impression was that she must have missed a button or two while getting ready that morning. Then I thought . . . Oh yes, must be those marketing people using the 'sex sells' tactic."

"THEY'LL INVITE YOU BACK, BUT THEY WON'T TAKE YOU SERIOUSLY"

Mark, the experienced executive and entrepreneur I mentioned previously, gave me an example that seemed fairly representative:

I had a meeting yesterday with some senior people who are looking for us to make an investment and talk about a strategic partnership. They had their COO with them, who had been a senior banker for [a major global bank] with some global responsibilities. And she's sitting across the table from me, leaning into me, and I'm trying *not* to see her bra. And I'm trying to figure out, is she *trying* to show me her breasts, or is she like clueless here?

I'm trying to have a conversation with her. And I don't even remember what she was talking about. Someone needs to get a hold of her and say, "Look, they'll invite you back, but they won't take you seriously." It's sort of like what I tell my daughters: You don't have to show your figure for guys to know you've got a good figure. They get it! It's their job to be always aware of that!! You don't have to wear that outfit for guys to notice.

"THAT DOESN'T BELONG IN BUSINESS"

The men I spoke with believe that "sexy" or revealing attire (including clothes that women would not perceive that way) belongs exclusively in one's personal life. The point of such clothes, to them, is to be eye-catching. They viewed such dress as not relevant to or appropriate in business, and as actually *distracting* to the purpose of business. As a result, they view this issue as they would any other example of bringing "Personal World rules" into the business world: They view the woman as less than business-savvy.

One senior executive described it to me this way: "For me, it creates a barrier immediately if a woman comes into a meeting showing cleavage. You as a woman have to get to the point that you realize, this isn't about sex, it's about business. Showing cleavage won't necessarily kill the deal, but it absolutely makes me question her judgment." This man's train of thought was telling—and all too representative. When he sees cleavage he automatically assumes the woman is immaturely trying to create an advantage by making the meeting "about sex."

When he sees cleavage he automatically assumes the woman is immaturely trying to create an advantage by making the meeting "about sex."

It should be noted here that although men often lose respect for such women, it doesn't necessarily mean that the approach doesn't work—at least in one of those infrequent-contact situations where certain men are fine with the "eye candy." One man who took the survey with the more revealing version of the video commented, "The reporter's busty attire distracted from the professionalism and credibility of the message, but it may have increased my attention."

One national sales director spent nearly an hour on a cross-country flight telling me the backstory of the sales practices in his large corporation. Prior to his arrival, the sales department had built teams of saleswomen who described themselves as "super hot" and dressed in vampy clothes. He acknowledged that when they began a substantial change to a more professional sales culture, they actually lost about a third of their sales in blue-collar environments! But interestingly, their more profitable white-collar sales increased by the same amount—because, he said, the customers felt that they were being respected rather than manipulated.

"SHE'S CLUELESS"

On the broader survey, just 37 percent of the men realized what is often the truth: that a woman who dresses revealingly "must not understand how she's being perceived." And the realization that a woman was "clueless" led them to respect her less, professionally.

One man I know attended a highly touted all-day corporate conference, and when I asked how he had enjoyed it, he described his reaction to one female speaker:

She was probably forty years old, very attractive and dynamic—but was wearing this top that sort of gaped and showed her breasts. I ran into her after her talk and she was telling me how she had spent ten thousand dollars on these high-level New York speaking coaches. And the whole time she's explaining this, these perfect golden boobs are staring at me. And honestly, I felt sorry for her. I'm thinking, *You just spent ten thousand dollars on learning how to be a better public speaker, and you just blew it all.* Because I doubt the men in there were really listening to what she was saying. And she could have been such a dynamite speaker.

EITHER NEGATIVE OR POSITIVE PERCEPTIONS CAN BECOME THE DEFAULT

Aidan, the global consulting partner I have mentioned earlier, is one of the top partners in his firm in terms of mentoring and promoting women. Among the advice he was eager to pass along to any up-and-coming woman who may occasionally dress in a way that shows off her figure:

> We as men don't just leave this [visual nature] in the parking lot. . . . Do you want the guy at work, when he thinks of you, to picture your legs, or picture your point of view? I think most women I know, I would put in one group or the other.
>
> You can be very attractive and that isn't a problem for a guy as long as everything is covered up, and not too close-fitting. If I see an attractive women being careful about it, the mental conclusion is that she's going to rely on her point of view instead of on her looks.
>
> But if I meet someone at work with a trendy, short skirt or close-fitting clothes, I know she must know that, so she's

relying on her body and the attraction factor to work in her favor.

Ramification 4: It Puts Men Who Want to Respect Women Professionally in an Awkward Position

Most of the men I spoke with wanted to be respectful of women. They didn't want the distraction or temptation that jumped to their minds—especially with regard to a female colleague they liked and respected. But when a woman colleague dressed in a revealing way, they couldn't easily avoid it without also avoiding that colleague. (Which was the choice some of them felt forced into.)

As a result, ironically, this dilemma was most challenging and demoralizing for the men who cared the *most* about honoring and respecting the women they worked with. Those who didn't care as much shrugged and said, essentially, "If she wants to show it off, I'll enjoy the show."

> *Ironically, this dilemma was most challenging for the men who cared the* most *about respecting women.*

SO WHAT DO WOMEN DO ABOUT IT?

Women in the workplace want to be taken seriously. My survey shows that few intend (or want) to create a visual dilemma that could hinder their effectiveness. Nonetheless, the simple reality is that some women are doing exactly that—and perhaps more than they realize.

Thankfully, more than any other subject in this book, the problem lends itself to a simple solution for the woman who decides to make a change based on this new knowledge. The visual distraction factor is triggered when a woman dresses in a way that overtly emphasizes or calls attention to her figure. And when she doesn't dress that way, the distraction factor isn't triggered.

In practice, however, we need to become a bit more educated and aware of what men see as "overtly calling attention to a good figure," or "revealing." There is a clear disconnect between what many women feel is "OK" and what men feel is "OK." Several times I have stood with a man I know at a busy pedestrian area, business district, or coffee shop and asked him to point out cases where he felt a woman's male colleagues would have a difficult time concentrating based on her choice of attire. And I was surprised at some of their choices. I'll bet that the woman in question would have been surprised as well.

This disconnect was evident on the survey, as well. Just 4 percent and 22 percent of women, respectively, said they "frequently" or "sometimes" wore work outfits that emphasized their figure. But men seemed to think that the visual dilemma occurred a lot more often.

Among men who have female colleagues and who don't have a strict workplace uniform, 58 percent of men say they see a female associate dressing in a way they find as distracting at least once a week. Twelve percent said they see examples of that "every day, multiple times a day."

Most of the women in question undoubtedly intend merely to dress professionally and attractively and are not aware that their attire is perceived as visually distracting.

Looking at the Specifics

On TheMaleFactorBook.com, my website for this book, I include some examples of the types of professional attire that many men have pointed out as a likely distraction. In general, the men pointed out that the more young and attractive a woman is, the more likely this is to be an issue and therefore, the more cautious she may want to be.

Here is what one of the men said with regard to outfits that tend to trigger a response in men:

> It's all about curves, bare skin, and, frankly, the sight of whatever is supposed to be covered. That is what a man's eyes will be drawn to. A tight outfit, a short skirt, a bra strap showing, low-cut pants in the back where you can see the top of whatever she is wearing underneath if she leans over a bit . . . any one of those things. And cleavage. Breasts are always distracting.
>
> It is so frustrating when I see in the morning that my one female colleague is wearing a button-down shirt, because she regularly has those types of shirts unbuttoned one button too low, and where it gapes or she turns sideways you can see everything. And I try to avoid looking, but I cannot put my hand up and go like this [he put his hand up as if to block his view of her chest] when I am talking to her, so that is a really difficult thing.
>
> And of course, I cannot tell her about her top. I think she trusts me, but no guy can ever talk about this with a woman. Unless she's his sister or something.

In several corporate events, I asked the person organizing the event to collect anonymous input on this issue from the men at the company beforehand. They raised quite a few specifics worth being aware of, which I am including on my website. (One example: "Tell the women to remember that men are taller than they are. The blouse may look fine straight on in the mirror, but think about what it will look like if someone is six inches taller and looking down.")

Help Other Women Understand This

Some readers of this book may want to pass some of this information on to female colleagues or female subordinates.

When I interviewed one senior female partner at a major consulting firm, she told me that the men in her practice had asked her several times to address this issue with specific women. The men explained that these women frequently went on client calls dressed in ways the men felt would be counterproductive. The men didn't feel that they could bring it up, but were anxious to correct the issue before it caused client problems. Yet the senior female partner was one of the top rainmakers for that practice. She was way too busy. Moreover, she told me she resented the fact that just because she was a woman, she was expected to "be a sort of babysitter to women who should know better." Because she was so busy, and didn't know how to address it in a nonoffensive way, she never followed up.

I know from experience that making other women aware of this issue can be awkward. It helps if you get the other person's permission in advance. For example, you might say, "I have something a bit awkward that I want to ask you about. But it's something that you might find important because it could affect how you may be perceived. Would you mind if I raised it with you?"

One senior female executive I know is always getting (in her words) "stuck" with having this conversation with female colleagues because she's one of the most senior women in the company, and no man feels able to raise the subject with the women in question. So the men go to my friend, and my friend has to raise it as part of her job.

When I asked her what approach she found to be the most effective, here's what she said:

It starts with ensuring you are respectful and discreet. You need to do it in such a way that no one else knows the conversation is happening. I have had to do this multiple times, and I basically ask the woman to come into my office, close the door, and say, "This is really awkward, but I have something I need to talk to you about. Let me just blurt this out, and we can clean it up later. I just have to address what you're wearing, and want to walk you through why it probably isn't the best choice for this work environment, or this meeting you're preparing for. It's both for your sake and the company's reputation. I'm so sorry, but I just have to bring this up."

"How do you explain the actual issue to the woman, though?" I ask. "If she's confused, or doesn't understand why this is an issue. Or if she's offended?"

I ask her, "When you do this meeting, what do you want to be remembered for?" She will almost always say, "My presentation! I've got the stats, I've been working hard on this, and now it's time to present it."

I then say, "OK, so if you want to be remembered for the presentation, then you want to do everything you can to ensure that the presentation is the focal point, and do everything you can to minimize any possible distractions, right? So you put together a great PowerPoint, and you decide how to emphasize these two main points you want them to remember. But you also think ahead of time about avoiding distractions—you silence your cell phone, for example, or close the conference room door so people don't get distracted by outside noise.

"We often don't realize it, but it works basically the same way with what we're wearing. If you want them to remember your presentation and not your feather hoop earrings, or your red stilettos, don't wear them. And if you want them to remember your two main points and not your cleavage, then you should probably consider changing your top before the meeting."

Sometimes I jokingly say, "You just happen to have a figure that I would kill for, so you may have to think more specifically about how to make it a nonissue, so the guys can concentrate on what you're saying."

A Tool That Might Help

As an aid for any managers, workers, or HR departments who want to address this with their female employees or colleagues, I have created a tool that might help: a short presentation that you can find on TheMaleFactorBook.com. The presentation summarizes the findings discussed in this chapter, in particular the results of the video experiment showing the "distraction factor," as a way of helping women understand how certain fashion choices may be perceived.

CHAPTER 11

"The Most Important Thing"

Men's Top Advice for Women in the Workplace

Of all the truths about men that intersect with us every day, there is one important truth I would like to highlight as we wrap up this book. After reading a few hundred pages about men's perceptions, it would be easy to assume that men expect women to set aside who they are and become "like a man" in the workplace.

But based on the surprising results to my final question on the survey, that is not the case at all. When I asked an entirely open-ended question about the single most important piece of advice men would offer women in the workplace, one resounding theme emerged:

Be competent and confident in who you are; you are re-spected and we're cheering you on.

THE FINAL QUESTION

As you know, I had asked the men two dozen multiple-choice sur-vey questions on a host of subjects, as well as the core question about whether (and how) they saw talented women unintention-ally shoot themselves in the foot. As the final question on the survey (that they were forced to answer before the survey would be

considered complete), I then gave the survey-takers a blank field in which they could write as much or as little as they liked, and asked this question: "Finally, if you could give one piece of advice to women in the workplace, what is the one most important thing you would say to them?"

Fully *half* of the men essentially gave something like these answers:

1. Be competent and you'll do well;
2. Just be yourself and confident in who you are; or
3. You're respected; keep up the great work

—or a combination of all three.

The fact that 51 percent of the men chose to offer one or more of those three very encouraging messages as their "most important advice" was astonishing for a question in which the men had a blank space and could say anything at all. The comments of the other half of the men were split among a dozen other types of substantive advice—in particular the suggestions that women be cautious about how they dress, and about how they display emotions. (You can see a broad sampling of the men's word-for-word answers at TheMaleFactorBook.com.)

I've listed the complete breakdown of their advice on the following page, assigning comments to their relevant chapter categories (where appropriate) for simplicity.

The fact that 51 percent said their top advice was "Be competent, be yourself, and keep up the great work" is astonishing, when they had a blank space and could say anything at all.

OPEN-ENDED COMMENTS	NUMBER OF ALL ANSWERS	PERCENTAGE OF ALL ANSWERS
	581[1]	100%
Be competent, and you'll do well	106	18%
Be yourself / confident in who you are	103	18%
You're respected; keep up the great work	87	15%
Visual / Sex (Be cautious of dress)	69	12%
Emotions	55	9%
Move past gender (Don't expect different treatment / Don't have chip on shoulder)	33	6%
It's not personal; it's business	30	5%
Respect / Be cautious of disrespect	30	5%
Let it go	27	5%
Be relaxed, genuine, forthright	12	2%
Suck it up	5	1%
Other subjects		<1%

The previous chapters have explained most of these areas of advice—except the three top categories. Let's look briefly at the three top comments that men would share with women in the workplace, starting with "Be Yourself," first.[2]

"BE YOURSELF; BE CONFIDENT IN WHO YOU ARE"

Many, many men in my interviews told me that they too often saw women believe that surviving in the marketplace required transforming their personality and becoming "like a man." And yet, they said, this approach usually backfired because they could tell the person wasn't being genuine; it created a subtle layer of distrust in their interactions.

Matthew, the North American sales manager for a medical equipment supplier, described it this way.

> I think sometimes the perceived need to survive takes over the personality or the natural disposition of some people. And my personal impression is that the effect is far more pronounced in women than it is in men. We had several thousand female sales reps at [his last company] and I often saw an overcompensation among women who felt like they had to change who they were in order to be successful. And that overcompensation often seemed to impact those characteristics that were decidedly female. But you can see strong female leaders who haven't done that—and haven't needed to. Margaret Thatcher was someone with the intellectual discipline and acumen to best any man in the room. She could be tough, but she maintained that characteristic that is distinctly female.

He paused for a moment and then said:

> You know what? I don't know that my favorable impression has anything to do, really, with a woman maintaining

feminine qualities, as much as with the fact that she is not changing who she naturally is. With Margaret Thatcher, you got the impression of honesty. Something that was not compromised. A truth in her speech and in her demeanor that said, "Look, I am tough, but I am also square with who I am."

People who change are not being themselves. It is like they are not in their own skin. That is not viewed well. Generally, people prefer to work with those who are genuine. There are a lot of people that would want to meet with a female account executive over a male account executive any day, because they appreciate their style. You don't want to lose that.

One partner in a major New York law firm told me, "Sometimes I have seen a woman try to overcompensate for the perception that she as a woman might not be a take-charge person. But by overcompensating she loses the natural strengths she has. She loses the ability to build a team, or lead a team in a less aggressive way, and she becomes almost obnoxious. A few days ago, I was sitting down with a team of lawyers from a potential M&A deal, led by a female partner. She was highly competent, and she knew what she was talking about, but she sounded and carried herself like a man. And I thought, *Whoa! I wonder what she must have gone through, to become like that.* Because the changes she had to force upon herself made her a strange person. Her body language, her coarse language, her tone. The words were abrasive. She was carrying a macho attitude like 'I'm in charge and I want everyone to know it.' A more overtly macho attitude, by the way, than most men have in a professional environment. I would have greater respect for her if she would just be herself. Trying to project a different image is not natural, for either a woman or a man."

As I was traveling to talk to a corporate women's network, one man cautioned, "Ironically, my female colleagues who try to 'be like men' tend to pick the most unattractive attributes of men—the hard personality traits that men dislike about each other."

One recently retired senior executive in the newspaper industry brought up several similar examples, but then contrasted those with this encouragement:

I grew up in publishing, so starting in the 1970s, I have encountered a lot of fantastically talented women in that industry, in the investment world, in the financial world, and in the advertising marketing world. And the ones that endured were women who had acquired a sort of confidence, a type of wholeness about them. They were sure of themselves and sure of their identity as women and very professional. They knew their borders, they knew their boundaries, but they did well because they knew they had to interact with men on a level that was extraordinarily professional, but human, extraordinarily human.

The men I interviewed brought up this "Don't feel you have to be like a man" point so frequently that I ended up including a related question on the survey and forcing the men into a choice. Essentially, the question was this: Would you trust and respect someone more if they were being themselves, instead of trying to create a persona? Or would you trust and respect someone more if they got the job done, period, even if in the process they put on the persona of someone they clearly were not?

Even though these men had clearly shown their "results orientation" on other questions, in the end, 77 percent of the male survey-takers had more respect for a person who was being authentic.

But What About All These Changes They Suggest?

Some women might wonder, as I did, *How can men say "Be yourself" when they also are clearly suggesting that it might be valuable for women to change their approach in certain areas?*

One survey-taker's top advice provided an answer that rang true with me: "Be your *professional* self. [Emphasis mine.] Don't try to be a man, because the fact is, you're not."

Another said, "Be yourself but realize that people, men and women, are different. There is sometimes a need to adjust to people, whether you want to or not."

Two men I interviewed made some particularly helpful distinctions. As one put it, "When men say 'Just be yourself,' they truly mean it—but it *doesn't* mean, 'so anything goes.' Men have all these professional expectations, right? Those rules essentially set their expected boundary for the workplace. And 'Just be yourself' essentially means, 'Within the rules, relax and be confident in who you are.'"

> "'Just be yourself' essentially means, 'Within the boundaries of the workplace, relax and be confident in who you are.'"

Another replied, "When you go to France, you are not going to be understood if you just speak louder in English. You have to speak French. This is like that. You learn to use a different language, but you don't have to be a different person."

And many men pointed out just how much is lost when someone does not leverage their natural strengths. As one survey-taker advised, "Be genuine. There's no need to be like a man to succeed. When there's too much masculine energy, sometimes we lose sight of other perspectives."

"BE COMPETENT, AND YOU'LL DO WELL"

One of the key themes running through all my interviews—as well as, obviously, the survey results—was summed up by this survey-taker: "Gender is irrelevant—be competent." (His comment was such a good summary that I included it in chapter 6, as well.)

When I went back through my interviews, I was struck by the fact that there were literally hundreds of quotes from men on this point. They emphasized it over and over, often returning to it several times in the same interview. I realized, in retrospect, that the men weren't sure I (or other women) would believe them or fully grasp the centrality of their perception—that the modern market was largely gender blind.

While several of my chapters show that "largely" is the operative word (in that some men were still, for example, more sensitive to criticism from women than from other men), this perception about competence is nevertheless worth highlighting—with one key caveat. As you have seen, part of what men view as "competence" includes the ability to fit into the rules and culture of the workplace, and all the other expectations addressed in this book. But that said, this perception was still encouraging.

It was extremely difficult for me to select just a few of the survey-takers' quotes on this, so I'm pulling out a few almost at random. As noted earlier, I will post the others on my website.

- "As far as I am concerned—and I am the CEO—results are what matter. Intelligent, efficient people of either sex deserve my full and complete support. I am male, but I would never even consider paying a female less than a male for the same work. My advice therefore is to stand up and demand full equality of sexes in the workplace.

Nothing less should be acceptable. Companies that cannot grasp this deserve to lose the quality female employees to more enlightened companies." (It is worth noting that this CEO has between 500 and 999 employees under him, according to the demographics given for each anonymous survey-taker.)

- "Performance speaks volumes. Work on being very good at your job, then adding value beyond your job in some way (through leadership or resolving thorny problems or bringing and implementing new ideas). Solid performance as well as adding value tends to help all men and women be given greater responsibilities in time."

- "Believe in yourself! It doesn't matter whether you're a man or a woman, it's how well you do your job."

- "Just be yourself and do the best job you can do. Your performance will speak for itself."

- "I believe a confident, warm, and capable personality is respected in almost every endeavor for both men and women. The woman who tries to be one of the men by being rough or crude or tough is often thought of as someone not being true to her natural gender, and hence disagreeable. Integrity, capability, and a secure personality are what is most respected and appreciated in a woman in *any* position."

> *"Integrity, capability, and a secure personality are what is most respected and appreciated in a woman in* any *position."*

With all these comments in mind, one survey-taker did provide an important caution:

Be yourself and work to the best of your abilities. In most situations that will be enough to enable you to have a pleasant and gainful work experience. And if it does not, then you should consider finding an environment that does allow you to be yourself and successful at the same time.

"YOU'RE RESPECTED; KEEP UP THE GREAT WORK"

Finally, a large number of the male survey-takers were very personally encouraging. It was almost as if they wanted to convey to the women reading the results of this "research project" (as it was described to the men), just how much they respected and were cheering on women in the workplace. ("Never give up!" "You go, girl!")

Even though many of the same men acknowledged that women still face certain disadvantages (despite the often-stated "You are equal" claim), the spirit behind their comments was encouraging. Here are just a fraction of the actual comments they wrote, in their own words.

- "All should be equal in the workplace. Don't let anyone tell you otherwise."

- "Always consider yourself as valuable as any other member of the workforce, if you are qualified for the tasks."

- "Always keep your confidence up."

- "Be confident in what you do, and let others know why what you do is important. Show that you are capable of responding to any situation in a positive manner."

- "Be professional and strong minded."

- "Be strong!"

- "Be strong. Not every man will be accepting of or act appropriately around women in the workplace, but there are a lot out there who do. It will keep getting better."

> *"Not every man will be accepting of or act appropriately around women in the workplace, but there are a lot out there who do. It will keep getting better."*

- "Continue to be compassionate and dedicated to your professional goals without letting the opinions and preconceptions of male coworkers get in the way."

- "Do not be intimidated by some men. You are probably smarter."

- "Do not let anyone treat you as a lesser person."

- "Don't be afraid to contribute."

- "Express your opinions. Don't be afraid to speak up!"

- "For both men and women in the workplace: You must perceive yourself as equal before anyone else will do so. Have the confidence, the dedication, and the professionalism to *know* that you are capable of working on an equal level of even the highest of authorities in your field. Carry this confidence *without* arrogance and without a standoffish attitude."

- "Have confidence in yourself and you will exude confidence to those around you."

- "I would tell the women that they are just as capable as men and should not feel like they have to work twice as hard to be recognized."

- "Keep doing what you are doing—eventually, the men in the workplace who don't 'get it,' will."

- "Keep it up!"

- "Keep standing up for your rights to be paid equally with men."

- "Keep up the good work and do not settle for the crap you get fed by men."

- "Never give up and don't believe you are inferior."

- "Strive to reach the top."

- "Take ownership of your opinions and work; never apologize for doing a good job."

MEN WANT TO BE OUR PARTNERS IN THE WORKPLACE

The bottom line for most of the men I interviewed is that despite their natural bent toward competition, they truly view women as equal partners in the workplace, working toward the shared goal of success for the organization. And they encouraged women to view things the same way. Both for the good of the company and—given an environment in which women still face some unique hurdles—for the good of the woman's career. As one survey-taker put it, "All things still are not equal in the corporate world. Keep working for equal respect, but try not to alienate the ones who reach out their hands as allies."

Another said, "Some men may still be prone to perceiving you in the 'typical male' way, but women can do a lot to create how they want to be perceived. Confident and direct communication will show your level of competency and talent, regardless of gender."

> "Some men may still be prone to perceiving you in the 'typical male' way, but women can do a lot to create how they want to be perceived."

A senior executive search leader I interviewed who had worked with many high-level female executives over the years strongly advised women to be keenly aware of the level of partnership and relationship needed as we rise to the top. He said that "the women who have tended to succeed" are those women who marshal their strength in relationship building and are willing to focus on others, rather than just themselves. He explained:

This is something that a lot of people—men or women—never understand. The very thing that may help a certain type of lower-ranking person fight toward the top of the ladder—like the sharp elbows and the willingness to step up on somebody else's hand—are the very things that prevent that person getting to the very top. Because the last three rungs of the ladder do not come as a result of that.

You might get through a pack of managers and a pack of directors and even a pack of senior directors in that way—but to reach the highest ranks of the company, there is a high level of emotional intelligence required. In the middle of the company, it is making the numbers work, it is making the customers happy; it is a lot of metrics that measure success. At the top of the company, it is extraordinarily relational.

What ultimately creates success is being able to create beneficial relationships with shareholders, stakeholders, customers, and key employees. Companies that succeed have figured out a way to have a very, very high trust factor at the top; people at the highest levels being willing to work together and really understand each other.

Women who operate that way, he concluded, "can be very, very effective."

When I was in the final stages of testing the survey, on one long coast-to-coast flight I handed out thirty or forty paper surveys to businessmen on the plane. While I was tallying the results I turned one survey over, and found the man had used the space to provide this summary of what he would "most want to tell women":

Men like confidence. Men are drawn to warm personalities. Men respect competence. Men like secure women who stand above the petty "din" of the gossip and fear that can often be in the workplace. Men want PARTNERS to build something together. [His emphasis.] The striving of competition in and out of the workplace stems from fear and hurt and insecurities on the part of both men and women. If these are done away with, the woman and man both can find their voices and rise equally according to achievement and contribution within an organization. Personally, I know the female energy within an organization adds to the richness of the environment. It would be nice to let the women know that they are noticed and appreciated, and it's not all a battle.

> ■ *"It would be nice to let the women know that they are noticed and appreciated, and it's not all a battle."*

Throughout this book, I have emphasized that the point of bringing these facts to light is having the information necessary to make an informed decision. Each reader will take something very different away from what they have read. Some women will feel comfortable that they already understand "the male factor" in the workplace, or that these things don't apply to them. Others may suspect the opposite. And our choices of what to do about it—if anything—will vary tremendously. If you are compelled to learn more, exchange ideas with other women in your field at your company, or explore different ways to move from information to application, you can find a few simple starting points at TheMale FactorBook.com

Over the last seven years of this research, I have been unexpectedly impacted by the intensity of the feelings of the men on many of these subjects—especially among those who most respect us as women and want to work with women in an effective way. For our sake as women, and for theirs as our allies and colleagues in the workplace, I hope that women will take this new knowledge seriously. I believe it presents an opportunity to address areas we may have never realized needed to be addressed, and to demonstrate that we respect not only ourselves, but those around us as well.

Acknowledgments

In a research project that spanned eight years, literally hundreds of people provided help, expertise, and insight along the way. While I cannot name them all here, some are acknowledged in earlier books, especially *For Women Only* and my novel *The Lights of Tenth Street*. All have my gratitude.

That said, I must thank several critical groups of people on this project.

To the women and men who provided so much information and insight: The content of this book springs largely from the generosity and goodwill of the hundreds of men I interviewed, and the dozens of people—men and women—who provided insight along the way, helped set up meetings, networked me into their contacts, and generally made the research possible. While I have promised to keep them and their organizations anonymous, they know who they are, and I am in their debt.

In addition to the research team named below, I want to thank the women who spent hours reading through chapters, giving me feedback, and/or helping with specific aspects of the research, including Susan Conley, Alison Darrell, Sue Deagle, Carrie Delong, Paula Dumas, Wendy Shashoua and Amy Smith. My deep thanks also to those such as Patti Ross, Nancy Chambers, Gary Smith, and the Transform Group team, who have recently been so willing to provide "beyond the book" help.

My thanks also to those who helped me conduct the "visual experiment," especially those at the InTouch studios in Atlanta and "Laurie Boss" for her time and talent. Special gratitude to Lisa Ryan who wielded the "virtual microphone" that started me on this road in the first place.

I am also deeply grateful to the generous group of women who spent hours brainstorming title and cover options, and receiving e-mails saying "What do you think of this one? . . . Oops, never mind." I lost track of how many "official" titles and covers we went through, but you never lost your patience.

To the Research Team and others who work with me: At the front of the book are photographs of the core team that helped me conduct the research; design, test, and conduct the survey; analyze the results; and advise me on many aspects of content. This has been a massive team effort, and there would be no book without them.

To Felicia Rogers, Ramiro Davila, Scott Hanson and the others at Decision Analyst: Over the years I have only grown more grateful for your outstanding work. After the years of research and testing that lead up to the critical moment of fielding the survey, each time you pull the trigger I'm very thankful that all that effort is in such skilled hands.

To Chuck Cowan and Mauricio Vidaurre-Vega at Analytic Focus: As always, thanks for willingly pouring so many extra hours of effort and personal interest into this project. Chuck, each time we work together, I'm immensely thankful for your belief in what I am doing, and your willingness to bring your considerable expertise to bear on the survey-development process.

To my personal team: Thanks for caring and investing yourselves so much, for your commitment to getting it right, and for going far beyond the call of duty.

My heartfelt admiration and thanks go to my outstanding research analysts Jenny Reynolds and Jackie Feit Coleman, who braved everything from, respectively, the minutiae of clinical neuroscience studies and detailed survey spreadsheets, to the prospect of being arrested while helping me test the survey (and nearly missing her graduate school graduation ceremony that night!). I'm grateful for other team members, such as Tally Whitehead, my column research assistant, and Suzanne Kaufman, Doreen Row, and Julie Fidler, whose great work in other areas allowed me to focus on the book. That is especially true of Lisa and Eric Rice, dear friends, coauthors, and partners on so many other books and projects that were unfolding at the same time as this one.

To Calvin Edwards, Kim Rash, and Jeff Feldhahn: the massive amount of personal energy, time, interest, and insight each of you was willing to invest over the last seven years has made an incredible difference to the content and, hopefully, usefulness of the final book. I am almost embarrassed when I look back and tally up the hundreds of hours the three of you poured into the process. Thank you for your willing gift of time.

To Ann Browne: thanks for bringing your personal and professional encouragement to bear over the years, and for being willing to step out of corporate America and partner with me in Human Factor Resources, to help readers go beyond the book and further develop the research.

And finally, most important, on my personal team I want to thank my director of operations, Linda Crews, for being so invested in this work and for her amazing way of keeping everything running. Also my assistants, Leslie Hettenbach, Karen Newby, and Vance Hanifen, who cheerfully listened to and read through even the most difficult of interviews; categorized subjects and arranged meetings, itineraries, and focus groups until neither they nor I knew what city I was in anymore; and generally did an amazing job of keeping this messy author organized.

To both publishers: A book that is co-published between two different divisions has had many skilled minds involved, and they all have my thanks. I am especially grateful for my primary editor on this project, Roger Scholl at Broadway, whose work and insight turned a big idea into a readable reality, and also for Dave Kopp at WaterBrook Multnomah, my editor on all my previous relationship books whose structural help, words, and advice since 2003 have so thoroughly influenced my ability to put such a project together in the first place.

I'm also grateful for, among many others, Anna Thompson, Talia Krohn, Meredith McGinnis, and Dennelle Catlett at Broadway; and for Ken Petersen, Carie Freimuth, and Tiffany Walker at WaterBrook Multnomah, who have been willing to jump through so many hoops in this effort. A special thanks also to Michael Palgon for his belief in and encouragement of this project.

And finally, a very personal note to those who walked the road with me: I think only my personal staff and a few family and friends truly know how challenging and draining the last few years have been: and their support, help, prayer, and encouragement has been vital in allowing me to come through this with family, sanity, heart, and most brain cells intact.

I'm so thankful for the dozens of men and women who committed to personally supporting me in thought, word, and prayer. Thank you for such an important act of friendship.

I'm grateful for the love and encouragement of my parents and Jeff's, Dick and Judy Reidinger and Bill and Roberta Feldhahn. I'm especially grateful for two little squirts who have loved and encouraged their mother through a much longer process than this was intended to be.

To Jeff, my husband and best friend: Bud, there is no way I can ever thank you enough. I'm awed by your unfailing, unflinching love, advice, encouragement, and intensely practical help to all of us. I'm so grateful I turned left instead of right that day.

Ultimately, to the One who matters most: all of this is because of and dedicated to You.

Appendix:
The Survey Methodology

By Dr. Charles Cowan, Managing Partner, Analytic Focus LLC

When Shaunti Feldhahn contacted me to help her with her first relationship book (*For Women Only: What You Need to Know About the Inner Lives of Men*), we began by discussing both her goals and my standards for conducting a quality survey. We agreed on many points; we're both researchers and wanted the facts, unvarnished and untainted.

Which is why it's been a pleasure to continue to work with Shaunti over the years as she has pursued her research and published on important issues regarding the interactions between individuals. But when Shaunti contacted me for help on the book you're now reading, she added another qualification: The sophisticated business reader must be comfortable that the research was of the highest quality and find the survey unassailable.

As with the other surveys we had worked on together, the reliability of results was paramount: It had to be statistically defensible. A survey or any research effort is a series of complex, interrelated steps, and at no point in the research process could biases be introduced.

That is why, for each survey, I have insisted that Shaunti start by writing down the hypotheses she would be testing. There are several reasons for this. The most important is that once we know the issues underlying the hypotheses, we can begin the arduous and time-consuming process of developing the questions that will be asked of every survey participant. Each hypothesis focuses on an issue to be examined and allows us to test it. It gives us a basis for discussing what the survey will be about and what the relevant population would be.

Once Shaunti began developing these hypotheses, we set up parallel tracks as we created the process that would eventually culminate in the survey: We had to develop the questions that would be asked and had to create the best mechanics for the survey itself.

Developing the Survey Questions

On the first track, Shaunti was responsible for starting to develop the survey questionnaire. Based on the feedback from her interviews with men in the workplace,

Shaunti wrote out a question or a set of questions that would get at each hypothesis she wanted to test (each area of "surprise" for the woman reader), and then submitted them to me. My job was to review the questions, push back on wording or content, and make sure they were unbiased. Any potentially leading questions were rewritten and the language clarified so that anyone from an entry-level staff person to a CEO could understand, find it relevant, and respond.

Then, as Shaunti explained in the opening chapter, she tested her questions in real-world environments, made changes, submitted the new questionnaire to me, and started the whole process over again. And again. Just this process of developing and testing the hypotheses and questions took at least six months of concentrated effort, and is a large part of why the research for this book (as well as her others) is precise and reliable.

Choosing the Survey Company and Developing the Survey Mechanics

On a parallel track, I worked with a team of experts to set up the survey mechanics. The first and most important decision was regarding what company would conduct the survey, and that choice was easy: Decision Analyst, which had conducted most of Shaunti's other surveys and has that "unassailable" reputation we were looking for. (On page 299, you will see a description by Decision Analyst of their work on this survey.)

One reason Decision Analyst is so well respected is that their rigorous methods and quality control ensure reliability for online surveys. For this survey, we knew that the respondents would have to be contracted and provided the survey online so they could complete the questionnaire on their own computer. It gave the respondents the necessary privacy to answer sensitive questions that otherwise might have been biased by the presence (either in person or on the phone) of an interviewer. Although the standardized nature of multiple-choice questionnaires can make them cost-efficient, the questionnaire format could limit a respondent's point of view to some extent and possibly force participants to opt for an answer. In order to provide for some flexibility without giving up the necessary standardization, our questionnaire consisted of a mixture of 38 open- and closed-ended questions (dichotomous, multiple response, multiple choice, nominal, and verbatim questions).

In order to increase response rates, lower participant drop-off levels, and maintain rigorous quality control of participants, most credible survey companies (including Decision Analyst) offer monetary as well as nonmonetary incentives to those who agree to take surveys. In this case, nonmonetary incentives included anonymity and confidentiality, as well as appeals to participants regarding the importance and magnitude of the research project that they would be part of. Monetary incentives included the opportunity to participate in a $10,000 monthly cash award sweepstakes, and a small check once the survey was completed.

When I worked with Decision Analyst to design the mechanics of the survey, we had to first determine a sampling frame that covers the population and then select a sample from that population to be questioned. For this survey, we did not draw a "simple" random sample. We set up controls on the sampling process to ensure a proportional distribution of the population across regions of the United States (northeast, central, south, and west) and across age groups. Our goal was to have completed surveys from 600 employed men (including 100 executives), ages twenty-five to sixty-five with a relevant mix of demographics (white-collar/blue-collar, full-time/part-time, across a spectrum of occupations, size of company, and seniority). We also needed to survey 100 white-collar women ages twenty-five to sixty-five, as a control group. Ensuring this sort of proportional distribution is much more time-consuming and expensive, but also delivers very reliable raw data. The sample is random, but it is not "simple"—it is complex and designed to meet a number of important goals.

Once the questionnaire was designed, it was programmed into a computer system that would allow the questionnaire to be taken online. Before the official survey was launched, Decision Analyst conducted a thorough quality-control process, including pretesting the online version of the questionnaire with a small group of randomly selected individuals who were not part of the overall sample. Several rounds of pretesting ensured that the programming was done correctly, that all answers could be recorded and collected, that there were no typos or ambiguous instructions, and that all "skip instructions" worked properly. (For example, if the respondent was a woman, Decision Analyst had to be sure that she would skip the male version of certain questions and see only the female version.)

Once the survey was good to go, invitations were sent out to the sample population and the survey was actually conducted. Here, I'll let Felicia Rogers of Decision Analyst explain a bit more about who they are and about their process.

CONDUCTING THE SURVEY
By Felicia Rogers, Executive Vice President, Decision Analyst

The survey fieldwork and data processing were carried out by Decision Analyst, Inc., a full-service marketing research and consulting firm.

Upon receiving the questionnaire from Shaunti, Decision Analyst programmed the survey instrument to be administered online with members of its American Consumer Opinion® online panel. This is a proprietary, double-opt-in panel of households that have agreed to participate in Internet surveys exclusively for Decision Analyst. The panel currently includes more than eight million men, women, and children throughout the United States, Canada, Europe, Latin America, and Asia. Decision Analyst's panels are recognized within the industry for their high quality of participants and the results they yield. For this project, approximately 50,000 panelists were invited to participate, with several thousand being screened for qualification.

The survey itself was very comprehensive, requiring twelve to fifteen minutes for respondents to complete, on average. Members of American Consumer Opinion® were invited via e-mail to complete a brief screening questionnaire. Qualified respondents (those who met the criteria for proportional distribution) were then invited to continue immediately through the full survey on Decision Analyst's secure Web server. Data was collected over a period of two weeks during late August and early September 2008, until each demographic quota was met.

Once data collection was complete, a set of complete cross-tabulations was provided via Decision Analyst's Logician® Online Reporting System, as well as to Analytic Focus in a raw format, for Shaunti to perform her comprehensive analysis.

Once the data was gathered, it was analyzed for accuracy and consistency. The data was processed using a statistical software package designed to tabulate the data and give reliability measures. Derivative variables were created by cross-tabulating the data. This in turn permitted us to group more than one variable into various subgroups, providing for a more specific characterization of participants and their responses.

My staff and I tabulated the survey results for Shaunti, providing both comprehensive Excel worksheets and specific requested cross-tabs as she proceeded in her analysis and uncovered facts she wanted to investigate further. We also gave Shaunti indicators for the reliability of the results.

Understanding What Is Statistically Significant

Reliability in this context does not mean that there was a question regarding the veracity of the respondents. Reliability for a survey has to do with the variation associated with responses because of the use of a sample. From a large population of men (several million), I can find millions of different samples of 600 men. However, each sample must be reflective of the overall population, but each varies from the overall population in some small way. The larger the sample, the less it is likely to differ from the general population, but it will still differ in some fashion.

Statistics and probability allow me to compute how much a sample is likely to differ from the underlying population. In the case of a sample size of 600, one would expect to have, worst-case, a variation of plus or minus 4 percent, with 95 percent confidence. This means on two separate questions (I prefer chocolate to vanilla and I prefer iced tea to coffee), if 52 percent prefer chocolate and only 48 percent prefer iced tea, I cannot say with 95 percent certainty that these numbers are statistically different, given my variation. A difference of 54 percent versus 46 percent, on the other hand, is one I can detect 95 times out of 100. This simply means that if I drew 100 samples independent from one another, each with 600 respondents, that if the true values in the population were 54 percent and 46 percent I'd be able to detect that difference ninety-five times out of the hundred. To achieve the desired reliability in the questionnaire, you have to select a large enough sample at the beginning of the survey to achieve that end.

One other key value to note is what happens to the reliability when comparing subgroups in the sample. If half of respondents are in one group and half are in the other, then the reliability decreases—but not by as much as you might expect. The variability for the results from a group of 300 is plus or minus 5.6 percent.

As we tabulated the survey results for Shaunti, and as she broke her analysis down into various subgroups (for example, the results among white-collar executives at large companies), we also gave her guidance on what constitutes a real difference versus what would not be statistically different for that subsample. In other words, what would be "statistically significant" and thus a reportable result, instead of results falling within the range of sampling variability for that subsample.

In the end, most of the main results were clearly statistically significant. Shaunti set aside those that weren't and did not pursue those areas of inquiry further.

It was a delight to work with Shaunti again. Although she is passionate about the subjects she is investigating, she has the researcher's desire to be true to the data. She also has the humility to understand that there are technical areas outside her knowledge base where I might be able to help. I hope I have.

CHARLES D. COWAN, PH.D., Managing Partner, Analytic Focus LLC

Notes

CHAPTER 3. "IT'S NOT PERSONAL; IT'S BUSINESS"

1. The tallied answer represents all men who actually did or didn't expect different behavior in the workplace, based on their answer(s) to several later questions. The tallied answer is comprised of those who gave one or more of the following answers on the survey (as seen at TheMaleFactorBook.com): (1) on Q1 (the original question noted here); (1) on Q2; (1) or (2) on Q4; (1) on Q18.1, Q18.2, or Q18.5; (2) on Q18.7; (1) on Q23 or Q23. This tallied answer isn't a perfect comparison, since the questions were not able to compare a man's response to a "personal" situation at work to that of a similar situation in his personal life. However, those answer choices would commonly be the opposite of those considered appropriate in a personal setting (such as not considering another person's feelings when making a decision that affected them). Thus, while the comparison isn't perfect, the tallied answer is likely a more realistic representation of how a man *actually* feels about whether the work and personal worlds function differently.

2. Ruben C. Gur, Bruce I. Turetsky, Mie Matsui, Warren Bilker, Paul Hughett, and Raquel E. Gur. 1999. "Sex Differences in Brain Gray and White Matter in Healthy Young Adults: Correlations with Cognitive Performance." *Journal of Neuroscience* 19(10): 4065–4072.

3. Rita Carter, *Mapping the Mind* (Berkeley: University of California Press, 1998).

4. Reuven Achiron and Anat Achiron. 2001. "Development of the Human Fetal Corpus Callosum: A High-Resolution, Cross-Sectional Sonographic Study." *Ultrasound in Obstetrics and Gynecology* 18(4): 343–347.

5. Ruben C. Gur, Bruce I. Turetsky, Mie Matsui, Warren Bilker, Paul Hughett, and Raquel E. Gur. 1999. "Sex Differences in Brain Gray and White Matter in Healthy Young Adults: Correlations with Cognitive Performance." *Journal of Neuroscience* 19(10): 4065–4072.

CHAPTER 5. "SHE'S CRYING—WHAT DO I DO?": HOW MEN VIEW
EMOTIONS IN THE WORKPLACE

1. Reuven Achiron and Anat Achiron. 2001. "Development of the Human Fetal Corpus Callosum: A High-Resolution, Cross-Sectional Sonographic Study." *Ultrasound in Obstetrics and Gynecology* 18(4): 343–347.

2. Ruben C. Gur, Bruce I. Turetsky, Mie Matsui, Warren Bilker, Paul Hughett, and Raquel E. Gur. 1999. "Sex Differences in Brain Gray and White Matter in Healthy Young Adults: Correlations with Cognitive Performance." *Journal of Neuroscience* 19(10): 4065–4072.

3. Michael Gurian, *What Could He Be Thinking?* (New York: St. Martin's Press, 2003), 83.

4. S. E. Taylor. 2000. "Biobehavioral Responses to Stress in Female: Tend-and-Befriend, Not Fight-or-Flight." *Psychological Review* 107(3): 411–429.

5. Michael Gurian, *What Could He Be Thinking?* (New York: St. Martin's Press, 2003), 84.

6. G. B. C. Hall, S. F. Witelson, H. Szechtman, and C. Nahmias. 2004. "Sex Differences in Functional Activation Patterns Revealed by Increased Emotion Processing Demands." *NeuroReport* 15(2): 219–22.

7. Z. Amin, C. N. Epperson, R. T. Constable, and T. Canli. 2006. "Effects of Estrogen Variation on Neural Correlates of Emotional Response Inhibition." *NeuroImage* 32(1): 457–464.

8. L. Cahill and A. van Stegeren. 2003. "Sex-Related Impairment of Memory for Emotional Events with ß-adrenergic Blockade." *Neurobiology of Learning and Memory* 79: 81–88.

CHAPTER 6. "IF I LET DOWN MY GUARD, THE WORLD WILL STOP
SPINNING": THE SECRET INNER BELIEF OF EVERY MAN

1. The full question listed eight actual quotes separately (included both in this chapter and chapter 9) and asked the survey-takers to separately evaluate each of them, as follows: "Below are several quotes from various successful businessmen about how they privately feel at times. Do you sometimes find yourself instinctively feeling this way? (When answering, please consider how you actually feel, whether or not you think it is logical, or whether you 'should' feel that way.)" Answer choices were "I feel like this regularly," "I feel like this sometimes," "I rarely or never feel like this." Responses to this particular question: 1) I feel like this regularly, 28%; 2) I feel like this sometimes, 52%; 3). I rarely or never feel like this, 20%.

2. Entropy. Dictionary.com. *The Free On-Line Dictionary of Computing*. Denis Howe. http://dictionary.reference.com/browse/entropy (accessed: February 25, 2009).

CHAPTER 7. THE LITTLE THINGS THAT DRIVE MEN CRAZY

1. Barbara and Allan Pease, *Why Men Don't Listen and Women Can't Read Maps* (New York: Broadway Books, 1998), 90.

2. From "Influencing Men, Influencing Women: Gender Strategies for Achieving Results," talk given by Jeffery Tobias Halter in Atlanta, February 5, 2009. Used by permission.

CHAPTER 8. "SUCK IT UP": GETTING IT DONE NO MATTER WHAT

1. Jeff Chu, "10 Questions for Meredith Vieira." *Time* magazine, Sunday, August 27, 2006. www.time.com/time/magazine/article/0,9171,1376220,00.html.

2. "Highlights of Women's Earnings in 2000," Report 952, U.S. Department of Labor, Bureau of Labor Statistics. August 2001.

3. See Denise Venable, "The Wage Gap Myth," National Center for Policy Analysis (www.ncpa.org), April 12, 2002. Also see "Behind the Pay Gap," by Judy Goldberg Dey and Catherine Hill, American Association of University Women (www.aauw.org), April 2007.

CHAPTER 9. THE CONFIDENCE GAME: MEN'S INNER INSECURITY— AND HOW IT CAN AFFECT YOU

1. See endnote 1 for chapter 6, for further explanation on the format of this survey question.

2. See endnote 1 for chapter 6 for further explanation on the format of this survey question.

3. The question was: In which of the following areas, if any, do you sometimes feel less than confident, or question how others view you? Of the men surveyed, 74% chose one or more of the different insecurities listed, while 26% chose "None of the above; I rarely struggle with confidence in any of these areas."

CHAPTER 10. THE VISUAL TRAP: WHY THAT LOW-CUT BLOUSE CAN UNDERCUT YOUR CAREER

1. Because there is no standard definition of what constitutes "being visual," there is no way to give a precise number for what percentage of women are visual. However, although estimates from different sources vary widely (from roughly 5% to 25%), the upper ranges appears to cluster around 20 to 25%—and since roughly 25% of people have what Michael Gurian calls "bridge brains" that are wired in ways similar to the opposite sex, that figure seems to be a safe upper estimate.

2. Tim Koscik, Dan O'Leary, David J. Moser, Nancy C. Andreasen, and Peg Nopoulos. 2009. "Sex Differences in Parietal Lobe Morphology: Relationship to Mental Rotation Performance." *Brain and Cognition* 69(3): 451–459.

3. L. Kilpatrick, D. H. Zald, J. V. Pardo, and L. Cahill. 2006. "Sex-Related Differences in Amygdala Functional Connectivity during Resting Conditions." *Neuroimage* 30: 452–461.

4. Michael Gurian, *What Could He Be Thinking?* (New York: St. Martin's Press, 2003), 107–109.

5. Itzhak Aharon, Nancy Etcoff, Dan Ariely, Chris F. Chabris, Ethan O'Connor, and Hans C. Breiter. 2001. "Beautiful Faces Have Variable Reward Value: FMRI and Behavioral Evidence." *Neuron* 32: 537–551.

6. John Stossel, "Lookism: The Ugly Truth About Beauty: Like It or Not, Looks Do Matter." August 23, 2002. ABCNews.com.

7. David M. Buss, *The Evolution of Desire* (New York: Basic Books, 1994), 71.

8. Stephan Hamann, Rebecca A. Herman, Carla L. Nolan, and Kim Wallen. 2004. "Men and Women Differ in Amygdala Response to Visual Sexual Stimuli." *Nature: Neuroscience* 7: 411–416.

9. Richard Restak, *The Brain* (New York: Bantam, 1984), 197.

10. Walt Larimore and Barb Larimore, *His Brain, Her Brain* (Grand Rapids: Zondervan, 2008), 46–47.

11. Joseph LeDoux. 1993. "Emotional Memory Systems in the Brain." *Behavioral Brain Research* 58; Ibid. 1994. "Emotion, Memory, and the Brain." *Scientific American*.; Ibid. 1992. "Emotion and the Limbic System Concept." *Concepts in Neuroscience*

CHAPTER 11. "THE MOST IMPORTANT THING": MEN'S TOP ADVICE FOR WOMEN IN THE WORKPLACE

1. Of the 602 male survey-takers, several men did not provide a substantive answer to the question, and several others provided advice in more than one area. The total number of substantive comments was 581.

2. Several of the survey-takers' quotes included in this chapter are edited for length, grammar, or clarity.

Index

Go Beyond the Book

If you want to learn more, or move from information to application, this is where you start!

TheMaleFactorBook.com

Find essential tools for personal development, peer coaching, mentoring, management or training; and exchange ideas and solutions with other women in the workplace.

- The Male Factor Workbook, including case studies and questions for individual and group application
- DVD resources, including the "visual" subject DVD for corporate or individual use
- Workplace blog
- Community forums
- Complete survey results, including verbatim answers to the final questions
- Research not included in the book
- Input from experts
- Links for training and speaking options

Come share your success "factors" and continue the journey!

TheMaleFactorBook.com

The ONLY Series
More Than 1.5 Million Copies Sold

Best-selling authors Shaunti & Jeff Feldhahn and Lisa & Eric Rice draw on groundbreaking national surveys and thousands of personal interviews to offer life-changing, eye-opening truths about all the people you care about most—truths that have now transformed millions of relationships.

For Women Only

What is he really thinking?

A thoroughly researched, yet easy to read book on the inner lives of men and what they are really thinking and feeling.

Discussion guide available separately.

For Men Only

A straightforward guide to the inner lives of women

Unlock the mysterious ways of women, and discover what you can do today to improve your relationship.

Discussion guide available separately.

For Parents Only

For every bewildered parent there's a kid longing to be understood

Insight from extensive research that addresses the things parents often don't "get" about their kids.

Discussion guide available separately.

For Young Women Only

Unlock the Mystery of Guy-World

Dive into the mysterious inner-workings of the teenage male mind and begin to understand why guys say and do what they do.

Discussion journal available separately.

For Young Men Only

A Guys Guide to the Alien Gender

Find out the real truth about what teenage girls think, what they want, and how average teen guys can build healthy friendships with girls.

Study guide included.

MULTNOMAH BOOKS
www.shaunti.com